Cats[illegible]
Mountain [illegible]
Trail & Guide

In the Footsteps of the Hudson River School

Voted "Best New Hiking Companion" by *Hudson Valley* magazine

"Researching a rich trove of old engravings, postcards, stereo-opticon views, and vintage trail guides, Robert Gildersleeve has retraced the 19th-century footpaths and plotted all the famous landmarks. ... He thoroughly documents his routes with GPS coordinates at nearly every turn. But his descriptions are so clear that you don't need a GPS at all." *TrailWalker*

"*Catskill Mountain House Trail Guide* ... is foremost a well-documented and accurate hiking guide to the surprising array of varied trails. ... Gildersleeve ... nails down details and identifying features of trails and rocks and natural formations that over the years and through the loose work of previous guidebooks lost any certitude they might have had. ... Gildersleeve has meticulously planned out lots of interesting one- to four-mile hikes in all kinds of directions." *Albany Times Union*

"Bob is adept at sifting Catskill fact from folly. His book, *Catskill Mountain House Trail Guide,* is a study in the ties that bind the area to legend and to luxury." *American Road magazine*

"We owe Bob Gildersleeve a debt of gratitude for ... showing us how much we can still enjoy of the scenery that aroused the admiration of America's Romantic writers, poets, painters, and landscape architects." Francis R. Kowsky, author of *Country, Park and City: The Architecture and Life of Calvert Vaux*

"It is good that we have just the right guidebook, to once again wander the old trails and see the forests through nineteenth-century eyes, exactly as they should be seen." Robert Titus, author of *The Catskills: A Geological Guide* and *The Catskills in the Ice Age*

"This book is highly recommended. ... The book is generously illustrated, filled with history and enthusiastic descriptions of trails. Gildersleeve is a clear writer and he captures the wonder and magic of the old resorts—and of the returning wilderness." *Kaatskill Life* magazine

"Hikers who can't get enough of the beauty and history of the Catskills, particularly the vicinity of the long-gone Catskill Mountain House, now have another resource for their enjoyment." *Kingston Daily Freeman*

This 1883 map from an edition of the Hotel Kaaterskill's souvenir publication, "Haunts of Rip Van Winkle," shows many of the traditional features of the region.

Catskill Mountain House Trail Guide

In the Footsteps of the Hudson River School

GPS Locations • Lost Places
Forgotten Paths • Historic Images & Accounts

Robert A. Gildersleeve

BLACK · DOME

Black Dome Press Corp.
1011 Route 296
Hensonville, New York 12439
www.blackdomepress.com
Tel: (518) 734-6357

First Edition Paperback 2005

ISBN-13: 978-1-883789-45-9
ISBN-10: 1-883789-45-1

Library of Congress Cataloging-in-Publication Data

Gildersleeve, Robert A.
Catskill Mountain House trail guide : in the footsteps of the Hudson River School / Robert A. Gildersleeve.—1st ed. paperback.
p. cm.
Includes bibliographical references and index.
ISBN 1-883789-45-1
1. Hiking—New York (State)—Catskill Mountains—Guidebooks. 2. Trails—New York (State)—Catskill Mountains—Guidebooks. 3. Catskill Mountains (N.Y.)—Guidebooks. 4. Hudson River school of landscape painting. 5. Catskill Mountain House (Hotel) I. Title.
GV199.42.N65C3824 2005
917.47'380444—dc22

2005005675

Outdoor recreational activities are by their very nature potentially hazardous and contain risk. See "Caution," page 15

Printed in the USA

Design: Toelke Associates
www.toelkeassociates.com

10 9 8 7 6 5 4 3 2

To my wife Maria

The title block from Thomas Nast's "Sketches among the Catskills," a double-page engraving published in Harper's Weekly, *July 21, 1866. The desk register of the Mountain House in the collection of the Greene County Historical Society shows that Nast, his wife, child, and a servant were guests there from September 12 through September 27, 1865. It was probably during those two weeks that Nast worked on the drawings that became the double-page engraving. Many of the illustrations in this book are details from that engraving. They capture not only the scenery, but the mood of the resort. Nast was America's most important political cartoonist of the nineteenth century, and is often credited with giving us our image of Santa Claus.*

Contents

Contents

Foreword

A Journey to Middle Earth

You can still walk right up to the front door of the Catskill Mountain House. Go to North–South Lake State Park and find your way to Otis Summit. Follow the sign that points to the Mountain House site and take the trail until you pass through the hotel's stone portals. Now it is your mind's eye that must take over.

You are on the circular driveway that once carried elegant people in elegant carriages. Ignore the drive. There, before you, is the hotel's front lawn. Find the bluestone slabs that make up the sidewalk that bisected the lawn, and walk east upon them. These are very large and once very fine bluestone slabs, and they must have been very expensive. A "who's who" of nineteenth-century feet once walked these stones. Follow them until you reach the front door of the hotel and … sadly it is gone.

I wish the hotel and its front door were still there. I can stand at the end of that sidewalk and look up at the Corinthian columns that supported the pediment above the main entrance of the old hotel. Below, still in my mind's eye, is that front door. It's not just any door; this one is of some importance. All the culture that we associate with the Catskills passed through it. And a great deal of America's culture followed.

That's a lot. That door witnessed Thomas Cole passing through it as a young man. He would soon establish himself as a major figure in the art world. Frederic Church, Sanford Robinson Gifford, Jaspar Cropsey, B.B.G. Stone, and many other artists would follow him through that door, and for a period of time the Catskills and the paintings they inspired would play a leading role in American art.

The writers would sit only one row back. James Fenimore Cooper's Natty Bumpo would stand on the ledge on the eastern side of the hotel and declare that he saw "Creation, all creation" from there. Washington Irving did not actually write *Rip Van Winkle* here, but he could have and should have. The surrounding slopes of North and South mountains seem to fit his descriptions to perfection. William Cullen Bryant would celebrate the area in poetry and prose. With time, John Burroughs would visit the hotel and take his turn entering through its front door.

During our nation's Victorian times, anyone who was anyone passed through that door. They all came here—the artists, writers, playwrights, actors, industrialists, politicians and general muck-a-mucks who made the country great.

And then, in the early twentieth century, the great Catskill Mountain resorts began a decline. The hotels closed, one by one, as did the railroads that served them. Then came the destruction; at first it was inadvertent, and then it was deliberate. The Hotel Kaaterskill accidentally burned in the 1920s. The Overlook Mountain House was purposefully burned in the 1950s. In 1963 the shell of what had, long ago, been the Catskill Mountain House was ordered torched by the New York State Department of Environmental Conservation. Soon the Laurel House joined the list of the lost. The great hotels of the Catskills had become disposable and were disposed of, one by one.

Surrounding communities suffered, and the Catskills sank into a time of decline. It is curious that just exactly as the last remnants of Catskill glories were disappearing, a renaissance began. In 1967 Roland Van Zandt published his book on the old hotel. Van Zandt, an academic scholar from Rutgers University, did much more than record the history of the hotel, he wove the hotel's history into the very cultural mainstream of nineteenth-century America.

In 1972 Alf Evers published his comprehensive history of the Catskills. Evers' book was broader in scope, but again it integrated the hotels into the very fabric of Catskill history and even, perhaps, American culture. Together the two books began to reawaken a communal sense of history. In recent years several more books have brought a sharper focus to this renaissance. Ray Beecher's study of Kaaterskill Clove has now been joined by Bob Gildersleeve's journey into what he likens to the "Middle Earth" that was once called Mountain House Park. These authors have taken us into the very heart of that early, summer tourist destination.

Collectively these books have reawakened our community's sense of its own value. The Catskill Mountains have always projected a warm and friendly image as a nice place to fall asleep for twenty years. The green forests and red sandstone ledges communicate comfortable and languid summer seasons. Rumor has it that this was a summer resort area, but that very soft image hid something far more important. The artists and writers probably began it. It was that sense of Nature with a capital N. The artistic and poetic renditions brought attention to Nature in what would come to be called its rawest or "sublime" state.

Masquerading as art, Nature had entered the nation's mindset, and eventually attitudes would need to be changed. That would take some doing. The hemlock forests of the Catskills had been early victims of the tanning industry. By the late nineteenth century the timber industry had joined in, and entire forests throughout the Catskills and Adirondacks had been cut down. The damage was enormous, and the devastated landscapes stood out in sharp contrast to the sublime that had come to be celebrated in art and writing. The contrast between the ideal and the real was too great to ignore.

Not surprisingly, the Adirondack and Catskill "parks" came to be established as wilderness preserves. Was this the birth of modern environmentalism? I do not pass judgment, but it certainly helped. Certainly, to the extent that our Catskills awakened a sense of the value of Nature, then they contributed, and the trails and carriage paths of Mountain House Park were central to all of this.

All the old trails of North and South mountains are still there, although many have suffered from age and are sometimes hard to follow. To hike any of these, and then to go off of them and enter the forest primeval itself, is indeed to journey into Middle Earth. My personal favorite is the steep slope behind the ruins of the Hotel Kaaterskill. It is, in the dark leafy green of late August, a spooky place. This forest has been here for tens of millions of years, and it feels it and shows it.

The area is in fact haunted, haunted by the people who came here and were affected by what they saw and what they experienced. You can really understand how Thomas Cole felt during his first Catskill wanderings, and you can find the same emotions that affected and still affect the generations of naturalists that have followed.

We have recently observed the centennial of the Catskill Park. The past century has allowed our Catskills to recover from much of the damage. It is good that we have just the right guidebook, to once again wander the old trails and see the forests through nineteenth-century eyes, exactly as they should be seen.

Robert Titus
Freehold, New York
February 9, 2005

Preface

With Romantic Eyes

Walking a mountain trail on a foggy day tightens focus, brings attention to the details at hand, and opens eyes to that nearby, quiet beauty that calms and refreshes. A nineteenth-century romantic would speak of the picturesque and would find it in forest glens, mossy brooks, and rocky ledges. The same romantic would be filled with awe at a vast panorama or a magnificent sunset, find the sublime in a sudden mountain thunderstorm, and always note the beauty of a mist-filled glen or the unusual effects of sunlight at dusk or dawn.

Now when we are familiar with the vast expanse of the Grand Canyon and when panoramic views from airplane windows are commonplace, we might not expect to be impressed with the scenery from a ledge a mere 2,200 feet above the surrounding countryside. That is not the case. Our experience with the vast beauty of this country does not diminish our appreciation of its near, quiet beauty. The classic Catskill Mountain landscape—that area within four miles of the Pine Orchard site of the Catskill Mountain House—still fills us with a sense of the picturesque and the sublime.

Today the area is home to North–South Lake Public Campground, and on a typical summer day it is filled with campers, day hikers, and other visitors who come to enjoy the lakes and the nicely wooded campsites. The public campground is one of the best in the state, and we are greatly indebted to New York State for preserving the beautiful and historic grounds of the Catskill Mountain House. Even campers who never leave the immediate area of the campsites and beach recognize this as a very special place. But those who venture out on its trails are often enchanted by the land and will return again and again.

The first vacationers that we know of came to the area over 180 years ago, in 1819, and camped near the Mountain House ledge. Led by Erastus Beach, they came by coach and horseback from Catskill. "Gathering boughs and hedging themselves in from the cool night wind, they made their beds upon the rock, and spent the night under the stars amid the grandeur of that virgin scene of solitude."[1] Within a few years the Catskill Mountain Association was formed, and in 1823 work on the Mountain House was begun. A year later it was ready to accommodate summer guests. People came. The land brought them and the land continues to bring them, long after the Mountain House deteriorated and was burned. They came first for the scenery, attracted by descriptions penned by James Fenimore Cooper and painted by Thomas Cole. Poets of the nineteenth century, including William Cullen Bryant, wrote of Kaaterskill* Falls and other wonders of the area.

The scenery of the Catskills, and especially that of South Mountain, also played a formative role in the design of many wonderful city parks that America's first generation of landscape architects created in the nineteenth century. I became aware of this through the insights of Ethan Carr while on a South Mountain walk with him and his students in landscape architecture at the University of Massachusetts at Amherst. Further communication with Francis Kowsky, author of *Country, Park and City: The Architecture and Life of Calvert Vaux,* reinforced this. The Kaaterskill region was well known to America's pioneer landscape designers, Andrew Jackson Downing, Calvert Vaux, and Frederick Law Olmsted.[2] Their attempts to arrange natural-feeling rural spaces within urban areas often evoked, directly or indirectly, the picturesque Catskill wilderness. Andrew Jackson Downing, who lived at Newburgh, wrote appreciatively of the area as early as 1837.[3] Calvert Vaux, who came to America from England at Downing's invitation in 1850, frequently walked the trails around the Mountain House. He knew well Moses Rock, Fairy Spring, Palenville Overlook, and other South Mountain sites to which visitors had given picturesque names—as he and Olmsted would do to features in Central Park and other parks that they designed. In 1857, the year that Vaux and Olmsted won the Central Park competition, Vaux, who often walked the Catskills with his brother-in-law, the painter Jervis McEntee,[4] proposed that an unobtrusive observation platform be built at the Kaaterskill Falls.[5]

Science, as well as art, is a creative process. The scientist observes and creates models and theories to better understand our world. By the end of the eighteenth century, the understanding that the Earth was extremely ancient had taken hold. Detailed studies of rock strata were undertaken. Early scientific writings on the geology of the Catskills coincided with the growth of the Mountain House, and by the 1840s W.W. Mather, a geologist with the Geological and Natural History Survey of New York, had created a detailed survey of each rock layer from the top of South Mountain to the valley below.

Evidence of glacial activity in the region exists in the scientific literature of the mid-1800s and the fact that it finds its way into Walton Van Loan's 1879 Catskill Mountain Guide shows that Mountain House guests were interested in the scientific as well as the aesthetic aspects of the area.

---

*The traditional pronunciation is Caw-ters-kill.

William Bartram (the pioneering American botanist), Arnold Guyot (the early geographer), and others explored the natural history of the region. Visitors were as aware of their work as they were of the works of painters and poets.

This book is intended to be a resource to visitors and Catskill Mountain enthusiasts who hike the area centered on Pine Orchard—the site of the Catskill Mountain House that is now part of North–South Lake Public Campground. It is also intended to show that the beauty of the area has survived and should be protected.

In preparing this book I endeavored to develop a firsthand intimacy with the Kaaterskill region. I hiked every trail and path and visited every site that I describe. I sought out locations that have been forgotten or ignored for many years, and came to conclusions that at times go against some recent guides. I chose to use location names as I believe they were used in the nineteenth century, which may cause some confusion when you compare this guide with its contemporaries. Where the current designations disagree with the traditional names, I explain my conclusions. To add precision to the location of these sites, I provide map coordinates. The tool that made this quest practical is the Global Positioning System receiver, or GPS unit. Use of a GPS unit is not required for most of the explorations in this book, but if you plan to use one, please read the setup instructions before you enter data.

Thomas Cole appealed to "lovers of Nature's works" in his poetry; Walton Van Loan suggested treks for "lovers of mountain rambling" in his guide. Today, as in the nineteenth century, both mountain ramblers and nature enthusiasts find countless reasons to love Pine Orchard and the Kaaterskill region.

Using the GPS

For little over a hundred dollars for a basic unit, it is now possible for a hobbyist to accurately record the position of virtually any point on earth and return to that spot with accuracy typically within fewer than thirty feet. GPS latitude and longitude readings are given (as they are here for the center of the Mountain House site on Pine Orchard) in degrees, minutes, and fractional minutes, with elevations in feet above sea level: **[N 42° 11.686′ – W 74° 2.076′ – elev. 2,225 ft.]**, using World Geodetic Survey 1984 (WGS 84) datum.

Elevation readings have been compared with topographic maps, and because the GPS is less accurate with elevations than with latitude and longitude, sometimes the maps were taken into consideration for the final recorded value. The map used as a base map is the 1997 edition of the Kaaterskill Clove Quadrangle 7.5-minute series. Topographical maps use a datum—a mathematical model of the shape of the Earth. Many GPS units, including the Garmin Legend that I used, are set by default to a datum named World Geodetic Survey 1984. The topographical map of the Kaaterskill Quadrangle uses a datum named NAD 27 for the continental United States. I decided to use the default datum, WGS 84, for this book. Most readers should be able to set a waypoint directly from the measurements recorded in this book without any changes to the settings of their GPS unit. Allowing for normal random errors, their GPS units should be in agreement with those coordinates. Those readers who need to correlate the coordinates with a topographic map should first be sure their GPS unit is set to WGS 84, and then they should enter the waypoints from this book. Finally, they should change the setting of their GPS unit to correspond to the datum of the map they are using. The coordinates will automatically change to reflect the datum they have set.

A GPS unit consumes batteries quickly, doesn't work well under heavy tree cover or in deep recesses, and can be incorrectly set. The direction arrow on most units is based on your movement and can be worthless if you are standing still. Elevation readings on units without a built-in barometer are not as accurate as latitude and longitude readings, but do seem to become quite accurate after several minutes in the same location. To improve the reading accuracy you may have to move to a location with a better view of the sky. Be sure large objects such as trees, rock ledges, or even your body are not blocking the unit's view of the sky. Use the GPS unit only as an aid. If it is working and properly set, it can give better directions than can your memory or common sense, but don't rely on it exclusively. Always carry a compass and maps.

CAUTION

Outdoor recreational activities are by their very nature potentially hazardous and contain risk. All participants in such activities must assume the responsibility for their own actions and safety. No book can replace good judgment. The outdoors is forever changing. The author and the publisher cannot be held responsible for inaccuracies, errors or omissions, or for changes in the details of this publication, or for the consequences of any reliance on the information contained herein, or for the safety of people in the outdoors.

Hiking Rules and Guidelines

1. Dress appropriately—cotton clothing and sneakers are the number one cause of illness and injury leading to emergency evacuation. Wear proper sun protection—hat, sunglasses, sunscreen—appropriate to the season. Wear and use appropriate snow gear when the trails are snow-covered.
2. Be prepared: have a first aid kit, whistle, flashlight, matches, small tarp, extra high-energy food, and water (at least twenty-four ounces per person). Do not drink untreated water from streams.
3. Respect private property rights. Do not trespass. Get permission before entering private land.
4. Sign in and out at trail registers. Never go off trail when hiking alone.
5. Overnight camping, except for the campsites within North–South Lake Public Campground, is not allowed in most of the area covered by this book.

In areas where camping is allowed:
A. Make sure all campsites are more than 150 feet from a trail or water, or in a designated site.
B. Hang all food and garbage from a tree at least fifty feet from the camp, fifteen feet or more above the ground, and eight feet or more from tree trunks and limbs.
C. Use pre-existing fire rings whenever possible. Make sure all fires are completely extinguished before breaking camp.
D. Camping permits are needed for groups of ten or more people, or for one or more people staying in the same place for more than three consecutive nights.
E. Camping and fires are prohibited above 3,500 feet each year between March 22 and December 20.

And remember: if you carry it in, carry it out!

Acknowledgments

There are many whose help, directly and indirectly, made this book possible.

My wife, Maria, and children, Diana and David, accompanied me on many rambles in the area and encouraged the writing of this book.

Ed West first introduced me to the historic spots on South Mountain on a hike with the Mountain Top Historical Society in July 1976. Ed's article in the historical society's book *Kaaterskill: From the Catskill Mountain House to the Hudson River School* is a nice discussion of the trail.

Every recent book on the northern Catskills credits Justine Hommel's contributions. This one is no exception. President of the Mountain Top Historical Society and longtime friend, Justine was consulted frequently throughout the writing, and it is Justine who loaned copies of the Van Loan and Rusk guides and many illustrations for inclusion here.

Larry Tompkins is a longtime friend, hiking companion, and co-leader of the hiking program of the Mountain Top Historical Society. Larry's enthusiastic good nature adds to every ramble in these mountains. His extensive collection of Catskill memorabilia provided crucial information and illustrations.

Dr. Robert Titus, "the Catskill Geologist," is the author of several books and articles on the geology of the Catskills. I've had the privilege to walk many of these trails with Bob. His insights have enhanced the geological comments in this book. Any geological errors presented here are certainly mine and not his. I am very honored that Bob agreed to write the foreword to this book.

Dr. Michael Kudish is the acknowledged authority on Catskill forest history. Kudish was a hiking leader and companion on many of my early walks in the Catskills.

Larry Gambon gave advice and instruction that allowed me to draw the maps. I used as a base map the U.S. Geological Survey *Kaaterskill Clove Quadrangle*–NY (7.5-minute series), 1997.

I thank the many individuals and organizations who provided materials and illustrations for this book: Jan and Steve Felter, Arlene Hoose, Scott Koster, Timothy Mallery of catskillarchive.com, Gary Slutzky, Raymond Beecher of the Greene County Historical Society, and the directors of the Mountain Top Historical Society.

Thanks also to the many people whose knowledge of the area and the time period gave me insights into the region and its influence on our history: Ethan Carr, John Ham, Frank Kowsky, William Rhoads, David Schuyler, and the many individuals who joined Larry Tompkins and me on hikes for the Mountain Top Historical Society.

I am especially indebted to Debbie Allen and Steve Hoare of Black Dome Press, who have been of great help throughout the development of this book, and to Matina Billias, Natalie Mortensen, Erin Mulligan, Eric Raetz, and Ed Volmar, who performed a very valuable service as proof-readers and copyeditors. The beautiful photographs on the cover of this book are the creative work of my friend, Catskill Mountain photographer Francis X. Driscoll. My gratitude goes to Ron Toelke who worked a complex mix of modern and historic text, technical data, and a variety of image styles into a very successful design.

My thanks to Dan Casucci, Michael Gross, Steve Jaffee, Don Shay, and Val Warren, childhood friends from the Carter Street days. The summer days we spent roaming the West Street woods in search of ERB's Jewels of Opar and Pal-lu-don were a precursor to my exploration of Kaaterskill.

The illustrations at the beginning of each part are from *Souvenir of the Catskill Mountains* (Portland, Me.: Chisholm Brothers, circa 1884).

SCHOOL No 9
TO WINDHAM
TO PRATTSVILLE
H
U
N
T
LOVERS GLEN
1609
SHANTY HOLLOW
COLD SPRING
Mossy Brook
COLONEL'S CHAIR
3165
HUNTER MOUNTAIN
TO STONY CLOVE
Entrance of the Notch
BREEZE LAWN W. T. VAN LOAN
HUNTER HOUSE
CENTRAL HOUSE
M.E. CHURCH
R.C. CHURCH
CHAIR FACTORY
BEDSTEAD FACT.
PRESB. CHURCH
MAP
OF THE HEART OF THE
CATSKILL MOUNTAINS.
Surveyed & Drawn by SAMUEL E. RUSK, to Accompany
RUSK'S Illustrated Guide to the CATSKILL MOUNTAINS.
ROADS,
1879.
PATHS.
SCALE OF MILES.
Copyright 1879, by Samuel E. Rusk.
T. Bonar, Lith. New York.
VIEW OF THE M
2978. OVERLOOK MT. HOUSE
Overlook Mountain 3150.
Plaaterkill Mountain
Indian Head 3581.
Plaaterkill Clove

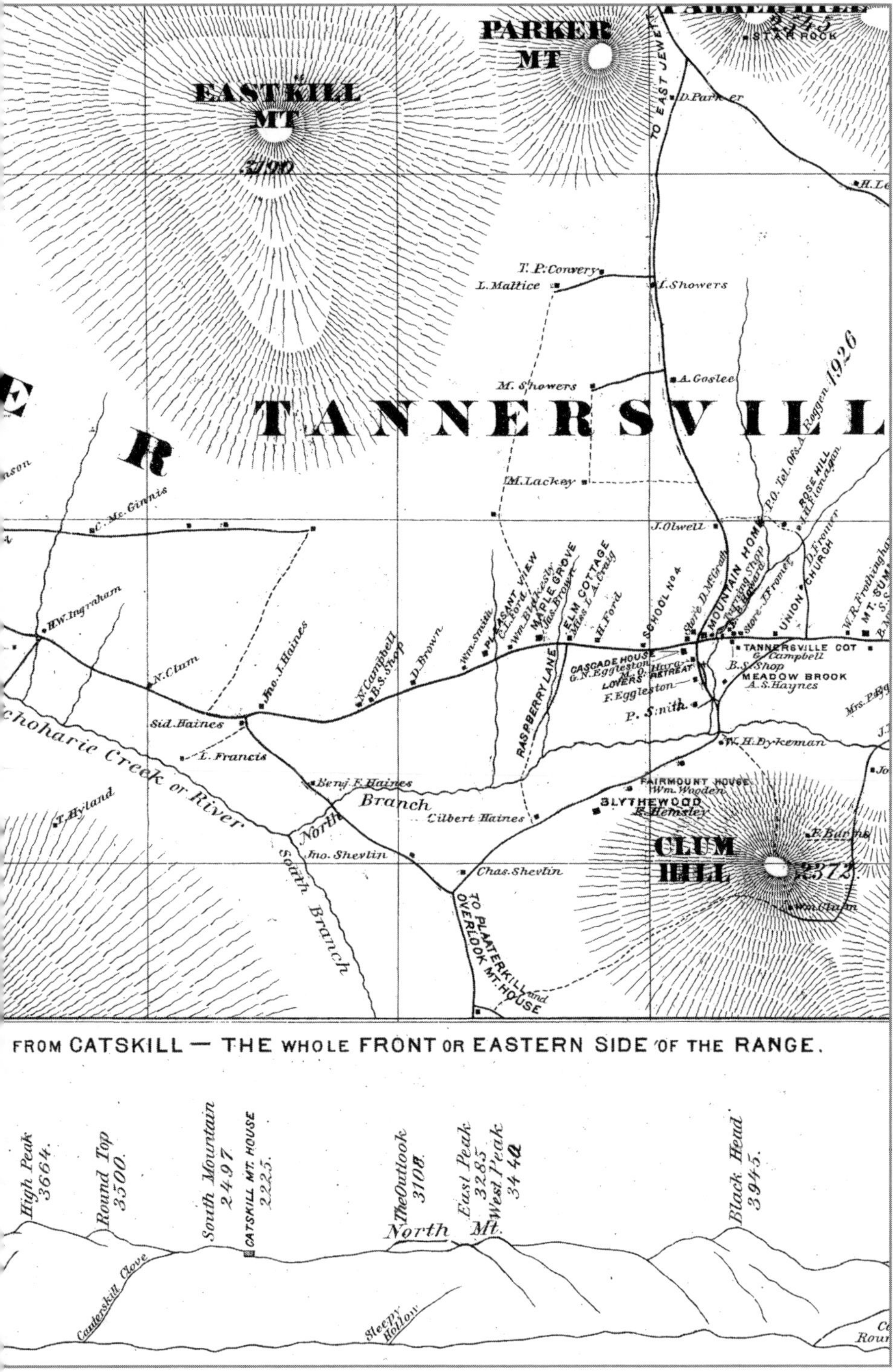
PARKER MT
EASTKILL MT
STAR ROCK
TO EAST JEWETT
D. Parker
T. P. Convery
L. Maltice
I. Showers
M. Showers
A. Goslee
TANNERSVILL
1926
M. Lackey
C. Mc. Ginnis
J. Olwell
H. W. Ingraham
N. Clum
Jno. J. Haines
N. Campbell
B. S. Shop
D. Brown
Wm. Smith
PLEASANT VIEW
MAPLE GROVE
ELM COTTAGE
H. Ford
SCHOOL No 4
MOUNTAIN HOME
P.O.
ROSE HILL
UNION CHURCH
TANNERSVILLE COT
C. Campbell
B. S. Shop
MEADOW BROOK
A. S. Haynes
CASCADE HOUSE
G. N. Eggleston
LOVERS' RETREAT
F. Eggleston
P. Smith
Sid. Haines
L. Francis
RASPBERRY LANE
W. H. Dykeman
FAIRMOUNT HOUSE
Wm. Wooden
BLYTHEWOOD
Benj. F. Haines
Branch
North
Gilbert Haines
Schoharie Creek or River
J. Hyland
Jno. Shevlin
South Branch
Chas. Shevlin
CLUM HILL
2372
TO PLAATERKILL and OVERLOOK MT. HOUSE
FROM CATSKILL — THE WHOLE FRONT OR EASTERN SIDE OF THE RANGE.
High Peak 3664.
Round Top 3500.
South Mountain 2497
CATSKILL MT. HOUSE 2225.
The Outlook 3108.
East Peak 3285
West Peak 3440
North Mt.
Black Head 3945.
Kaaterskill Clove
Sleepy Hollow

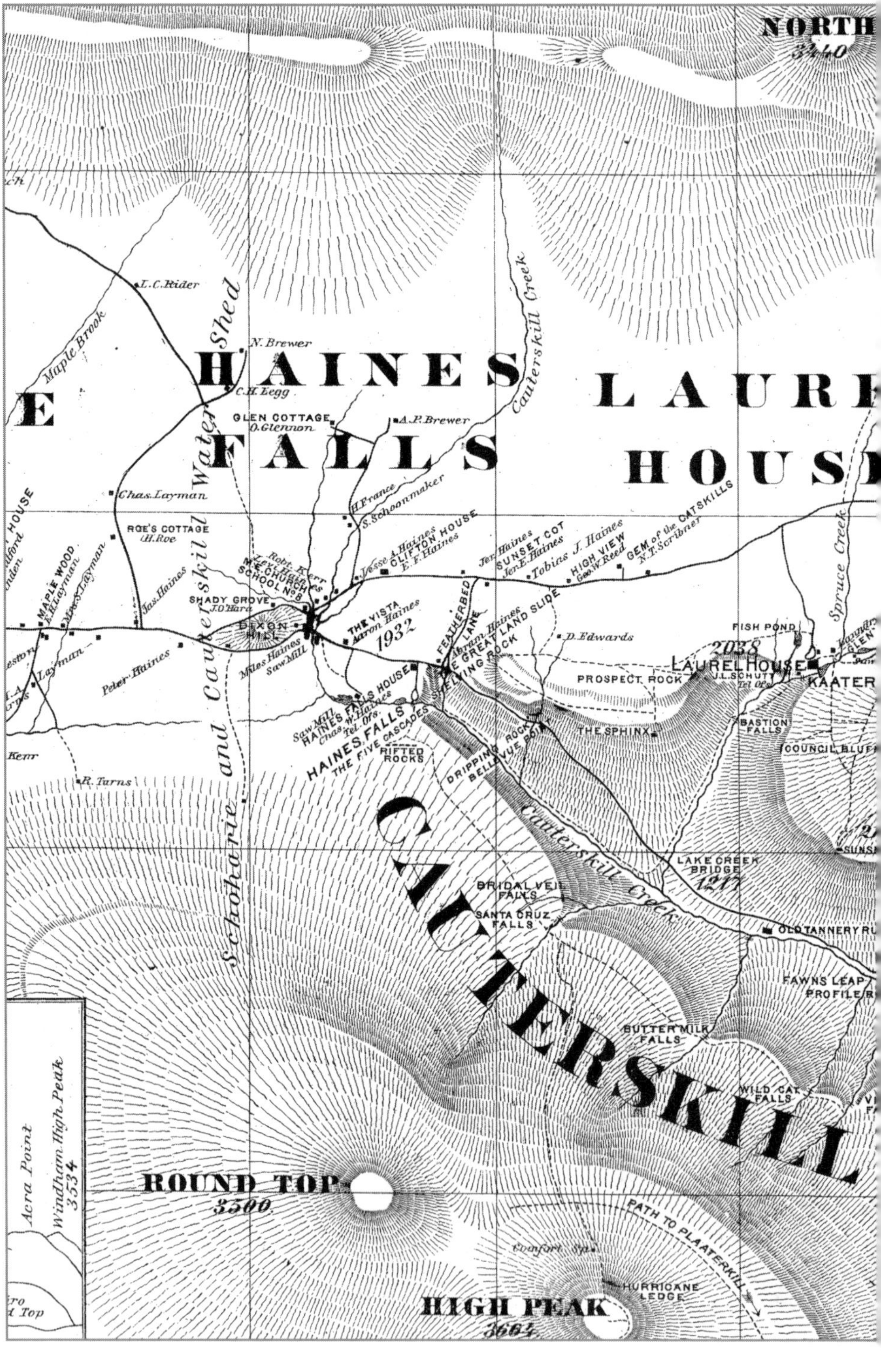
NORTH
3440
HAINES
FALLS
LAUREL
HOUSE
Water Shed
Schoharie and Cauterskill
Cauterskill Creek
Maple Brook
L. C. Rider
N. Brewer
C. H. Eegg
GLEN COTTAGE
O. Glennon
A. P. Brewer
Chas. Layman
ROE'S COTTAGE
H. Roe
MAPLE WOOD
Jas. Haines
H. France
S. Schoonmaker
CLIFTON HOUSE
E. F. Haines
SUNSET COT
Tobias J. Haines
HIGH VIEW
Geo. W. Reed
GEM of the CATSKILLS
N. T. Scribner
M.E. CHURCH
SCHOOL No. 8
SHADY GROVE
J. O'Hara
DIXON HILL
THE VISTA
Aaron Haines
1932
FEATHERBED LANE
THE GREAT LAND SLIDE
FLYING ROCK
D. Edwards
Peter Haines
Layman
Miles Haines
Saw Mill
HAINES FALLS HOUSE
Tel. Ofs.
HAINES FALLS
THE FIVE CASCADES
RIFTED ROCKS
DRIPPING ROCK
BELLEVUE POINT
FISH POND
2038
LAUREL HOUSE
J. L. SCHUTT
PROSPECT ROCK
KAATER
THE SPHINX
BASTION FALLS
Spruce Creek
Kerr
R. Tarns
CAUTERSKILL
LAKE CREEK BRIDGE
1217
BRIDAL VEIL FALLS
SANTA CRUZ FALLS
OLD TANNERY
FAWNS LEAP
BUTTER MILK FALLS
WILD CAT FALLS
ROUND TOP
3500
Acra Point
Windham High Peak
3534
PATH TO PLAATERKILL
Comfort Sp.
HURRICANE LEDGE
HIGH PEAK
3664

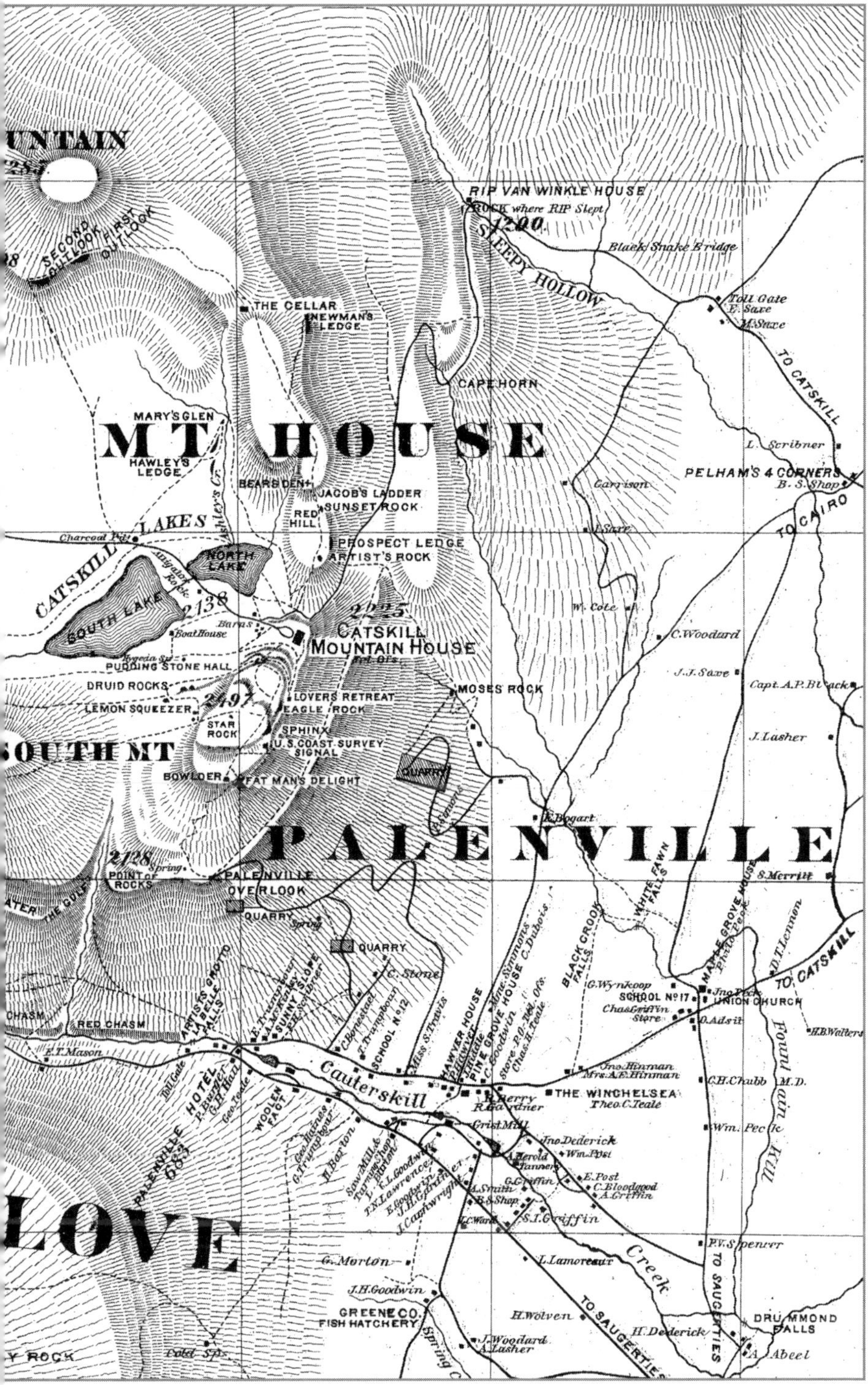
RIP VAN WINKLE HOUSE
ROCK where RIP Slept
SLEEPY HOLLOW
Black Snake Bridge
Toll Gate
E. Saxe
M. Saxe
TO CATSKILL
THE CELLAR
NEWMAN'S LEDGE
CAPE HORN
MARY'S GLEN
MT HOUSE
HAWLEY'S LEDGE
BEARS DEN
JACOB'S LADDER
SUNSET ROCK
RED HILL
L. Scribner
PELHAM'S 4 CORNERS
B. S. Shop
Carrison
TO CAIRO
LAKES
Charcoal Pit
PROSPECT LEDGE
ARTIST'S ROCK
CATSKILL
NORTH LAKE
SOUTH LAKE
2138
2225
CATSKILL MOUNTAIN HOUSE
Boat House
W. Cole
C. Woodard
PUDDING STONE HALL
DRUID ROCKS
LEMON SQUEEZER
J. J. Saxe
Capt. A. P. Black
LOVERS RETREAT
EAGLE ROCK
MOSES ROCK
STAR ROCK
SPHINX
U.S. COAST SURVEY SIGNAL
J. Lasher
SOUTH MT
BOWLDER
FAT MAN'S DELIGHT
QUARRY
E. Bogart
PALENVILLE
2128
Spring
POINT OF ROCKS
PALENVILLE OVERLOOK
S. Merritt
QUARRY
WHITE FAWN FALLS
BLACK CROOK FALLS
MAPLE GROVE HOUSE
D. T. Lennon
TO CATSKILL
C. Stone
HAWYER HOUSE
PINE GROVE HOUSE
SCHOOL No 12
G. Wynkoop
SCHOOL No 17
UNION CHURCH
Chas. Griffin Store
D. Adsit
RED CHASM
CHASM
E. T. Mason
Cauterskill
Jno. Hinman
Mrs. A. E. Hinman
THE WINCHELSEA
Theo. C. Teale
C. H. Chubb M.D.
HOTEL
WOOLEN FACT
Grist Mill
Jno. Dederick
Wm. Post
Wm. Peck
Fountain Kill
E. Post
C. Bloodgood
A. Griffin
PALENVILLE 683
LOVE
S. I. Griffin
G. Morton
L. Lamoreaux
Creek
P. V. Spencer
TO SAUGERTIES
J. H. Goodwin
GREENE CO. FISH HATCHERY
H. Wolven
TO SAUGERTIES
H. Dederick
DRUMMOND FALLS
J. Woodard
A. Lasher
A. Abeel
Spring

Introduction: The Unique Kaaterskill

All of the material in this introduction has been presented in greater detail in other sources, but if you are about to begin exploring the area there are a few things that it would be helpful to know. I will outline some essential information and then point you toward additional resources in the conclusion.

Geology and Topography

The essential thing to know is that the Catskill Mountains consist of sedimentary rock layers that were laid down during the Devonian period about 380 million years ago. This period was the age of the fishes, meaning that it was the time when fish evolved and proliferated. The sediments that formed the rocks now in the North Lake area were deposited in a large river delta. The rivers flowed out of a towering mountain range to our east and entered an extensive inland sea. A trained eye can see indications of streambeds and ancient floods. As sediments were deposited, their weight depressed the Earth's crust and allowed further sediments to accumulate until sedimentary layers were stacked thousands of feet deep.

Much later, the sediments were lifted up in perhaps two separate phases. As water and ice eroded the elevated plane, it became the Catskills. The sediments now lie essentially flat (though they are tilted slightly to the west) and are cut by valleys and cloves (the local term for gorges) that create a picturesque beauty.

Fossils are present, though not abundant, in the Kaaterskill region. It is common to see indications of the ancient fern tree forest first identified at Gilboa. Small, snakelike, scaly imprints of branches and roots are not uncommon and can be readily seen in stone quarries. (These are not snake fossils; there were no land vertebrae in the Devonian period.) Fragments of fish fossils are also common, but not as easily identified.

In much more recent times (thousands, rather than millions of years ago), glaciers flowed down from the north, scouring the landscape and leaving many indications that are easily seen and identified. The last of these glaciers retreated about 14,000 years ago. Even after the Hudson Valley glacier receded, local glaciers persisted in the valleys and cols (mountain passes) between the highest mountains.

Forests

Any Catskill forest that existed before the ice age was scoured away. As the ice receded, new forest returned to the land—first alpine plants, then trees adapted to the cold, and eventually the forest we know today. Forest historian Michael Kudish documents two alpine plants that have survived along the Catskills' escarpment on rocky areas that apparently have never been reforested. It is also worth noting that the escarpment hosts "the widest diversity of plant species of any area of similar size in the Catskills."[6] This is because of the sudden elevation change and corresponding temperature differences between the base of the escarpment and the tops of South Mountain and Kaaterskill High Peak.

Much of the abundant hemlock were cut down in the mid-nineteenth century and stripped of bark, which was a source of the tannin used in the local leather tanneries. The region was also subject to forest disturbances from blowdowns, fires, recreational use, logging, and stone quarrying. With the acquisition and protection of the land by New York State, much of the disturbed forest is recovering.

The Resorts

There were three major resorts in the area we will walk. The Catskill Mountain House, at Pine Orchard, opened in 1824 and was intentionally destroyed in 1963 when it was beyond repair and a danger to visitors. The Hotel Kaaterskill, on the more western summit of South Mountain, opened in 1881 and was accidentally destroyed by fire in 1924. The Laurel House, at the brink of Kaaterskill Falls, opened in 1850 and was destroyed—again intentionally—by New York State in 1967. Other smaller boardinghouses were in the area, notably Scribner's Glen Mary Cottage near the Laurel House, and the Dodd House on Palenville Overlook. Many of the trails that we enjoy today were created for the guests of these hotels.

The Railroads

Four passenger railroads operated in the region.[7] All began in a flurry of activity and competition in the early 1880s.

The Kaaterskill Railroad ran from Kaaterskill Junction near Stony Clove, where it met the Stony Clove & Catskill Mountain Railroad, a narrow-gauge subsidiary of the Ulster and Delaware Railroad that ran from Phoenicia to the Hunter line through Stony Clove notch. From Kaaterskill Junction outside of the village of Hunter, the Kaaterskill Railroad ran through Tannersville and Haines Falls and on to the Laurel House, ending at the Kaaterskill station near the South Lake dam. It was built as a narrow-gauge railroad in 1883.[8] It was converted to standard gauge in 1899 and ceased operation in 1940. Parts of the right-of-way are now used as a biking trail developed by the village of Tannersville.

The Catskill Mountain Railway opened for service in 1882. It was a narrow-gauge line running initially from Catskill Landing on the Hudson River to the base of the escarpment near the Mountain Turnpike. A year later it was extended into Palenville. It originally met the stage line for the final trip up the mountain. In 1892, when the Otis Elevating Railway opened, the base station—now named Otis Junction—was moved to meet that railway.

The Otis Elevating Railway, with its two odd cars connected together by a long cable, carried people up the front face of the escarpment to within a short distance of the doors of the Mountain House. The cable ran around a large wheel in the power station at the summit. Passengers sat facing down the mountain in benches that reclined sharply. As the car began its uphill trip, the benches straightened out, giving the passengers a view of the valley below. Halfway up the mountain, the upward-bound car passed its descending twin. One early tourist wrote, "It is like riding up to the moon to make this trip going up backwards by cable in a car carrying 75 people."[9]

All that is left of the Otis is the scar cut along the escarpment, now used for power lines, and remnants of trestles along the right-of-way. How many years will those remnants exist, compared to the less than thirty-year operation of the Otis? Similar railways could be found at Mount Beacon along the Hudson in Dutchess County, and on Prospect Mountain near Lake George.

A connecting line was built in 1893 between the Otis summit station and the Ulster & Delaware's Kaaterskill station at South Lake. Initially owned by Charles Beach and run by the U&D, the line soon became independent and was extended to Tannersville. This line was officially named the Catskill & Tannersville Railway, but it is often called the Huckleberry. It ceased operation in 1918.

There are fervent hopes that the paths of these mountaintop rail lines will become trails that connect the communities with the existing trail system. Such a connection would establish a resource for Hudson Valley and Catskill Mountain residents that would benefit all for years to come.

The Artists

The Hudson River School, America's first school of landscape painting, had its beginnings with an 1825 visit to the North Lake area by Thomas Cole.

His paintings sparked interest in the region and the American wilderness at a time when there was great emphasis in the arts on the connection between landscapes and the impact of human history on them. The new continent lacked that connection.

Many other landscape artists who are identified with the style that has become known as the Hudson River School chose subjects that we will see on our walks. They include Frederic Church, Jasper Cropsey, Asher Durand, Sanford R. Gifford, John Frederick Kensett, and B. B. G. Stone.

Recreation

Skiing, hiking, camping, hunting, rock and ice climbing, mountain biking, ice fishing, and geo-cacheing (a recently invented game in which a small cache of items is hidden for others to find using a GPS unit and clues posted on the Internet) all bring people to the Kaaterskill region. Local stores and individuals provide services and information on all of these activities and more.

Suggested Reading

A good starting point is the Mountain Top Historical Society's *Kaaterskill: From the Catskill Mountain House to the Hudson River School.* I was involved in the production of that book, which is an anthology of articles by experts on various aspects of the Kaaterskill region including artists, resorts, geology, forestry, and railroads. Many of those articles are referenced in this book.

Roland Van Zandt's definitive volume, *The Catskill Mountain House: Cradle of the Hudson River School*, is much more than a history. Van Zandt's perspective brings to light the lasting influence that this small area has had on American culture.

In *Kaaterskill Clove: Where Nature Met Art,* Greene County Historian Raymond Beecher explores the close relationship between the artists of the Hudson River School of painting and the scenic domains of Kaaterskill Clove, as well as providing insights on the building of the clove road ("The Rip Van Winkle Trail"), the legend of Rip Van Winkle and its ties to the clove, the grand hotels, and the nineteenth-century harvesting of the forest products of the region.

Those interested in learning more about the region's geology will want to read *The Catskills: A Geological Guide* and *The Catskills in the Ice Age,* both by Robert Titus; any of Titus's articles in *Kaatskill Life* magazine; "Geology of the Eastern Catskill Escarpment" by Constantine Manos, in *Kaaterskill: From the Catskill Mountain House to the Hudson River School*; and *Geology of*

New York State: A Simplified Account, from the New York State Museum.

For more information on the forests of the Kaaterskill, read Michael Kudish's *The Catskill Forest: A History* and his article "Forest History of the Kaaterskill Region" in *Kaaterskill.*

The region's railroads are documented in *Rip Van Winkle Railroads* by William Helmer, as well as in his article "Rails to the Peaks" in *Kaaterskill;* also see *Light Rails and Short Ties through the Notch* by John Ham and Robert Bucenec.

Full references for all books recommended can be found in the bibliography.

PART I

Into the Mountains

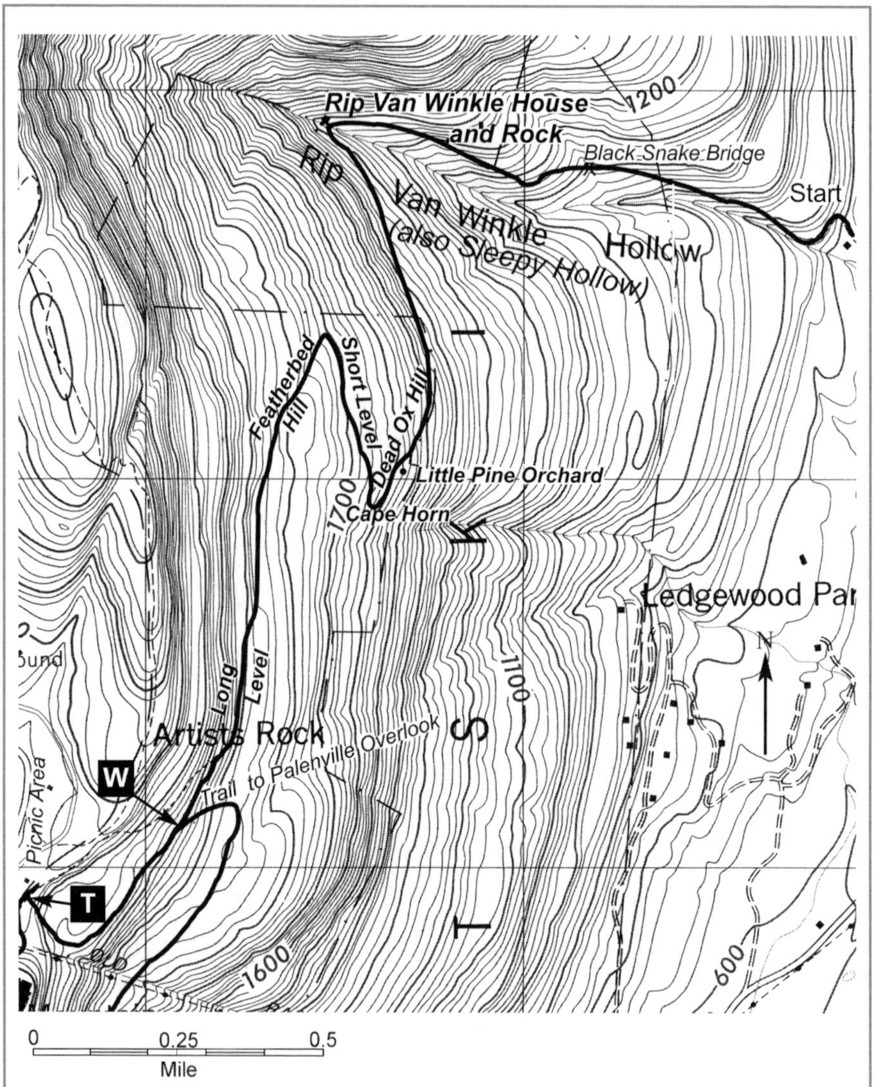

Rip Van Winkle House and Rock
1200
Black Snake Bridge
Start
Rip Van Winkle Hollow
(also Sleepy Hollow)
Featherbed Hill
Short Level
Dead Ox Hill
Little Pine Orchard
1700
Cape Horn
Ledgewood Par
1100
Long Level
Artists Rock
Trail to Palenville Overlook
W
Picnic Area
T
1600
600
0
0.25
0.5
Mile

Hike 1:

The Old Stage Road

Distance: 3.5 miles one way
Type of Trail: Carriage road, most of which is suitable for foot, snowshoe, trail bicycle, or horse. Check New York State publications for restrictions on use.
Difficulty: Moderate to difficult
Elevation Gain: 1,470 feet from start to Pine Orchard
Comments: Leaving a car parked at North Lake beach makes this a one-way hike. Returning the way you came doubles the length of the walk.

Typical nineteenth-century Catskill Mountain vacationers arrived at the village of Catskill on "elegant" Hudson River Day Line steamers from New York City, a trip of about seven hours. Some may have journeyed overnight by Catskill night boat, having breakfast aboard before disembarking. Still others came by a three to four-hour rail trip on the east shore's Hudson River Railroad, followed by a short ferry ride across the Hudson.

However they reached Catskill village, the travelers would then board a stagecoach to begin a classic journey to the base of the mountain and then up to the Mountain House over "the best mountain road in the country." We can follow their path today. The road from Catskill to the Mountain House was called Mountain Turnpike.[10] If you want to drive the portion of the route that approaches the base of the mountain, you can take Route 23A west from the village of Catskill. Before you reach Route 32 at Story's Corners, turn right onto what is still called Mountain Turnpike. You will reach Route 32 near the Friar Tuck resort. From there, the old route continued directly toward the base of the mountain. That section is no longer open. You can find where it continues if you turn south on Route 32 to Route 23A at Story's Corners. Turn right onto 23A and drive into Palenville. Pass through the traffic light and turn north (right) when you reach Bogart Road.

As you drive along Bogart Road, keep your eyes open for the route of the Otis Elevating Railway. In the summer of 2002, extensive clearing of the power line right-of-way was done and the railway grade is more visible than it has been in years.[11] Continue past the intersection of Bogart with Pennsylvania Avenue. A short distance beyond, turn left onto Mountain House Road. Drive the old road to the base of the escarpment, where you

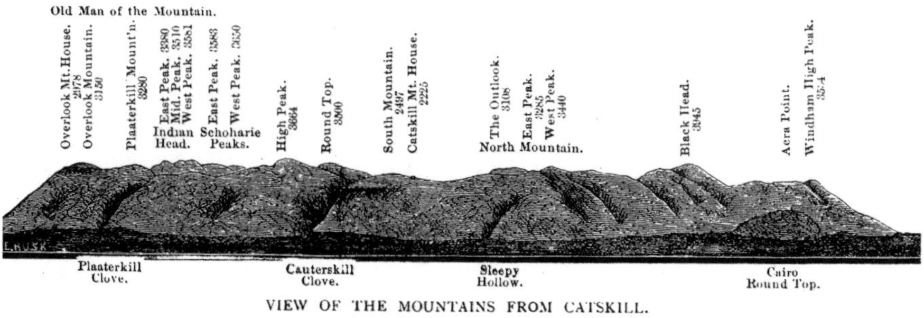

Samuel Rusk's diagram of the Catskill escarpment from his 1879 Illustrated Guide to the Catskill Mountains. *Courtesy of Justine and Hillard Hommel.*

will be able to park [N 42° 12.757′ – E 74° 0.467′ – elev. 690 ft.]. Take care when you park not to block the access of other hikers or the local residents.

This is the area of the turnpike's tollbooth. Travel on the road was not cheap, as we learn from the experience related by R. Lionel DeLisser, who drove his carriage down the road in 1893 and encountered this "remnant of barbarism"—DeLisser's term for tollbooths.

"At the foot of the Hollow I come upon another of those 'r. b.'s,' a very immodest one this time—seventy-five cents demanded. Words fail, my feelings are too deep for utterance. There is no help—I must pay, so I try to get a small part of my money's worth in playing with the tame coon that lives here, a cute little fellow. I had no sooner taken a seat than he proceeded to search every one of my pockets for something to rob me of. It was useless, for his master had left nothing."[12]

We need not pay to walk the remaining three miles to the North Lake beach. Although the tame coon is gone, Cody, the friendly dog of one of the residents, has taken great pleasure in following hikers up the trail. This has been a real inconvenience for its owner, who sometimes has to drive the ten miles or so up the mountain to North Lake to retrieve his pup.

You are now ready to begin the classic approach into the mountains.

Leave your car and—hopefully—the local dog behind. Pass through the gate and follow the old road, which is now marked as a horse trail. It soon turns to the left and begins a moderate ascent. You can hear the sound of the stream below you to the left. Also below are small private roads. Continue uphill. At about 960 feet in elevation, the road crosses a small tributary at Black Snake Bridge [N 42° 12.860′ – W 74° 0.966′]. The trail continues its uphill climb to the west. Years of erosion have made the trail rocky along this section. The road was undoubtedly groomed to a smoother surface when Charles Beach's stagecoaches were the main means of transportation to the Mountain House. By the time a four-horse team had pulled the passenger and luggage-laden coach up another 300 feet, passengers and team alike were ready for a rest stop at the Rip Van Winkle House [N 42° 12.920′ – W 74°1.479′ – elev. 1,260 ft.]

This was the site of two buildings—a small shanty dating to 1828 and a larger boardinghouse built sometime between 1865 and 1870.[13] In 1886 *Harper's New Monthly Magazine* serialized a travelogue written by Charles Dudley Warner that featured several interesting and opinionated characters. They passed by this spot on their approach to the Mountain House. Observe the reactions of some young, fellow passengers:

> When the stage reached the Rip Van Winkle House, half-way, the shy school girls were for indulging a little sentiment over the old legend, but the boy, who concealed his ignorance of the Irving romance until his cousins had prattled the outlines of it, was not to be taken in by any such chaff, and though he was a little staggered

A night boat advertisement from "Kaaterskill Mountains," circa 1893. Courtesy of Justine and Hillard Hommel.

by Rip's own cottage, and by the sight of the cave above it which is labelled as the very spot where the vagabond took his long nap, he attempted to bully the attendant and drink-mixer in the hut, and openly flaunted his incredulity until the bar-tender showed him a long bunch of Rip's hair, which hung like a scalp on a nail, and the rusty barrel and stock of the musket. The cabin is, indeed, full of old guns, pistols, locks of hair, buttons, cartridge-boxes, bullets, knives, and other undoubted relics of Rip and the Revolution. This cabin, with its facilities for slaking thirst on a hot day which Rip would have appreciated, over a hundred years old according to information to be obtained on the spot, is really of unknown antiquity, the old boards and timber of which it is constructed having been brought down from the Mountain House some forty years ago.[14]

The Rip Van Winkle House. *This 1866 illustration doesn't show the larger structure with two full floors seen in later illustrations and photos. Thomas Nast, "Sketches among the Catskills," 1866.*

There was probably nothing above the house that we would call a cave (other references refer to "Rip's Rock"), but this passage shows us an example of the commercialism of the time. All that is left of Rip's house and the next-door tavern is a stone foundation. Retaining walls on both sides of the stream, and photos of the cabin and tavern indicate that the two structures were on opposite sides of the stream and connected by a platform bridging it. Rip's House and Rock are depicted in the illustrations taken from early-twentieth-century postcards.

Rip's Rock [N 42° 12.911′ – W 74° 1.496′ – elev. 1,290 ft.], which was featured in photos and postcards, can still be located. Stand at the center of the bridge and face the southwest corner. Straight ahead and a little uphill is a stone retaining wall with a flat area at its top. Rip's Rock is along the same line and partway up the hill beyond the flat area. It rests alone on the side of a hill below a rock ledge. Some weathering has occurred, but it closely matches the nineteenth-century photos. Initials carved in the top further support the idea that it was an important local landmark. Should you attempt the climb to the rock, be careful; the hillside can be slippery and some of the rocks are loose.

Beyond Rip's house, the trail leaves Sleepy Hollow and gradually ascends the side of North Mountain. We can see rock ledges above to the right, and another private road to the left. A view of the valley partially opens up and we can see the long, narrow chicken barns on Cauterskill Road in the valley. Soon the trail gets a good deal steeper as we climb Dead Ox Hill. Partway up the hill, about 250 feet higher than Rip's, is Little Pine Orchard [N 42° 12.440′ – W 74° 1.312′ – elev. 1,520 ft.] The spot still bears the same name, and with its good view of the valley, picnic table, and privy, it is good for a short break before continuing up to North Lake.

Rip Van Winkle House as it appeared toward the end of its service. Postcard, circa 1907.

Rip Van Winkle House, Catskill Road. *Harry Fenn, 1870, engraving in* Picturesque America, *William Cullen Bryant, ed. This illustration, showing a stagecoach crossing the bridge in front of the Rip Van Winkle House, captures the wild feeling of Sleepy Hollow.*

At the top of Dead Ox Hill is a hairpin turn in the road. This is Cape Horn [N 42° 12.379′ – W 74° 1.395′ – elev. 1,620 ft.] Rounding the horn, we are on Short Level and soon come to another hairpin turn and begin to climb Featherbed Hill, a tongue-in-cheek name suggesting that this was a rough stretch of roadway. The hill levels off at about 1,750 feet above sea level. Van Loan's map shows a path heading north from this point, which he tells us is the path to Rip Van Winkle's Ledge.[15] We are now at the elevation of the most dominant ledge on the eastern escarpment. Farther south this same ledge holds the Old Wood Road that leads to Palenville Overlook. This stretch of road is called Long Level and provides a leisurely path.

As the road again begins to rise, an old road enters from the left [N 42° 11.917′ – W 74° 1.800′ – elev. 1,980 ft.] This descends a steep hill to the Old Wood Road and is the easiest path to Palenville Overlook. Van Loan's map shows a trail at the bottom of the hill leading to Moses Rock. Because of the rock cut for the Otis Elevating Railway, that trail is no longer recommended as the approach to Moses Rock and a different approach is discussed elsewhere.

We postpone the trip to Palenville Overlook for another time and continue toward North Lake and the Mountain House site. Soon, before the road takes a sharp turn to the right, we come to the spot where the Mountain

Rip woke up and moved on, but his rock bed can still be found. Postcard, courtesy of Ron Hoose.

Nearing the Mountain House.
Thomas Nast, "Sketches among the Catskills," 1866. The first good view of the Mountain House from the stagecoach road. This famous turn was probably moved several hundred feet north when the Otis inclined railway was built. Traces of the route of the old road before the construction of the Otis forced it to be relocated can still be seen.

House made its first dramatic appearance to the approaching stagecoach. Numerous engravings, paintings, and photos captured the famous view. (See Thomas *Nast's Nearing the Mountain House* from his two-page "Sketches among the Catskill Mountains" in the July 21, 1866, issue of *Harper's Weekly.*) Yet a modern-day hiker may note something wrong here. The photos, and especially the descriptions, imply that the Mountain House was almost directly overhead at the turn. The turn that we meet is not below the Mountain House site; it is a little too far north. The explanation is probably that the builders of the Otis Elevating Railway cut through the stage road and moved the turn to its present location. Remnants of the original path of the road lie just beyond the Otis cut, and part of the original road's path is apparent to the left as we climb this final hill.

At the base of this last hill, a careful observer will also notice a raised mound of dirt snaking its way through the woods to the right. This is the bed of the rail ride at Rip's Retreat, a small theme park that occupied the area near the North Lake picnic grounds in the 1950s.

From here the road becomes very steep. Weary travelers were often asked to leave the coach and walk in order to spare the even more weary horses. Nast's image, *The Last Mile or*

So, captures the scene with the humor that made Nast one of the most noted cartoonists of the nineteenth century.

We come, at last, to the top of the hill and find ourselves at the edge of the picnic area at North Lake [N 42° 11.839′ – W 74° 2.071′ – elev. 2,150 ft.] Ahead to the right is a comfort station; the beach is just across the parking lot. A handicapped-accessible platform for viewing the valley below, located near the comfort station, is set for completion in 2005.

If you want to continue the trek to Pine Orchard, turn left and follow the blue trail markers. We enter an open area, and after crossing it find that the road climbs diagonally up a hill. At the top, the road curves around to the left and passes between the original stone pillars that marked the entrance to the immediate grounds of the Mountain House. Crossing the open field at the top of the hill, we take in the magnificent view of the Hudson Valley so familiar to generations of hotel guests. This is Pine Orchard [N 42° 11.687′ – W 74° 2.076′ – elev. 2,225 ft.], the spiritual center of the classic Catskill Mountains. Although the Mountain House is gone, we can almost imagine ourselves in Nast's illustration, *The Piazza,* looking at the view that brought thousands to this spot for over 180 years. It is from here that we will, as did our nineteenth-century ancestors, set out to explore the "most picturesque mountain region on the globe."[16]

The Last Mile or So. *Thomas Nast, "Sketches among the Catskills," 1866. The last hill of the Mountain Turnpike was so hard on the team that the men were asked to get out of the coach and walk.*

GPS and Map Data	Description	Directions and Comments
0.0 mi. N 42° 12.757′ W 74° 0.467′ Elev. 690 ft.	The hike begins in the area of the nineteenth-century tollbooth for the then privately owned Mountain Turnpike.	Drive to the end of Mountain House Road off of Bogart Road in Palenville and park on the shoulder before the red barn. Be careful not to interfere with the access of local residents. Begin uphill climb following markers for the horse trail.
0.5 mi. N 42° 12.860′ W 74° 0.966′ Elev. 960 ft.	Black Snake Bridge crosses a tributary of the main Sleepy Hollow stream.	Continue on the horse trail.
0.9 mi. N 42° 12.920′ W 74° 1.479′ Elev. 1,260 ft.	Rip Van Winkle House site at Sleepy Hollow. The main house was on the north side of the bridge; a small cabin was on the south side. A walkway bridged the creek between the two. (Conclusion based on map and photos.) Nearby is Rip's Rock.	Still on the horse trail, you come to a hitching rail and another, larger bridge. This is the deepest part of Sleepy Hollow. Explore and then continue on the horse trail.
N 42° 12.911′ W 74° 1.496′ Elev. 1,290 ft.	Rip's Rock, one of several spots where Rip was said to have spent his twenty-year sleep. To find the rock, stand on the bridge and face southwest along the diagonal of the bridge. Directly in front of you is a retaining wall and beyond that, halfway up the hill before the base of the cliff, is a large boulder. Several initials are cut into the top. The shape of the rock matches the nineteenth-century photo in DeLisser's *Picturesque Catskills.*	You may want to scramble uphill to Rip's Rock before you continue. See middle column for the exact location.
	Dead Ox Hill	Leave the area of Rip's House. The trail soon begins to climb.
1.5 mi. N 42° 12.440′ W 74° 1.312′ Elev. 1,520 ft.	Little Pine Orchard. A modern picnic table and not-so-new privy are located here.	The clearing and flat area to the left of the trail provides a view of the valley.

GPS and Map Data	Description	Directions and Comments
1.6 mi. N 42° 12.379′ W 74° 1.395′ Elev. 1,620 ft.	Cape Horn	Trail turns sharply to the right.
Elev. 1,690 ft.	Short Level	Continue over this relatively flat stretch.
1.9 mi. Elev. 1,700 ft.	Featherbed Hill—a short climb of about 100 feet. Van Loan's map shows a trail to Rip Van Winkle Ledge above the north side of Sleepy Hollow.	Trail turns back to the left and begins a climb.
2.1 mi. Elev. 1,800 ft.	Long Level. About a half-mile of level walking. This stretch is along a dominant 1,800-foot elevation ledge that extends along much of the eastern escarpment.	
2.9 mi. N 42° 11.917′ W 74° 1.800′ Elev. 1,980 ft. **Location W**	This is the Old Wood Road on Van Loan's map. This was a road that led to Moses Rock and Palenville, and to a road to Palenville Overlook and Point of Rocks. That walk is Hike 6. The USGS map seems to show a path to the right that comes out just north of the picnic area at North Lake. This is most likely an error.	A trail—actually an old road—enters diagonally from the left. Continue on main trail.
3.1 mi. N 42° 11.759′ W 74° 1.993′ Elev. 2,120 ft.	Final hill to North Lake picnic area. Van Loan's maps indicate that before the Otis Elevating Railway was built, the road continued south without turning here. The turn to the right was in the path of the Otis and was relocated to this area.	Trail makes an abrupt right turn and begins to climb hill. Near the top, note the ramp on the left. It seems to have been the path of the Mountain Turnpike before the construction of the Otis Elevating Railway.
3.2 mi. N 42° 11.839′ W 74° 2.071′ Elev. 2,150 ft. **Location T**	Picnic area and top of Mountain Turnpike. Right along fence to rest-rooms.	Left to top of Otis and the final short climb to Pine Orchard.
N 42° 11.687′ W 74° 2.076′ Elev. 2,225 ft.	Pine Orchard	

The Piazza. *Thomas Nast, "Sketches among the Catskills," 1866. A welcomed peace must have enhanced the mood as these visitors looked out over the famous Pine Orchard view a year after the end of the Civil War.*

PART II

South Mountain—the Classic Catskills

Our next series of walks includes the most popular nineteenth-century sites—those on South Mountain. The trails on North Mountain may be more popular with modern hikers, but the South Mountain trails feature some of the best views and most romantic spots in the Catskills, and they were the walks favored by Mountain House and Hotel Kaaterskill guests. The next few walks will in fact start at the site of the Mountain House (now commemorated by a historic marker) and end at the site of its rival, the Hotel Kaaterskill. The climbs are short, but have an impressive concentration of diverse and interesting stops.

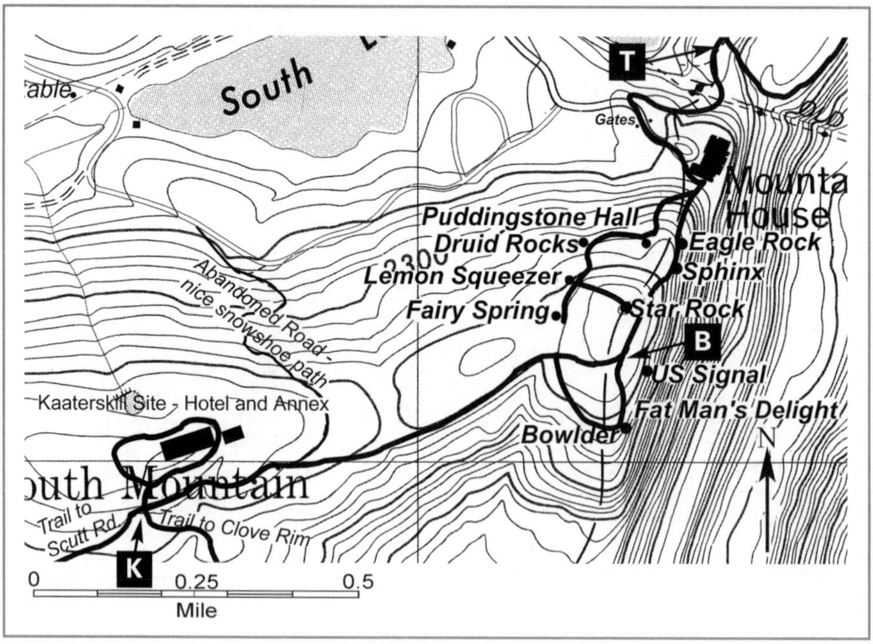

Hike 2:

Pine Orchard to Hotel Kaate

Distance: 3.0 miles round-trip
Type of Trail: Marked footpath and nineteenth-
roads
Difficulty: Easy to moderate
Elevation Gain: 280 feet, North Lake beach parking to top of South Mountain
Comments: Check the maps and decide before you go what options you may want to take on your return. With a little planning, you can place a second car for a convenient return trip.

This orienting hike is the most direct path to Boulder Rock and the Hotel Kaaterskill. It serves to familiarize the hiker with the locations of the lesser-known spots on South Mountain. Highlights include extensive views of the Hudson Valley; a variety of geological features, including thick conglomerate beds and glacial markings; one of the most diverse forests in the Catskills; the ruins of the Hotel Kaaterskill; and—after an initial steep climb—a long, level walk on an old carriage road.

To get to Pine Orchard, enter North–South Lake Public Campground (fee required) and take the first right-hand turn after the gatehouse. Pass the earthen dam at the end of South Lake and drive past the beach parking area to the parking area near the picnic pavilion. A sign will direct you to the Mountain House site in Pine Orchard.

As described, this is an easy to moderate, one-way hike of about 1.5 miles, or 3.0 miles round-trip. You will have to walk back to the starting point, or you can park a second car at either the Scutt Road parking area or near the South Lake dam.

The Catskills are composed of sedimentary rock layers, and these layers stand out clearly to anyone who approaches the eastern escarpment after a light snowfall. They also are very apparent to all of us who hike these mountains. Most ascents in the Catskills consist of a series of steep uphill climbs ascending strata, alternating with short distances of level walking along the surfaces of the layers—not unlike climbing an enormous staircase. The climb up South Mountain is such a staircase. There are a number of small ledges, but two distinctive conglomerate layers stand out. They are the Pudding-Stone Hall ledge and, above it, the Fairy Spring

Keeping these two layers in mind will help us locate the sites on South Mountain.

Our first hike follows the blue-marked trail that is part of the Escarpment Trail maintained by New York State. The trail has been in use since approximately 1891[17] and will help us orient ourselves for a more detailed exploration of older walks that are no longer marked.

As we follow the blue-marked trail from near the historic marker at Pine Orchard to Boulder Rock, we first go up a steep hill by way of a zigzag path around the eroded trail that was here until fall 2003. The hill ends at the top of what Van Loan calls "the second ledge."[18] The blue trail levels off a bit at the top of the second ledge and then starts a gradual climb over what appears to be a very old path. Note the low stone wall that supports the left side of the path and possibly dates from the 1891 trail construction. At the end of this short stretch, the blue trail encounters the Pudding-Stone Hall ledge. The exposed face of this conglomerate layer nearly encircles South Mountain, and we will explore it thoroughly on Hike 3. Cracks and breaks in the layer allow us to negotiate the ledge at several interesting places, including Pudding-Stone Hall and Fat Man's Delight as well as this unnamed slope on the blue trail. In one spot large fragments of the ledge have weathered away to create Druid Rocks. A view of the cliff itself at the Sphinx was the destination of a noteworthy scramble for nineteenth-century hikers.

A "realphoto" postcard of the Catskill Mountain House circa 1907.

Looking South from South Mountain. *Harry Fenn, 1870, engraving in Picturesque America. The location is somewhere along the ledge below the direct path to South Mountain, probably in the area of Eagle Rock.*

Boot Jack Rock, on the west side of the trail near Eagle Rock, has several antebellum initials. Postcard, courtesy of Scott Koster.

When we climb to the top of the conglomerate layer, the "new" 1891 section rejoins an older part of the trail and we are now on what Rusk and Van Loan call "the direct path to South Mountain." Our eyes catch an imposing rock to the right of the trail here—a glacial erratic. It seems to be thrust upward at an angle, creating a dramatic appearance. A Herman Bickelmann postcard from the early 1900s names this Boot Jack Rock.[19] The several old, nicely engraved initials on this rock date back to the 1850s.[20] Careful observers have pointed out that many of these names and initials recur in important sites throughout the Kaaterskill area. To our left is the first good view of the valley since we left the Mountain House site. This is Eagle Rock [**N 42° 11.555´ – W 74° 2.148´ – elev. 2,410 ft.**]

Continue south on this level section of trail. A little beyond the view at Eagle Rock, the ledge to the left changes to a steep, wooded hillside before we reach a second outlook ledge called the Sphinx [**N 42° 11.527´ – W 74° 2.152´ – elev. 2,410 ft.**] This slope between the two ledges was the location of the path that led to a shelf below Eagle Rock on the north and the Sphinx on the south. Fenn's illustration *Looking South from South Mountain* may depict the ledges below this outlook. It is still possible to scramble down the slope and go to the base of either ledge. The conglomerate is particularly thick here, and the size of the embedded cobbles indicates that a strong current deposited them. The cliff that makes up the Sphinx still juts out, but a twenty-first-century eye may have great difficulty seeing any resemblance to that Egyptian monument. The top of this layer provides still another spectacular view—from Boulder Rock farther along—but first we need to climb the next level before we return to this level.

Leaving the top of the Sphinx and continuing south along the blue trail, we walk over hemlock roots that spread across this often muddy section of the trail, and soon climb uphill over the next conglomerate layer. This is the layer of the Lemon Squeezer and Fairy Spring, but here the layer is mostly covered by soil. At the top we reach the eastern summit of South Mountain (or as near to the top as the blue trail allows). From here our trail takes us along the east face of South Mountain toward the junction with the trail to Boulder Rock. South Mountain is now covered with forest, but in the 1870s it had been denuded of trees by forest fires. If we were to have walked along this area at that time, we would have been able to see the top of South Mountain to our right. On the top was the largest of many nearby glacial erratics. It was distinguished by a star painted on it and was named Star Rock [**N 42° 11.487′ – W 74° 2.254′ – elev. 2,483 ft.**] We'll see it later.

A pleasant little moss-covered hollow and shallow pool is just off the blue trail to the west, before we reach the junction to Boulder Rock. It is not mentioned in the earlier guides; without the forest, perhaps, direct sunlight may have evaporated the water that now collects there and prevented the growth of moss. Thankfully the forest has returned and we again recognize the debt we owe to New York State. If you leave the trail, tread carefully so as not to disturb these special places.

On the left of this section of trail, we pass an eroded slope. With a careful look below you may see an iron pipe in the rock. Van Loan shows this as a landslide and something called US Signal (US Coast Survey Signal) [**N 42°11.444′– W 74° 2.192′ – elev. 2,400 ft.**] Surveys were taken of the area in the early 1800s, and this is most likely related to those early surveys. Don't go down the slide to see it; it is possible to reach the spot easily from Boulder Rock without contributing to the erosion of the slope.

Walk the short distance to the junction [**N 42° 11.439′ – W 74° 2.250′ – elev. 2,470 ft.**] of the trail to Boulder Rock. This was the boundary of the Hotel Kaaterskill and Mountain House properties. If you continue straight (the red trail to the right), you will be walking along Sugar Loaf Drive—a carriage road operated by the Kaaterskill. We will take the left, blue trail

View of the Hudson Valley, from South Mountain. *From an 1884 picture folder published by Wittemann Bros., courtesy of Larry Tompkins. Looking down on Palenville Overlook and the Dodd House from Boulder Rock. Palenville is at the foot of the clove, with the Hudson River in the distance. The road depicted on the ledge below is the path traveled on Hike 6.*

downhill 0.1 mile to Boulder Rock [N 42° 11.361′ – W 74° 2.256′ – elev. 2,374 ft.] and then rejoin the carriage road by an interesting detour. The Boulder Rock area is another must-see and a great spot for lunch. It has been a favorite destination from North Lake for 180 years and deserves special consideration. The view is magnificent, the boulder makes a good photo backdrop, and the warm sun is welcome on all but the hottest days. The Hudson Valley, Palenville, Kaaterskill High Peak, and Round Top are in view. Looking south, see if you can pick out Sky Top and Bonticou Crag in the Shawangunks near New Paltz.

A small set of two or three steps placed against the boulder in the 1870s made climbing it much less difficult than it is today, but an amusing illustration in Warner's "Their Pilgrimage" shows that it was still a challenge for some. Today the south side is a relatively easy climb even without the steps, but the north side is quite dangerous.

The top surface of the ledge is what Robert Titus calls a "dance floor," a ledge polished and striated by a passing glacier. Titus discusses the feature in his book *The Catskills in the Ice Age* and in an article written for the winter 1998–99 issue of *Kaatskill Life.* Look here, and on the ledge just south of the boulder, for signs of glacial movement. The view of the valley below also shows signs of glacial erosion. The complexity of glacial activity in the area is an interesting story that is still being written.

North of Boulder Rock, on the same ledge, we will find a narrow crevice called Fat Man's Delight [N 42° 11.370′ – W 74° 2.237′]. The crevice makes a good access route to the area below the boulder, and in days past was part of a trail to Palenville Overlook. (The old trail could be reopened and would make an interesting addition to the hikes on South Mountain, but for now it is best to reach Palenville Overlook by other routes.) It is fun to descend through the crevice and explore the area a short distance south from the bottom of Fat Man's Delight. Stay next to the ledge until you pass below the boulder. Walk between the wall of the escarpment and a huge rock that has split away. Beyond this passageway and a few yards downhill, another large boulder—split in two—supports a smaller rock bridging its two parts. Postcards of the early twentieth century gave this minor formation the rather grandiose name "Natural Bridge of the Catskills." After exploring this and some of the other detached rocks along the ledge, return to the level of Boulder Rock by way of Fat Man's Delight.

For the few who want to see the iron post known as US Signal, the easiest way is from this spot at the top of Fat Man's Delight. Walk a short distance north until you are directly below the eroded slope that we passed as we walked along the blue trail at the top of South Mountain. The post is near the edge of the escarpment. It is shown on Van Loan's map near a landslide on the east face of South Mountain just north of the boulder. Ed West pointed out and identified the iron post for me many years ago.

Excursionists. *C.S. Reinhart engraving in Charles Dudley Warner's 1884* Harper's Monthly *romance, "Their Pilgrimage." Two young women sit pensively while a more active group of working-class day excursionists explore Boulder Rock and the Natural Bridge. The story traces the summer wanderings of several well-to-do travelers of the 1880s. "Their Pilgrimage" has been recently republished, and the full text can be found on the Internet.*

The best course from this point is to retrace our steps back to Boulder Rock. Any descent below this ledge is very dangerous, and the climb up the hill from US Signal merely leads us back to the trail that we passed earlier and will further erode the already fragile slope.

Back at the boulder take a last look at the view before you continue your walk to the Hotel Kaaterskill site. Concentrate on things nearer at hand. Photos and drawings of the area prove that it was once much more open than it is now. One drawing shows the ledges below with so few trees that Palenville Overlook and the house that stood on the brink of that dramatic cliff were easily visible. Several old postcards of Boulder Rock show Hotel Kaaterskill clearly visible to the southwest. Trees would now obscure our view of the hotel if it still stood.

The great success of the Catskill Mountain House spawned many smaller hotels and boardinghouses, and one resort—the Hotel Kaaterskill, built in 1881—that hoped to surpass the premier hotel of the Catskills. According to legend, the Hotel Kaaterskill was built because George Harding, a wealthy lawyer from Philadelphia who was staying at the Mountain House, was unable to get fried chicken for his daughter who was ill and on a special diet. If the legend is correct, less than a year passed between the July 1880 chicken incident and the opening of the new hotel on South Mountain on June 27, 1881. Only forty-three years later, on September 8, 1924, workers making soap with the grease collected from the just-completed season's cooking accidentally set a fire that soon roared out of control and destroyed the hotel.

The stairway from Boulder Rock to the base of the ledge. This was the beginning of a trail that passed the Natural Bridge and led to Palenville Overlook.

During its short life the Hotel Kaaterskill—with its modern lighting, telephone service, and superior facilities—attracted many notable guests, including playwright Oscar Wilde, former president Ulysses S. Grant, and then-president Chester A. Arthur, but it never did eclipse the Mountain House in historic stature or as the premier hotel of the region.

The site of the Hotel Kaaterskill still shows many signs of the resort and of the fire. Be careful not to get injured on sharp objects or rusty metal. As you explore the area please don't move or take artifacts. They are of no value except for historic research and, consequently, are best left in place. All you will find are broken pieces of toilets, miniscule chips of old plates, rusted pipes, electrical cable, and heat-distorted chunks of metal.

To get to the site, follow the blue trail along the top of the conglomerate ledge. Several pieces of the ledge beyond Boulder Rock have split away and stand like islands. The ledge shows interesting signs of glacial action that are described in Robert Titus's later editions of *The Catskills in the Ice Age.* As the trail climbs gently we may see signs of an airplane crash off to the left. Soon we come to a junction with Sugar Loaf Drive, the Hotel Kaaterskill carriage road. Directly ahead, a few hundred feet through the woods is the marsh at Fairy Spring. To the right is the red trail back to the point on the blue trail where we turned to go to Boulder Rock. To the left is the road to the Hotel Kaaterskill.

Natural Bridge, just below Boulder Rock on the original trail to Palenville Overlook. Postcard, circa 1905.

Continue southwest along the level carriage road, following the blue markers. The road was once much wider, as we will see in places where the built-up stonework defines the edges. In the heyday of the Hotel Kaaterskill, elegantly dressed, wealthy patrons of

Note the lack of forest on South Mountain in this view of the Hotel Kaaterskill from Boulder Rock. Postcard, circa 1908.

the hotel rode in carriages along this route. The cleared forest allowed views of the Hudson Valley and the mountains above the clove to the south. The illustration *On the Road from Kaaterskill Hotel* from A.E.P. Searing's *The Land of Rip Van Winkle* depicts this road in the 1880s. Today a more diverse mix of visitors finds this an excellent stretch of trail to walk, bike, snowshoe, and cross-country ski. About 0.3 mile from the area of Fairy Spring, we will pass an unmarked carriage road on the right [N 42° 11.358′ – W 74° 2.723′ – elev. 2,420 ft.] This is the most direct way down to the road from the dam at the outlet of South Lake and the South Lake beach and parking area. In winter it makes a nice snowshoe walk, but obstacles in the path make it dangerous for cross-country skis.

Continue past this junction until your path approaches four other paths. This is an important crossroads that we pass through on several hikes [N 42° 11.292′ – W 74° 3.016′ – elev. 2,430 ft.] I've labeled it "Location K" (for Kaaterskill) on the hike charts. To the immediate left a path drops down to the trails on the clove rim and the spectacular views from Sunset Rock and Inspiration Point. It also connects with a trail to Palenville Overlook and the road, built for the Hotel Kaaterskill, that can take you to White Road in Palenville (see Hike 9: The Road That Couldn't Be Built). To the right of that, a path leads to the foot of Scutt Road. The next two paths are actually opposite ends of a single path circling the Hotel Kaaterskill site. Take that path and select the right branch. You will want to explore the area; a general outline may help get you started.

The path around the site soon approaches a stand of scrub trees on a small hill to your left. This is the site of the main building of the Hotel Kaaterskill [N 42° 11.356′ – W 74° 2.941′ – elev. 2,470 ft.] Several timbers and some hardware on the right may have been part of a bridge between the hotel and its annex. Proceed a short distance ahead and follow the road as it turns to the left. We now stand between the main hotel on the left and the annex on the right. The bridge connecting the buildings would have been above our heads. Downhill to the right are a clearing and the remains of the stone footings of the annex [N 42° 11.415′ – W 74° 2.891′ – elev. 2,460 ft.] and what appear to be fragments of toilet fixtures. You may want to trace out the size of the annex. It is less disturbed than the main building. Please respect the site and leave it undisturbed.

Return to the road that circles the main building and continue until you see a foot-worn path on the right. This leads to a small pond [N 42° 11.430′ – W 74° 3.029′ – elev. 2,440 ft.] and large stone cistern. The pond, like North Lake, seems to be in a glacially scoured basin. A sloping, stone shoreline is covered with glacial markings showing the northwesterly motion of the glacier as it moved over South Mountain. (Several of the scratches deepen to the northwest and abruptly stop—a sign that the glacier moved in that direction.) Scratches of this type are not uncommon in the area, but this is one of the best places to see them. A man-made dam

On the Road from Kaaterskill Hotel. *A.E.P. Searing's* The Land of Rip Van Winkle, *1884. Sugarloaf Drive, now part of the blue trail on South Mountain, makes a superb cross-country ski and snowshoe trail.*

holds the water in place. On the other side of the dam is a surprisingly large, well-like structure of stone and concrete that was obviously part of the water system for the hotel. There is quite a lot of old barbed wire here; be careful.

At the site of the main building, small trees grow amid old stone footings, which hardly seem adequate for what was said to be the largest

NEW HOTEL IN THE CATSKILLS.

HOTEL KAATERSKILL,

THE LARGEST MOUNTAIN HOTEL IN THE WORLD.

Open from June 25 to October 1, 1883.

Three Thousand Feet above the Sea. Commands Sixty Miles' View of the Hudson River.

THE PURE, COOL AIR AFFORDS CURE FOR MALARIA AND HAY FEVER.

TOLL'S GERMANIA ORCHESTRA BAND.

EVERY MODERN CONVENIENCE—BATHS, CLOSETS, GAS, ELEVATORS, ETC.

FOR TERMS, MODES OF ACCESS, etc., address

E. A. GILLETTE,

HOTEL KAATERSKILL, KAATERSKILL P. O., GREENE CO., N. Y.

Route from New York, via Stony Clove and Kaaterskill R.R. Route.

Via New York Central and Hudson River Railroad, or Day Boat, to Rhinebeck and Rondout, thence *via* Ulster and Delaware Railroad and Stony Clove and Kaaterskill Railroad to Kaaterskill Station; or take the New York, West Shore and Buffalo Railway to Kingston; thence *via* Ulster and Delaware Railroad, Stony Clove and Kaaterskill Railroad to Kaaterskill Station; half-mile distance from Hotel.

An 1883 advertisement for the Hotel Kaaterskill still shows elaborate observation towers. The final towers were of a much more modest design—if anything about the Kaaterskill could be called modest. Van Loan's Catskill Mountain Guide, *1883 edition. Courtesy of Justine and Hillard Hommel.*

The road in the foreground is the trail that loops around the Hotel Kaaterskill site, which is now covered with small birch and white pine. Postcard, circa 1915, courtesy of Mountain Top Historical Society.

mountain hotel in the world. It is interesting to trace out the shape and imagine what this magnificent hotel must have been like.

From here we can return the way we came or take an alternate route back. See the maps or check the mile-by-mile trail list.

Lovers' Retreat: Unadvisable Path

A popular short walk from the Catskill Mountain House was to a spot named Lovers' Retreat, where the roots of two trees entwined to form a seat where a romantic couple could gaze at the Hudson Valley below. The path started at the south edge of Pine Orchard ledge.

An unmarked trail still exists here, but after a short distance it becomes precarious at best and could spell real danger.[21] I suspect that ladders, railings, or some other aid may have been provided for Mountain House guests, and that a path may have existed that joined with the built-up section of the blue trail just below the Pudding-Stone Hall ledge.[22]

A hollowed-out stratum along this path supports tales that vacationers dug caves in the softer ledges in search of gold. The dig has a column of stone left in place for support. At least one apparent chisel hole can still be seen.

GPS and Map Data	Description	Directions and Comments
0.0 mi. N 42° 11.686′ W 74° 2.076′ Elev. 2,225 ft.	Pine Orchard and the Catskill Mountain House site. This is the center of our exploration of the Kaaterskill region. From here, James Fenimore Cooper tells us we can look out over "all creation." Trails started from this location as early as the 1820s, making these among the oldest recreational mountain trails in the country.	Start at the historic marker at the south edge of the clearing.
	Trail starts uphill. I suspect that the present trail is to the east of the nineteenth-century trail. A bushwhack uphill to the right approximates my best guess of the original trail. For now, stay on the marked trail.	From the historic marker at the Mountain House site, follow the blue trail south as it climbs a steep hillside. As of fall 2003 this was eased by creating a zigzag in the trail.
	Boulders in the path. Keep an eye out to the left for indications of an old path that I believe came from Lovers' Retreat.	Continue on blue trail past some boulders as the trail levels off.
	The current path is built up with stones that apparently made the going easier for elegantly dressed nineteenth-century walkers. Even so, this was not the original, direct path to South Mountain, but a path constructed sometime around 1891.	Trail approaches the base of a ledge.
	Pudding stone, or conglomerate, formed from sediment in very rapidly moving water. This is the site of a 350-million-year-old flood. On a later hike we will pass through Pudding-Stone Hall on this same ledge.	Stay on blue trail as you ascend the ledge to the area of Eagle Rock. Once at the top, there is one more ledge to go to the top of South Mountain.
0.2 mi. N 42° 11.555′ W 74° 2.148′ Elev. 2,410 ft.	To the left of the trail, Eagle Rock has another fine view of the Hudson Valley with Palenville below to your right. To the right of the trail is Boot Jack Rock. Note the carved names from the 1850s on it and the smaller rock nearby.	Take in the view from Eagle Rock, then continue south on the blue trail. In a few feet you pass a wooded slope to the left of the blue trail. This was the site of a path to the ledge below.

GPS and Map Data	Description	Directions and Comments
0.21 mi. N 42° 11.527´ W 74° 2.152´ Elev. 2,410 ft.	The Sphinx—a ledge on South Mountain— not to be confused with Sphinx Rock on Prospect Mountain near the Laurel House. The face of the cliff when viewed from below was said to resemble the Sphinx, but you would need a vivid imagination.	A few more paces and you pass another ledge. Known as the Sphinx, it is just off the blue trail on the left. The view is nearly identical to that at Eagle Rock.
0.24 mi.	Top of South Mountain. (The actual top is at Star Rock, which is part of Hike 3.)	Beyond the Sphinx, the path climbs to the highest point on this South Mountain trail.
0.25 mi. N 42° 11.444´ W 74° 2.192´ Elev. 2,400 ft.	US Signal below on left. Mossy pool in woods on right.	Continue on blue trail.
0.3 mi. N 42° 11.439´ W 74° 2.250´ Elev. 2,470 ft. **Location B**	Junction of blue escarpment trail with red trail to Hotel Kaaterskill site. This was the boundary of Catskill Mountain House and Hotel Kaaterskill properties. The carriage road from the Hotel Kaaterskill ended here in a cul-de-sac.	Turn left and follow the blue trail to Boulder Rock.
0.4 mi. N 42° 11.361´ W 74° 2.256´ Elev. 2,374 ft.	Boulder Rock. Both Van Loan and Rusk use an alternate spelling—"bowlder"—which I intentionally use on the map. Trail continues to the right (west), but you will want to explore this area. Nearby sites: Fat Man's Delight [N 42° 11.370´ – W74° 02.237´] is just 200 feet or so north of the boulder on same ledge. Natural Bridge. Go down through Fat Man's Delight and follow the ledge until you are just south of the boulder. The bridge is just downhill. US Signal [N 42° 11.444´ – W 74° 02.192´] is about 0.1 mi. north on top of the ledge.	The trail turns right at Boulder Rock, but you will want to explore the area before you continue. See description of nearby sites in the middle column.

GPS and Map Data	Description	Directions and Comments
0.45 mi.	Split Rocks. To the left, rocks have split away from the conglomerate ledge. Glacial polishing of the rocks of the trail is pronounced. Blueberries grow along the right side of the trail, and mountain laurel abounds.	Return to the trail where you first encountered Boulder Rock. Turn right at Boulder Rock and continue south-west, walking along the blue trail, with the top of the ledge on your left.
0.6 mi. N 42° 11.479′ W 74° 2.386′ Elev. 2,445 ft.	Junction on right with the other end of the red trail that we met at Location B (above). The blue trail turns left and follows the old car-riage road to Hotel Kaaterskill site. Maps published by the hotel call this road Sugar Loaf Drive. Note the American chestnut saplings and mountain laurel along the trail.	Turn left at junction to go to the Hotel Kaaterskill site. (If you wish to cut the hike short, take the red trail to the right. You will soon come to the spot where you turned off to go to Boulder Rock, and you will be able to retrace your steps back to Pine Orchard.)
0.95 mi. N 42° 11.358′ W 74° 2.723′ Elev. 2,420 ft.	An unmarked and unmaintained trail comes in from the right. This old road dates from the earliest days of the Hotel Kaaterskill. It descends to the modern vehicle road that leads to the South Lake beach. The trail is fairly open and makes a good snowshoe walk, but obstructions could cause problems for skiers. (If you left a car at the South Lake dam, this is the most direct bailout route but may not be easy to follow.) From the South Lake dam, this is the second trail on the right as you drive toward the beach. It may be difficult to follow, because at least one side trail joins from the east.	Junction with unmarked trail to the road to the South Lake beach. Continue on blue trail.

GPS and Map Data	Description	Directions and Comments
1.15 mi. N 42° 11.292′ W 74° 3.016′ Elev. 2,430 ft. **Location K**	A rather confusing junction of three marked and two unmarked trails. To the left a carriage road (marked blue) goes downhill and will provide access to the clove rim area at Location V. To the right of that, a second carriage road (marked red) leads past another route to the clove rim (Location R) and then to the bottom of Scutt Road. To the right of that, an unmarked trail goes a short distance, then branches in two. The two branches are opposite ends of a loop around the site of the main building of the Hotel Kaaterskill. Take the right-most trail and then the right branch of the loop. This was the roadway in front of Hotel Kaaterskill.	Trail junction. Take right-most trail to Hotel Kaaterskill site. See middle column for detailed description.
1.25 mi. N 42° 11.356′ W 74° 2.941′ Elev. 2,470 ft.	Hotel Kaaterskill site. Stone footings, BX electrical cable, and assorted shards and debris mark the location of the once-magnificent hotel.	Uphill on the left side of the trail, small trees are growing amid the stone footings of the Kaaterskill main building.
1.3 mi. N 42° 11.415′ W 74° 2.891′ Elev. 2,460 ft.	Hotel Kaaterskill Annex. Rarely visited, this site is less disturbed than that of the main building.	The trail turns to the left and passes between the main building (on the left) and the annex (on the right).
N 42° 11.430′ W 74° 3.029′ Elev. 2,440 ft.	Pond and water-holding tank.	Path continues, turns left, and passes between the back of the old building site and a small pond.
N 42° 11.430′ W 74° 3.029′ Elev. 2,440 ft.	The hike ends in the middle of the woods! You have several options: 1. Retrace steps to Pine Orchard. 2. From the trail junction at 1.15 mi. (above), take the trail leading to the bottom of Scutt Road. From the junction at the bottom of the hill, you can follow the path to the right back to the South Lake dam, or cross the footbridge and walk uphill to the Scutt Road parking area. 3. Combine this walk with a walk along the Clove Rim (see Hike 4).	Back to the loop path and continue past a modern shale bank to the other end of the loop at Location K.

View of the Central Façade of the Hotel Kaaterskill from the Esplanade.
A detail of the façade of the Kaaterskill, from "Kaaterskill Mountains", an advertising brochure circa 1893. Courtesy of Justine and Hillard Hommel.

Sites in the North Lake Area

This is not really a hike, but a list of sites within the campground that you will want to see. If you are a day visitor, you can park at the North Lake Beach parking area and see most of the sites within less than an hour.

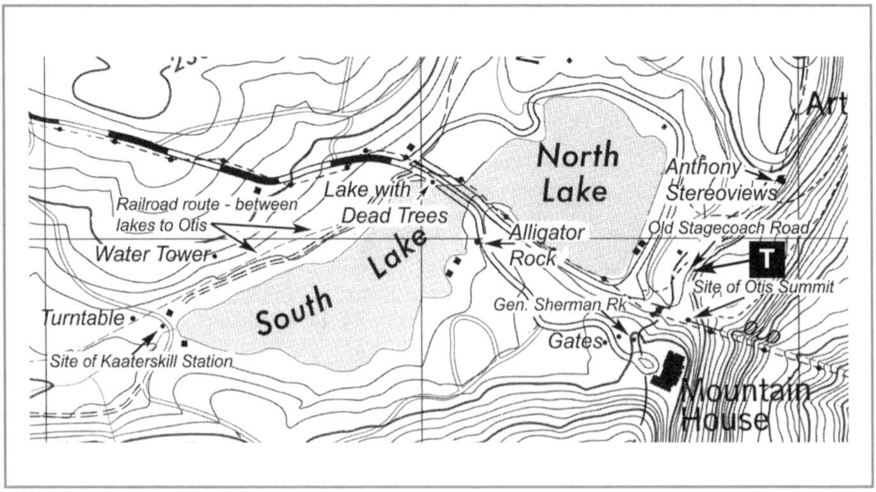

"It's like riding up to the moon," says the note on the back of this postcard sent in 1915. Courtesy of Justine and Hillard Hommel.

GPS and Map Data	Description	Directions and Comments
N 42° 11.880′ W 74° 2.145′ Elev. 2,130 ft.	North Lake beach area.	Walk across the parking lot, pass the restrooms, and come to the fence at the ledge. Turn south (right) and pass the fence.
Location T N 42° 11.839′ W 74° 2.071′ Elev. 2,150 ft.	Mountain Turnpike. The old road to the east (left) is the carriage road to Palenville. Don't descend the road. That's part of another walk.	Continuing south, pass the old road and go down a slight hill into an open area. Turn left and walk to the log rail at the top of the escarpment where power lines come up from the valley.
N 42° 11.781′ W 74° 2.059′ Elev. 2,140 ft.	Summit Station and head of Otis Elevating Railway. The Otis had two cars connected by a cable the length of the descent in front of you. The engine was housed in the Summit Station at this location.	Turn around and walk west. Follow the paved trail next to North Lake until the path ends at the spot where North and South lakes meet.
N 42° 11.936′ W 74° 2.446′ Elev. 2,140 ft.	This is where the Huckleberry Railway along the south side of North Lake crossed between the lakes and then continued west toward Haines Falls. At the water's edge the view to the left is approximately that of Thomas Cole's 1825 painting *Lake with Dead Trees.* The mountain in the distance is Round Top. From here it is not lined up as it is in Cole's painting. To see the view aligned as the artist depicted, you will have to go to the other side of the lake, directly across from this spot.	Until recently the path crossed between the lakes at this point. Now, it will be necessary to walk around the lake. The path is directly across from the caretaker's cabin in Loop 1 of the campsites.

GPS and Map Data	Description	Directions and Comments
		Turn left and follow the connecting trail toward South Lake parking area.
N 42° 11.852′ W 74° 2.413′ Elev. 2,150 ft.	Alligator Rock on the right is unmistakable. Maintaining the "teeth" is a job that has been taken on by many generations of Catskill vacationers.	Alligator Rock
	Mountain House access parking area and South Lake picnic pavilion. The South Lake beach parking area is along the road beyond the pavilion. Should you want to walk around the lakes, a trail leads from the west side of the beach along the shore of South Lake to the dam at the end of the lake.	At the parking area, turn left, walk through the lot to the gate at the old road, and follow the path toward the Mountain House site.
N 42° 11.726′ W 74° 2.162′ Elev. 2,190 ft.	Stone gateposts of the original entrance to Mountain House grounds.	Follow this road, always bearing right. This is the approach to the Mountain House.
N 42° 11.739′ W 74° 2.143′	General Sherman's Rock (author's designation). Around 1890, just months before he died, General William Tecumseh Sherman visited the Mountain House. While there, he posed in front of this rock with several children. The photograph was published in Roland Van Zandt's *The Catskill Mountain House.*	As you pass between the stone gates, look off to the left. There you will see a large rock. In 1890 the rock had its moment of fame.
N 42° 11.687′ W 74° 2.076′ Elev. 2,225 ft.	Pine Orchard, the site of the Mountain House and its spectacular views.	Follow the blue escarpment trail north to return to the North Lake parking area.
		Walk around North Lake to the caretaker's cabin, or drive to the parking area near the South Lake dam and follow the trail on the north side of the lake to the caretaker's cabin.

GPS and Map Data	Description	Directions and Comments
N 42° 11.967´ W 74° 2.530´ Elev. 2,140 ft.	Site of Thomas Cole's painting *Lake with Dead Trees,* one of three paintings executed by Cole in the fall of 1825. If Cole's depiction is accurate, South Lake must have risen beyond its earlier bank, flooding and killing several large trees near the lake's shore and creating the picturesque scene that Cole captured. The painting captured the attention of the art community in New York City and launched Cole and the Hudson River School.	Follow the path toward the channel between North and South lakes. The Cole painting site is on the right.
N 42° 11.855´ W 74° 2.938´ Elev. 2,170 ft.	For railroad buffs, foundations of some of the old buildings associated with the two rail lines that were on the northwest shore of South Lake can be found just off the tracks between here and the South Lake dam.	Turn around and follow the yellow trail west (left) along the shore of South Lake. This trail parallels the path of the Catskill & Tannersville Railway.
N 42° 11.870´ W 74° 2.928´ Elev. 2,175 ft.	Water tower. Still standing near the path of the narrow-gauge Catskill and Tannersville Railway, this is one of the best preserved remnants of the days of the railroads.	You'll need a GPS or a bit of luck to locate the water tower in the woods above the yellow trail.
N 42° 11.773´ W 74° 3.040´ Elev. 2,140 ft.	Auto access to this area is available year-round. It is a popular staging area for cross-country skiing, snowshoeing, snowmobiling, and ice fishing. It also provides access to the old railroad grade.	Dam at foot of South Lake.
N 42° 11.773´ W 74° 3.169´ Elev. 2,140 ft.	Ulster and Delaware turntable. Alongside the path toward the wastewater treatment facility, you will find a hollowed-out area on the right. This was a turntable for the Ulster & Delaware railroad.	From the north side of the dam, find the path that goes west toward the wastewater facility. This was the old Ulster & Delaware railroad bed. The site of an old turntable is nearby.

Looking down the Otis tracks. The location is not far from the new picnic pavilion in the lower North Lake beach parking area. Postcard, courtesy of the Mountain Top Historical Society.

The ornate depot of the Kaaterskill Railroad (a division of the Ulster & Delaware Railroad) near the dam at South Lake. Postcard, circa 1907. Courtesy of Justine and Hillard Hommel.

Hike 3:
Circuit of South Mountain (A Twenty-First-Century Variation)

Distance: 1.75 miles round-trip
Type of Trail: Bushwhack, with portions along marked trails
Difficulty: Moderate because of terrain
Elevation Gain: 280 feet, North Lake beach parking to top of South Mountain
Comments: This hike is a bit of a bushwhack. It involves going off the beaten track and should only be taken with a companion who can seek help in case of an emergency, since others may not pass by. Please try to minimize impact on the area.

Both Rusk and Van Loan describe two routes up South Mountain from the Mountain House. (A third route near Lovers' Retreat is mentioned also, but the trails have changed since then and to protect the fragile soils, the best way to the top of South Mountain is by the state-maintained blue trail.)

The direct path led hikers through Pudding-Stone Hall, past Star Rock, and on to Boulder Rock. Today's blue escarpment trail up South Mountain dates from about 1891 and is east of the direct path.

The circuit of South Mountain went to the bottom of Pudding-Stone Hall and then circled counterclockwise around South Mountain, passing several interesting places before arriving at the escarpment rim. We will now attempt to retrace the Mountain House–era climb of South Mountain, and in doing so will discover several lost sites with charms that recall a more romantic time. Highlights include Pudding-Stone Hall, Druid Rocks, Fairy Spring, and what I think was known as the Lemon Squeezer.

From Pine Orchard west of the historic marker, take the blue-marked Escarpment Trail uphill. Rusk and Van Loan speak of climbing two ledges. If we stay on the state trail, we will have trouble finding where the first ledge ends and the second begins. This is the first clue that we are not exactly on the original trail. Follow the blue trail past the registration kiosk until the trail levels off.[23] Along this marked trail, the two ledges described in the old guides and distinguishable to the west are merged into a single hill. At the top of the hill you have reached the top of the second ledge. Turn right and walk a short distance without climbing. You will soon find the collapsed ruins of a water tower [N 42° 11.660′ – W 74° 2.170′ – elev. 2,310 ft.]

Markings on the valves indicate an early-twentieth-century manufacture. Please do not disturb the site.

Just to the west of the water tower, climb diagonally uphill to the base of the next ledge. I have seen indications that the path may have existed up this hill. The conglomerate ledge at the top of the hill will stop your progress. Turn to the right and walk a very short distance. You will come to Pudding-Stone Hall [N 42° 11.623′ – W 74° 2.212′ – elev. 2,407 ft.] It is an unmistakable crevice in the rock directly in front of you and is virtually unchanged since the accompanying stereoview was taken.

Pudding-Stone Hall, South Mountain. The cleft in the ledge not far from Eagle Rock is virtually unchanged from when this J. Loeffler stereoview was taken circa 1870. Note the two men in the cleft.

In an article in the summer 1996 issue of *Kaatskill Life,* Bob Titus indicated that he could not find Pudding-Stone Hall. His quest for the elusive outcrop formed the backdrop for an explanation of pudding stone (now called conglomerate), a sedimentary rock made up of pebbles and larger stones in a matrix of fine-grain material. Conglomerate is easily recognized. It looks like concrete with a great deal of embedded gravel. There are massive layers of it on South Mountain. The rock of Pudding-Stone Hall was formed in a rapidly moving stream coming from an enormous mountain range that once loomed to the east of the Catskills.

Before Titus's article and the accompanying stereoview, I was happy to believe that the Escarpment Trail passed over this layer at Pudding-Stone Hall south of the Mountain House. That's what Ed West had told me years ago when we walked the area. Harry Fenn's illustration from *Picturesque America* was just a romantic exaggeration, or so I believed.

But here in the Titus article was a photo—a Pudding-Stone Hall, not as grand as Fenn's, but definitely a match for Rusk's description of "a huge block of pudding-stone broken and separated" from the ledge. The location that for years I had mistakenly called Pudding-Stone Hall is just a steep climb up the conglomerate ledge at a different point. It is pudding stone, yes. But a hall? No!

Pudding-Stone Hall. *Harry Fenn, 1870, engraving in* Picturesque America. *This well-known illustration contributed to the difficulty in finding Pudding-Stone Hall. The hall is not this large, and the rocks are not tilted.*

Armed with a copy of Titus's article, my GPS unit, and a digital camera, I set out and finally found the famous outcrop. A few weeks later I had the good fortune to hike the area with Bob Titus. Together we searched for Prospect Rock, he led me to Sphinx Rock, and I brought him to Pudding-Stone Hall.

William Cullen Bryant's *Picturesque America* describes the scene:

The World-Famed View. *Postcard, circa 1915. Courtesy of Gary Slutzky. The famous view was at the doorstep of the Mountain House—a claim that the Hotel Kaaterskill could not make.*

> You have reached the level of a stratum of conglomerate of many feet in thickness, which lies across the top of this and the North Mountain. Some convulsion of Nature has riven off a piece of it, which now lies on the hill-side, many feet in thickness, and eighteen or twenty feet high. Between this and the solid rock is a passage several feet in length and two or three in width, to which someone has given the name of "Pudding-Stone Hall." Ferns are growing in the dark recesses of the rock, and water drips constantly into the cavity. Your path leads through the chasm, and by means of a pile of stones at the farther end … you climb up to the top of the ledge of conglomerate.[24]

If you turn east from the top of Pudding-Stone Hall and walk along the top of the ledge, you will find the blue trail near Eagle Rock. We will not climb through the hall, but instead continue west along the base of the ledge in our Circuit of South Mountain. Our intent here is to stay at this level (follow the contour) in search of Druid Rocks, climb to Fairy Spring, and then work our way up the ledge to the eastern crest of South Mountain.

The forest here has recovered from the fires that had denuded it in the nineteenth century. Any trail that existed here exists no longer. Rocks are moss-covered, the soil is often damp, and the undergrowth is cluttered with fallen branches. The most challenging task is not to find Druid Rocks or Fairy Spring, but to recognize that you have found them. We can only try to match the rocks that we see with the vague descriptions, fanciful drawings, and rare photos of that era, but taken together the photos, drawings, and descriptions do give pretty convincing evidence.

A few hundred feet past Pudding-Stone Hall, keeping the ledge at our left, we see the large boulders of Druid Rocks [**N 42° 11.624′ – W 74° 2.260′ – elev. 2,360 ft.**] below us to the right. If we look at these large boulders, we can probably find the rock depicted in Fenn's woodcut.

Druid Rocks. *Harry Fenn, 1870, engraving in* Picturesque America. *Fenn accurately captured one of the several boulders known as Druid Rocks. They are only a few hundred feet beyond Pudding-Stone Hall.*

These are large fragments of the conglomerate ledge that have broken loose by the action of frost, glaciers, or gravity and lie on the hillside. Once you are here, you'll need to judge what these rocks look like. They were seen as resembling many varieties of creatures in the nineteenth century, and were very popular among resort guests and excursionists. But not all who saw them joined in the game. Listen to the cynical comments of Philip Quilibet from an 1877 issue of *The Galaxy:*

> The greatest object of interest to the ordinary summer tourist is some rock, mound, or tree bearing a fancied resemblance to something which it could not by any possibility be. The grandest spectacle of nature—the majestic ocean, booming upon the beach at the base of a cliff and shone upon by the full-orbed moon; the snow-capped pinnacle piercing the clouds, the cataract roaring in the lonely glen, the yawning gorge between two vast mountains—these, I say never seem to excite as much interest in the average traveler as a stone that looks a little like a square box, or a hill that is backed a little like a turtle. … These chance physical resemblances are the unintentional puns of nature; they find profound admirers in all famous resorts. … So, in the Catskills we find remarkable interest developed in the Druid rocks, one of which is said to "resemble a gigantic toad—or rabbit," and also in "Alligator rock"—a boulder that by fortunate cracking apart gave the appearance of huge open jaws.[25]

I include Quilibet's comments so that we don't fall into the trap of oversimplifying the attitudes of early tourists to the mountains. But just as we are asked to suspend disbelief when we watch a play, we should put ourselves into a nineteenth-century romantic frame of mind as we seek these forgotten places. We may feel a connection with nature or begin to discover the sublime. We may even find that rock that looks like a bear. What better place to start than Druid Rocks?

We can ascend the ledge in several places near Druid Rocks to reach the top of the conglomerate ledge. We may encounter a bike trail that has been recently cut by mountain bike enthusiasts. If you turn east, you will be able to walk to the blue trail, which is about at this level. We will pass over the bike trail and continue on our circuit moving south and west until we reach the bottom of the next and final ledge. Our directions are unavoidably vague here because this is open woods, but the ledge circles most of the top of South Mountain and cannot be missed.

At that ledge turn right and follow the base of the cliff. Here, again, there is no clear trail. The ground is covered with forest debris. A GPS unit will be very helpful in relocating the points I describe, but be sure to use your compass to help keep your sense of direction. Batteries go dead rapidly in a GPS unit.

The first stop is at what is likely the Lemon Squeezer [**N 42° 11.521′ – W 74° 2.329′ – elev. 2,426 ft.**], sometimes known as Elfin Pass—a pass through the ledge to the top of South Mountain. This spot is in the location described by Van Loan and Rusk. The only problem is that it does not look like the only photo I've seen of the Lemon Squeezer—a stereoview[26] by Loeffler from the late 1800s. I've scoured the ledge and itemized at least seven possible passes, but none fit that photo!

Continue along the base of the ledge to Fairy Spring [**N 42° 11.497′ – W 74° 2.347′ – elev. 2,419 ft.**] This is easier to identify—the ledge at your left overhangs a quiet trickle of water, and there are several boards scattered around. This site was extremely popular in the nineteenth century, but it is virtually unheard of today. Years ago, on a hike with the Mountain Top Historical Society, we came across a mossy ledge with a number of weath-

Always a favorite photo background, Alligator Rock is just a short walk from the South Lake picnic pavilion. The tradition of placing rock teeth in the jaw continued from the earliest days. Postcard, circa 1908.

ered boards scattered on the ground. There had been some structure there at one time, and we suspected that we might have found Fairy Spring.

Years later, on a beautiful late-spring Saturday in 2002, my suspicions were confirmed. This was the first site that I located by using the GPS. Van Loan's map shows Fairy Spring to be at about the same latitude as Eagle Rock, and the same longitude as Boulder Rock. Using those two coordinates, I set a way-point in the GPS receiver and, starting from the trail junction near Boulder Rock, navigated to a ledge that looked promising. When I descended the ledge, I recognized the spot we had visited years before. I had arrived at Fairy Spring by a totally different route. My confidence was building. It didn't take long to match the scene with a nineteenth-century stereoview of the spot. Make the comparison for yourself and visit the site, for in the words of "a visitor" in one of the earliest guides to the area, "A view of this gem of the mountains compensates for any fatigue that may be encountered in the ramble."[27]

There is no view from here, yet the spot evokes a romantic sense of primitive forest. A short distance downhill, water gathers in the hollow between the two crests of South Mountain and forms a moss-covered basin. Small trees grow amid the scattering of rocks, extending their roots into the moist soil. This is the world of *A Midsummer Night's Dream.* Little wonder that our nineteenth-century forebears named a nearby rock cleft Elfin Pass, and the spot itself Fairy Spring.

Make your way back from Fairy Spring to the Lemon Squeezer (Elfin Pass), and climb through it to the top of South Mountain. Neither Rusk nor Van Loan mentions climbing through the Lemon Squeezer. That approach to the top of South Mountain comes from the earlier, anonymous *Guide to Rambles from the Catskill Mountain House,* which states: "after visiting the Spring, retrace your steps a short distance and turn to the south through a small fissure in the rock, and ascend to the summit of the South Mountain. This pass is known among the mountaineers as the 'LEMON SQUEEZER,' and among artists as the 'ELFIN PASS.'" [28] Walk to the southeast (a GPS unit is very handy here) and look for the boulder at the highest point on the mountain. This is Star Rock [N 42° 11.487′ – W 74° 2.254′ – elev. 2,483 ft.], which is a little harder to find now than in 1879 when, according to Rusk, "The summit of South Mountain and much of its sides [were] nearly barren." Star Rock is at the very top of the eastern summit of South Mountain and is now off trail and out of sight. There are inscriptions carved on top of its slanted surface. Farther to the east you will come upon the modern blue trail, not far from the junction to Boulder Rock. To continue the nineteenth-century itinerary of the Circuit of South Mountain, turn left on the blue trail and

Note the man standing at the opening of the Lemon Squeezer. The passage leads through the final ledge to the top of South Mountain. We have yet to find the location depicted in this J. Loeffler stereoview circa 1870.

return toward the Mountain House. (Refer to Hike 2 for other options from this point.)

On our way north, back to the Mountain House, we will descend a hill and arrive at the area of the Sphinx ledge. We passed this area on Hike 2. The top of the ledge is a little off to the east and down a three-foot-high rock step. The ledge is supposed to look like a sphinx when viewed from below. Van Loan suggests that a path to the north of the ledge led down to a spot to view the face. From below, the ledge overhangs a narrow shelf of a path with a steep, tree-lined slope below. The protruding exposure and a nineteenth-century imagination may allow you to see the Egyptian statue. The conglomerate that makes up the layer is particularly thick here, and the size of the embedded cobbles indicates that a strong current deposited them.

North of the Sphinx on the blue trail is Eagle Rock. The views here are similar to those at Pine Orchard—so much so that hikers are often so complacent that they pass this by. Back from the ledge, on the western side of the trail, the rather striking boulder projecting at an angle looks as if it should have a name. Just recently, a postcard surfaced showing the rock and giving it the name Boot Jack Rock. This is the only reference to this rock that I have ever seen. Some of the inscriptions on the rock date before the Civil War.

From this point we can either follow the blue trail back to Pine Orchard, or turn left before we descend the pudding stone ledge and return by way of Pudding-Stone Hall [N 42° 11.623′– W 74° 2.212′ – elev. 2,407 ft.], which is a few hundred feet to the west. When we reach Pine Orchard, we have completed the Circuit of South Mountain, a walk that is the essence of nineteenth-century Catskill romanticism.

Fairy Spring has changed very little since this J. Loeffler stereoview from the 1870s. Courtesy of Timothy J. Mallery.

GPS and Map Data	Description	Directions and Comments
0.0 mi. N 42° 11.686′ W 74° 2.076′ Elev. 2,229 ft.	Van Loan directs us to climb to the top of the second ledge. Since the trail was relocated around 1891, it is nearly impossible to distinguish two ledges. Farther to the west, where the original trail was, the two ledges are more distinct. Here, they blend together. Just climb until the trail levels off, and stop before you reach the conglomerate ledge. An old water tower is off in the woods to the right of the trail. It is perched at the top of the second ledge and makes a good landmark.	Start at the Mountain House historic sign at Pine Orchard. Follow the blue trail as it goes uphill and passes the registration book. Continue until the trail levels off. Turn right and leave the marked trail. Without climbing, walk along above the ledge. You will soon see the ruins of an old water tower.
0.1 mi. N 42° 11.660′ W 74° 2.170′ Elev. 2,310 ft.	Water tower ruins. Apparently a water supply tower for the Mountain House. Markings on some of the pipes indicate early-twentieth-century construction. Look, but don't touch. A little to the west, it appears that the trail may have started uphill to the base of the Pudding-Stone Hall ledge. Climb the hill. The conglomerate ledge at the top will cause you to stop. Turn right and follow the ledge.	From the tower continue diagonally uphill until you reach the next ledge. The pudding stone ledge is unmistakable. Turn right and walk along the base of the ledge. You will soon come to Pudding-Stone Hall. *Note: If you are uncomfortable with this type of walk, don't do it. The easiest thing to do is return the way you came. There are many other walks along more clearly marked trails. Check the Mountain Top Historical Society's website (*www.mths.org*) to see if there is a guided walk scheduled.*
0.16 mi. N 42° 11.623′ W 74° 2.212′ Elev. 2,407 ft.	Pudding-Stone Hall was the junction of the two popular climbs of South Mountain. The "direct path" went up through the crevice to the top of the ledge, turned east and returned to the blue trail near Eagle Rock. It then went on to Boulder Rock by what is now the state-marked trail. We could choose to do that now—the route is still easily passable. The Circuit of South Mountain went around Pudding-Stone Hall without climbing the ridge, stayed at the bottom of the pudding stone outcrop, and continued on to Druid Rocks and the other sites we are about to search out.	Pudding-Stone Hall looks exactly as it does in the old stereoview. When you reach it, don't climb through. Stay at this level and walk around the right of the crevice. Keep the pudding stone ledge at your left hand and walk along through the brush at the base of the ledge. In a few hundred feet you will see a large accumulation of boulders split off from the ledge. These are the Druid Rocks.

GPS and Map Data	Description	Directions and Comments
0.2 mi. N 42° 11.624′ W 74° 2.260′ Elev. 2,360 ft.	Druid Rocks. Take time to explore these once-popular moss and fern-covered megaliths.	
	The directions are necessarily vague here because GPS readings are difficult to make under heavy tree cover, and there is no marked trail.	There are several locations at and just beyond Druid Rocks where you can ascend the ridge; climb up. You are now at the level of the top of Pudding-Stone Hall.
	The ground here has a variety of low ridges, scattered boulders, and flat boggy areas. You may encounter a mountain bike trail that has recently been blazed by bike enthusiasts. If you've had enough, turn east (left) and follow the bike trail back to the blue trail and familiar ground. If you are up for more, cross the bike path and continue until you reach the base of the next (and final) ledge on South Mountain.	From the top of the ledge, walk south until you are stopped by a ledge very much like the one you just climbed. Then turn right and continue toward Fairy Spring and the Lemon Squeezer.
0.5 mi. N 42° 11.521′ W 74° 2.329′ Elev. 2,426 ft.	A pass through the Fairy Spring ledge to the top of South Mountain. This seems like a good possibility for the site. It doesn't look like the one photo I've seen—but neither does any other place I've found.	The Lemon Squeezer (my best guess)
0.55 mi. N 42° 11.497′ W 74° 2.347′ Elev. 2,419 ft.	A gentle trickle of water from the rock ledge under an overhang that looks nearly identical to the stereo photo from the mid-1800s. The beautiful and fragile moss-covered bog below conjures images of *A Midsummer Night's Dream.* In 2003 and on earlier visits, a number of boards were scattered on the ground under this ledge. On the chance that they may be of value to researchers, please leave them there.	Fairy Spring

GPS and Map Data	Description	Directions and Comments
0.6 mi		Backtrack to the Lemon Squeezer and climb through to the top of the ledge.
0.7 mi. N 42° 11.487′ W 74° 2.254′ Elev. 2,483 ft.	Star Rock is a boulder at the highest point of the eastern top of South Mountain. The rock is near a small ledge and its top surface is slanted. There are still names carved in its surface, but no sign of the painted star has survived the years since Van Loan described it. To get to the blue trail, make your way to the southeast, finding the easiest way down the nearby low ridge. You should come out near the junction leading to Boulder Rock.	Continue to the highest point on the mountain. A GPS unit is very useful here. The general compass direction is just south of east.
0.8 mi. N 42° 11.439′ W 74° 2.250′ Elev. 2,470 ft. **Location B**	Blue trail at junction to Boulder Rock. To complete the classic circuit, turn north and follow the blue trail to the Sphinx and Eagle Rock. From Eagle Rock you can either continue on the modern trail back to Pine Orchard, or turn west and follow the ridge back to the top of Pudding-Stone Hall and retrace your steps from there	If you don't have a GPS unit, a compass heading east will take you to either the blue or red trail near the Boulder Rock junction. When you reach either of those trails, a turn to the left will take you back to Pine Orchard.

Hike 4:
The Clove Rim—
Laurel House to Hotel Kaaterskill

Distance: 4.0 miles, approximately, round-trip
Type of Trail: Marked footpath and carriage roads
Difficulty: Easy to moderate
Elevation Gain: 490 feet, from Laurel House to Hotel Kaaterskill site
Comments: Parts of the trail along the clove rim are rocky. The ledges can be dangerous and should not be traveled by bike or cross-country skis.

This walk is one of the most beautiful in the Catskills. You will see more scenic views with less effort than is possible anywhere else in the Catskills. The hike is done in a loop, so one car is sufficient, but you may wish to take a second car and park it at the North Lake beach parking area so that you can combine this hike with Hike 1 (done in the opposite direction). There is a fee to enter North Lake.

Highlights include Kaaterskill Falls, Layman's Monument, Sunset Rock, Inspiration Point, and the Hotel Kaaterskill site. There are blueberries in summer and outstanding displays of mountain laurel in June, as well as extensive glacial markings showing that the local mountain topography actually caused the glacier to flow in a northwesterly direction. There is truly something for everyone along this amazing trail.

(For an alternate start and easier hike, see Hike 5: Scutt Road to Hotel Kaaterskill.)

Take Route 23A to Haines Falls and turn north onto County Route 18 (North Lake Road). In about 1.5 miles turn right onto Laurel House Road, go downhill and park your car at the parking area at the foot of the road [**N 42° 11.737′ – W 74° 3.790′ – elev. 2,085 ft.**] Railway buffs will want to poke around on either side of the road near the parking lot for signs of the two railroads that passed through here.

Walk through the gate and down the old road toward the site of the Laurel House. The Laurel House was the smallest of the three well-known hotels in the area, but commanded the most famous of the waterfalls. Rusk and Van Loan include an illustration of the Laurel House as it appeared in the 1880s. That illustration is reprinted later in this book. You may want to

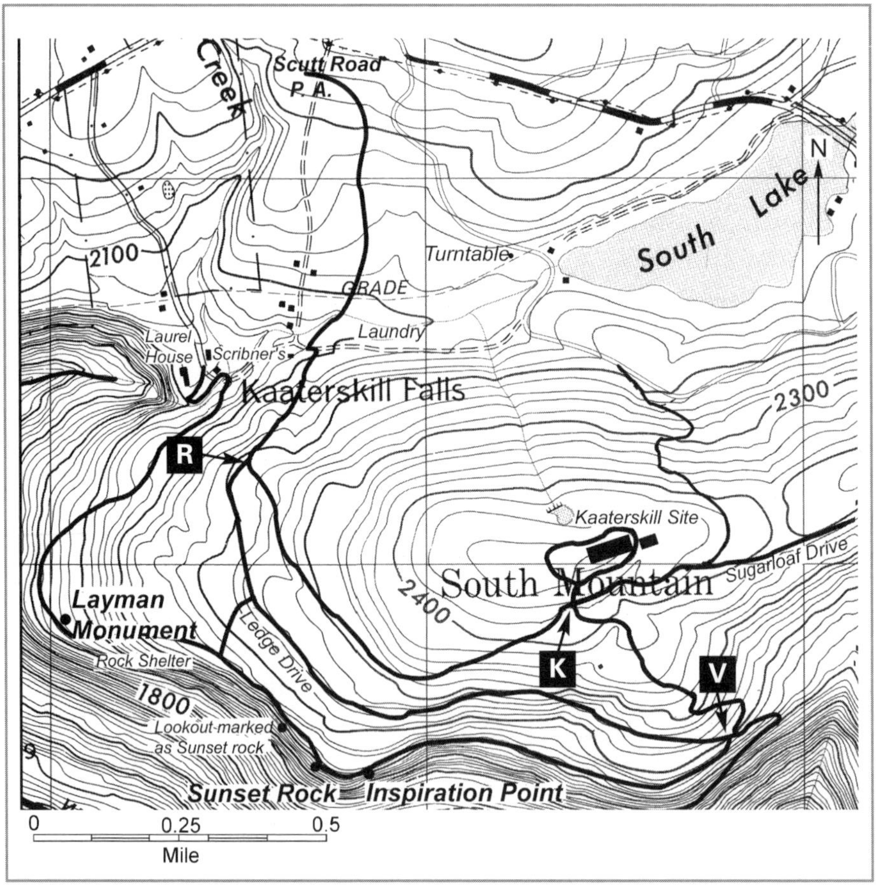

explore the area around the Laurel House site, but the main point of interest here is the top of Kaaterskill Falls [N 42° 11.604′ – W 74° 3.796′ – elev. 1,980 ft.]

First, a word of caution. The drop is 167 feet. The rocks at the top of the falls and in the streambed can be slippery, and you don't want to join the many that have fallen to their deaths. A small building known as the "spray house" and an observation platform were built on the large boulder at the top of the falls. The boulder is still a popular lookout point. You may notice the inscription S. R. Gifford, for Sanford Robinson Gifford (1823–1880), carved in the top of that boulder. Gifford was a well-known Hudson River School painter.

A dam held back the water of Lake Creek, the stream that feeds the waterfall, so it could be released to enhance the waterfall during the dry summer season. Guests were charged a fee of twenty-five cents and then would descend a stairway that started a few hundred feet west of the falls. Descending, they must have passed near the memorial to Vite, "The Bayard of Dogs." Once at the base of the falls, they could enjoy refreshments that were placed in a basket and lowered from the observation platform above. Fenn's illustration of the *First Leap of the Falls* shows the spray house and the basket. The stairs are long gone, and the trail that once led to the base of the falls became so badly eroded that the state found it necessary to close it. We will reach the bottom of the falls by the trail from Route 23A as part of Hike 10.

Follow Lake Creek upstream until you reach the remnants of the bridge that once crossed the stream. Make your way across the stream near this point. (If high current makes this too difficult, you may need to change plans and start at Scutt Road, where the state has provided a footbridge.)

Once across the stream, climb the hill and find the blue trail. Turn right (southwest) on the trail, which will lead through flat open woods, then downhill toward Layman's Monument. Layman's Monument [N 42° 11.344′ – W 74° 4.093′ – elev. 1,840 ft.] was not on any of the original trails of the area.[29] The monument was constructed to honor Frank D. Layman, who lost his life fighting a forest fire here on August 10, 1900. This is an appropriate spot to remember that local residents are often put in danger attempting to aid hikers, campers, and climbers. Your caution in a wilderness area not only protects your safety, but also avoids putting others into unnecessary danger. Layman's Monument commands a view of the upper clove, Haines Falls, and the parking area on Route 23A.

Continue past Layman's Monument and shortly the trail turns left and starts uphill. (It is easy to miss this turn.) About 0.1 mile past the monument you will come to a good lookout with a glacial erratic that forms a rock shelter. This is probably Council Bluff [N 42° 11.282′ – W 74° 4.060′ – elev. 1,937 ft.]

The Laurel House at the Kauterskill Falls. *Thomas Nast, "Sketches among the Catskills," 1866. The Laurel House before the additions transformed it into the third major area hotel. Note the top of the spray house at the right end of the fence.*

View from the Laurel House Piazza. From an 1884 picture folder published by Wittemann Bros. Courtesy of Larry Tompkins.

Before the 1900 fire, a trail went straight from the Laurel House to Sunset Rock. A side trail led from that trail to this lookout.

Continue uphill. The trail climbs a ledge and passes through a rift between the ledge and a separated rock, notable in that you can easily see how the two surfaces fit together. Continue uphill and you will soon reach the side trail [**N 42° 11.226´ – W 74° 3.730´ – elev. 2,190 ft.**] to the left that leads to Ledge Drive, a carriage road built by Harding as part of what the Hotel Kaaterskill called "Kaaterskill Park." It is now a horse trail. About 0.1 mile beyond this, you will come to the outlook [**N 42° 11.182´ – W 74° 3.623´ – elev. 2,190 ft.**] mistakenly labeled Sunset Rock. This spot probably never had a name, and it is certainly not the Sunset Rock of the nineteenth century. The original Sunset Rock [**N 42° 11.081´ – W 74° 3.522´ – elev. 2,120 ft.**] is ahead and downhill—it may be labeled Inspiration Point, but it is without question the original Sunset Rock.

More than any other spot, the original Sunset Rock inspired me to write this guide. The guidebooks of the Mountain House era praised Sunset Rock as the most spectacular view on the rim of Kaaterskill Clove. It was engraved, painted, and photographed, and was the major destination along the clove rim. Yet when I walked the rim to the ledge marked with a signpost pro-

The basket suspended from the end of a pole attached to the spray house's observation platform was used to lower refreshments to visitors who had descended the nearby stairway to the base of Kaaterskill Falls. Stereoview, 1870s.

claiming it to be Sunset Rock, I wasn't nearly as impressed as I was by other, nearby locations. When I looked over photos on postcards, stereopticon views, and the engravings of Harry Fenn and others, I discovered the reason. The spot now marked Sunset Rock was never depicted in those images.

Starting sometime after 1910, some postcards of Sunset Rock began to be labeled Inspiration Point, while others retained the original name. The earliest example I've found is a linen-finish postcard for sale on Ebay that was said to be postmarked 1916. By the 1950s the change of name was all but complete.

The misnaming of Sunset Rock was the first of many name changes of which I became aware. As I looked over the old maps and guides, I began to discover that nearly half of the popular spots of the nineteenth century were misnamed, relocated, or simply ignored. The beauty of each spot doesn't depend on its name, of course, but using the same names as in the past helps us to understand what early vacationers saw and why they were so impressed.

The original Sunset Rock on South Mountain is impressive on many levels. The view encompasses most of Kaaterskill Clove and part of Haines Falls. Round Top and High Peak tower above, while the Kaaterskill Creek flows below. The spot was described in *Picturesque America:*

> As you stand upon Sunset Rock and look westward up the Clove, you have one of the most picturesque views in the range of mountain scenery. The rock is broad and flat, projecting far out over the precipice. An old pine tree stands, like a sentinel, upon its very verge. In front of and behind you, as you sit by the old tree on the dizzy edge, the mountain pushes two great, gray cliffs, bald and ragged, far out over the glen, and then falls in broken lines a scarred and frowning precipice.

The Spray House at the top of Kaaterskill Falls. J. Loeffler stereoview circa 1870. Courtesy of Gary Slutzky.

The large rush of water probably means that the waters were released from the dam. This E.&H.T. Anthony stereoview was taken from the top of the stairway that led to the base of the falls. Note the observation platform and pole.

The lines of the South Mountain and of the spurs of High Peak and Round Top blend so gently together, as they meet beneath, that it is difficult to trace the bed of the Kauterskill or its tributary even by the shadows in the dense forest of green. Directly in front of you the table-land, which is formed by the shoulders of these mountains, rolls off toward the westward, where the sharp lines of Hunter Mountain are clearly defined against the sky among its sister peaks. Over the edge of this table-land leaps Haines's Fall. As in the accompanying engraving, it looks, from Sunset Rock, like a white spot in the dark forest—glittering for an instant in the sunlight, and then plunging down behind the waving tree-tops.[30]

Kaaterskill Falls. *Thomas Nast, "Sketches among the Catskills," 1866. Nast's engravings set a standard for the remainder of the nineteenth century.*

The surface of the bedrock here is scoured by glacial action, forming a surface sometimes called a "dance floor."[31] The direction of the glacial markings indicates that the ice that once filled the clove was moving northwest, deflected by High Peak and Round Top and forced up into the clove by the pressure of the continental glacier in the valley. Stand here and imagine the forces that shaped the land, and how the land shaped our nation. This spot was known throughout the world. It is one of those places that helped give America its identity.

So was there an Inspiration Point in the days of the Mountain House? Yes, and it was nearby. An image of the view from Inspiration Point showing the Hudson Valley, Point of Rocks, and the Harding Road to the Hotel Kaaterskill appeared (along with an image of the view from the original Sunset Rock) in an 1884 souvenir album of "Photo Views by Louis Glaser's Process." Inspiration Point also appears on Van Loan's map (though not on Rusk's). Van Loan shows it on the clove rim at the western tip of the cirquelike curve in the clove's north rim known as the Amphitheater. The location is about 500 feet to the east of Sunset Rock. Here the view opens to the east allowing us to see the Hudson Valley and the cliffs above the entrance to the clove—a view identical with the 1884 illustration. This is the original Inspiration Point. With few exceptions, later postcard images claiming to be Inspiration Point are actually the original Sunset Rock of earlier images.

This has caused great confusion among many of us interested in the Catskills, and we all like to take a stand. Here, in summary, is mine. The small ledge uphill and to the west of the original Sunset Rock is incorrectly labeled Sunset Rock today. It was most likely unnamed in the nineteenth century. The original Sunset Rock on South Mountain is the large open ledge [**N 42° 11.081′ – W 74° 3.522′ – elev. 2,120 ft.**] with a fine view of the upper part of the clove and Haines Falls to the west—a great place to see the sunset. The original Inspiration Point [**N 42° 11.066′ – W 74° 3.422′ – elev. 2,123 ft.**] is 500 feet east of the original Sunset Rock. It has a view down the clove to the east. The upper part of the clove is concealed, but a view of the valley floor and Point of Rocks has opened up.

Beyond Inspiration Point the trail continues along the clove rim through a beautiful mountain laurel patch until it reaches Belle View [**N 42° 11.129′ – W 74° 2.834′ – elev. 2180 ft.**] (apparently a fairly modern name) and, immediately afterward, the junction with Ledge Drive, the

The Sunset Rock ledge is very broad. This photo was taken from the western portion looking east. Postcard, circa 1906.

Sunset Rock. *Harry Fenn, 1870, engraving in* Picturesque America.

A rare early photo of Inspiration Point shows that it provided a view not possible from Sunset Rock. The same view is possible today from the trail along the clove rim about 500 feet east of the original Sunset Rock. From a J. Loeffler stereoview. Courtesy of Gary Slutzky.

Hotel Kaaterskill carriage road that is now a horse trail [N 42° 11.080′ – W 74° 2.764′ – elev. 2200 ft.] From here, if you've had enough, you can turn left, follow Ledge Drive until it meets the red trail at Location R, then turn left and go downhill to the foot of Scutt Road, where you can make a final left turn onto the blue trail and walk back to the point where you crossed Lake Creek by the ruins of the old bridge near the Laurel House.

If you have decided to continue to the Hotel Kaaterskill site, turn right and walk the short distance to the junction I designate as Location V [N 42° 11.129′ – W 74° 2.706′– elev. 2,210 ft.] This junction is the eastern end of Ledge Drive. Ahead the Harding Road descends into Palenville and is marked as a horse trail. To the left, the last stretch of the Harding Road makes its final climb to the hotel site. Turn left and climb that blue-marked trail. After a climb of about 225 feet in less than 0.5 mile, we reach the major trail junction (Location K) [N 42° 11.292′ – W 74° 3.016′ – elev. 2,430 ft.] near the site of the old hotel.

VIEW FROM SUNSET ROCK.

A view of the upper clove from Sunset Rock on South Mountain. Note the size of the ledge and the path uphill to the right. From an 1884 picture folder published by Wittemann Bros. Courtesy of Larry Tompkins.

Take a minute to orient yourself before you go to the hotel site. To your immediate right is a long, flat, blue-marked trail that leads to Boulder Rock, Fairy Spring, and other sites on South Mountain—the subject of Hike 2 and Hike 3. If you have a car at North or South Lake, you may want to do Hike 2 (in reverse) from this point. Straight ahead the trail splits. The right branch is the unmarked loop around the Hotel Kaaterskill site (see the detailed description in Hike 2). The downhill path to the left of the hotel loop is marked red and will take you past the carriage road at Location R [N 42° 11.480′ – W 74° 3.617′] and then to the foot of the trail near Scutt Road. From there, turn left and follow the blue trail that parallels Lake Creek back to the point where you crossed the creek by the ruins of the old bridge near the Laurel House, and on to the starting point of this hike.

VIEW FROM INSPIRATION POINT.

This image of the view from Inspiration Point is from the same picture folder as the previous view from Sunset Rock. Note the Harding Road as it passes through the Amphitheater. The road can still be seen from this spot today, especially when there is a light snow cover. Courtesy of Larry Tompkins.

GPS and Map Data	Description	Directions and Comments
0.0 mi. N 42° 11.737′ W 74° 3.790′ Elev. 2,085 ft.	Laurel House Road parking area. From North Lake main gate take North Lake Road toward Haines Falls. Laurel House Road is the second road on the left. The parking area is at the bottom of the hill.	From the parking area pass through the gate and follow the wide path downhill. Be particularly careful on the eroded slope to the top of the falls and near the edge.
0.15 mi. N 42° 11.604′ W 74° 3.796′ Elev. 1,980 ft.	Top of Kaaterskill Falls. The large rock on this side of the stream was the site of an observation platform known as the spray house.	Walk upstream on this side of the stream until you reach the man-made stone wall that was part of a bridge.
0.25 mi. N 42° 11.623′ W 74° 3.702′ Elev. 1,980 ft.	Remains of the bridge on the road to South Lake. A dam once used to collect water for dramatic release over the falls was nearby. Make your way across the stream, climb the hill at the bridge, and continue uphill through the woods to the right. The more open path to the left goes toward the foot of Scutt Road.	At this writing, there is no maintained crossing before the footbridge above Scutt Road. If you can't cross here, you will have to go to Scutt Road (see Hike 5).
	The original trail through this area most likely followed a higher route. It is possible to set a course south from this area and bushwhack over this shoulder of South Mountain following the approximate route of the old trail. You will intersect the blue trail in the vicinity of Sunset Rock. The forest is pretty, but you will miss several nice lookouts. Another lost side trail descended to Council Bluff. The spot was identified on the early maps, but little was written about it.	Follow the blue trail southeast. After a short climb the trail levels off and enters an open forest. The trail remains level until it starts downhill toward Layman's Monument.
0.6 mi. N 42° 11.344′ W 74° 4.093′ Elev. 1,840 ft.	Layman's Monument. Nice views of the western head of Kaaterskill Clove. The parking area locally known as Molly Smith's (for the souvenir shop that was there in the 1950s) is below.	Trail turns east and in a short distance begins a steep uphill climb to the level of the clove rim.

GPS and Map Data	Description	Directions and Comments
0.7 mi. N 42° 11.282′ W 74° 4.060′ Elev. 1,940 ft.	The name of this spot is not documented. It may be that it was off of any trails and hence unnamed.	Good lookout with a sheltering rock—too good, in fact, not to be known to Laurel House guests. Continue uphill.
1.0 mi. N 42° 11.226′ W 74° 3.730′ Elev. 2,190 ft.	Yellow trail on left from carriage road (see Hike 5).	Pass side trail and continue on blue trail along the clove rim.
1.1 mi. N 42° 11.182′ W 74° 3.623′ Elev. 2,190 ft.	Outlook mistakenly called Sunset Rock. This small outlook was not named in the nineteenth century.	False Sunset Rock. Pass the small outlook now labeled as Sunset Rock. Continue a short distance east and proceed downhill to the real Sunset Rock, which is mistakenly labeled Inspiration Point..
1.25 mi. N 42° 11.081′ W 74° 3.522′ Elev. 2,120 ft.	The most popular view from the clove rim, this spot has been visited and captured in art since the earliest days of tourism in the Catskills. The confusion over the name of this site inspired this book. I have no doubt that this is the original Sunset Rock and that a different, nearby location that now bears no name was called Inspiration Point.	Original Sunset Rock (called Inspiration Point in some images and in postcards from the 1920s and later).
1.33 mi. N 42° 11.066′ W 74° 3.422′ Elev. 2,123 ft.	Views of the Amphitheater, Hudson Valley, and Point of Rocks (Indian Head). This is the view depicted in the early illustrations of Inspiration Point.	Original Inspiration Point
N 42° 11.129′ W 74° 2.834′ Elev. 2,180 ft.	Belle View	
1.9 mi. N 42° 11.080′ W 74° 2.764′ Elev. 2,200 ft.	You are now on part of the carriage road system of the Hotel Kaaterskill. Some of these are now used as horse trails.	Junction with Ledge Drive, a carriage road (marked as a horse trail). Left will lead you back to Scutt Road. Turn right and walk a few hundred feet to a marked junction.

GPS and Map Data	Description	Directions and Comments
2.0 mi. N 42° 11.129′ W 74° 2.706′ Elev. 2,210 ft. **Location V**	Kaaterskill Turnpike is one of many names applied to the road that George Harding built from Palenville to his Hotel Kaaterskill atop South Mountain. We've come to call it "The Road That Couldn't Be Built." We travel this road on Hike 9. A short distance ahead, at a right-hand turn in the road, a horse trail to Palenville Overlook branches off from the road. Palenville Overlook is visited in Hike 6.	Junction with Kaaterskill Turnpike. Ledge Drive ends here. Straight ahead, Kaaterskill Turnpike leads to Palenville; to the left, the turnpike climbs to the Hotel Kaaterskill site. Turn left and ascend.
2.35 mi. N 42° 11.292′ W 74° 3.016′ Elev. 2,430 ft. **Location K**	Confusing junction (see Hike 2). The first trail to left (red) is the most direct route to Scutt Road. Straight ahead leads to the Hotel Kaaterskill site. Trail to right (blue) leads to Boulder Rock and Pine Orchard.	Stop here and get your bearings. Look over the map and decide how you want to proceed.
	For the most direct route back to the starting point of the hike, take the red trail to Scutt Road. At the end of the red trail, turn left and follow the blue trail back to the dam above Kaaterskill Falls. See Hike 5 for details and mileage. To go on to North Lake, take the blue trail. Refer to Hike 2: Pine Orchard to Hotel Kaaterskill. You are now at the end of that hike (also indicated as Location K in that chart). Do that hike in reverse to return to North Lake.	

Hike 5:
Scutt Road to Hotel Kaaterskill

Distance: 3.0–4.75 miles round-trip, depending on option taken
Type of Trail: Marked footpath and carriage roads
Difficulty: Easy to moderate
Elevation Gain: 450 feet, from Scutt Road to Hotel Kaaterskill site
Comments: The route from the Scutt Road parking area to the bridge crossing the stream can be very muddy.

This is an alternate approach to the Hotel Kaaterskill and the ledge along the north rim of Kaaterskill Clove. This hike does not include a detailed description because the details are included in Hike 4. You may, however, want to consider some options on this hike.

If your main interest is reaching the Hotel Kaaterskill site, follow this hike as far as Location R, then continue straight ahead about 0.75 mile to Location K. The unmarked trail to the immediate left circles the site of the once-spectacular hotel. This is the most direct route to the hotel site.

To find the original Sunset Rock, again proceed to Location R and turn right onto the carriage road known to Hotel Kaaterskill visitors as Ledge Drive. At 0.82 mile a yellow foot trail leads down to the blue rim trail. Turn left, pass the small outlook falsely labeled Sunset Rock, and descend to the original Sunset Rock. This is the most direct route to the original Sunset Rock.

GPS and Map Data	Description	Directions and Comments
0.0 mi. N 42° 12.037′ W 74° 3.512′	On nineteenth-century maps this road was called the road to Scribner's.	Trailhead at Scutt Road parking area. The trail starts on the east side of the road across from the parking area. Follow blue markers.
0.37 mi.	The Catskill and Tannersville (narrow-gauge) and, a short distance further, the old Ulster and Delaware (standard-gauge) railroads came through here.	Trail crosses two old railway beds and passes a path that leads to the Hotel Kaaterskill laundry ruins.
0.38 mi.	Footbridge across Lake Creek followed shortly by a path from the left and then a second footbridge.	Cross the two footbridges.
0.4 mi. N 42° 11.656′ W 74° 3.505′ Elev. 2,080 ft.	Junction with carriage roads. Left leads to South Lake dam; right (blue) leads to Laurel House area and the hike described as Hike 4: Laurel House to Hotel Kaaterskill. Also to the right, near the foot of Scutt Road, is the approximate location of Scribner's Glen Mary cottage.[32] Our path is marked red. It is straight ahead and takes us uphill.	At the junction cross the old road and follow the red trail uphill.
0.41 mi.	Registration booth. Please register. Funding for trail maintenance is better justified if the trails are well used.	
0.65 mi. N 42° 11.481′ W 74° 3.617′ **Location R**	This is a key crossroads. The red path is the most direct route to the Hotel Kaaterskill site. The yellow path is nearly level and can lead to Sunset Rock, or Palenville Overlook, or loop back to this junction after passing the Hotel Kaaterskill.	Junction. Take yellow trail (carriage road) to the right.

GPS and Map Data	Description	Directions and Comments
0.82 mi. N 42° 11.288´ W 74° 3.660´	The trail ahead and the footpath rejoin each other about a mile ahead. If you are on bike, horseback, or skis, continue straight ahead. The footpath leads to the blue trail and a cliffside walk.	Junction. Take footpath on right (yellow) for the best views.
0.9 mi. N 42° 11.226´ W 74° 3.730´	Junction with (blue) Escarpment Trail.	From this point, the hike is identical with Hike 4. Turn left.
1.0 mi. N 42° 11.182´ W 74° 3.623´ Elev. 2,190 ft.	Outlook mistakenly called Sunset Rock. This small outlook was not named in the nineteenth century.	False Sunset Rock. Pass the small outlook now labeled as Sunset Rock. Continue a short distance east and proceed downhill to the original Sunset Rock, which is mistakenly labeled Inspiration Point.
1.15 mi. N 42° 11.081´ W 74° 3.522´ Elev. 2,120 ft.	The most popular view from the clove rim, this spot has been visited and captured in art since the earliest days of tourism in the Catskills. The confusion over the name of this site inspired this book. I have no doubt that this is the original Sunset Rock and that a different, nearby location that now bears no name was called Inspiration Point.	Original Sunset Rock (called Inspiration Point in some images and in postcards from the 1920s and later).
1.2 mi. N 42° 11.066´ W 74° 3.422´ Elev. 2,123 ft.	Views of the Amphitheater, Hudson Valley, and Point of Rocks (Indian Head). This is the view depicted in the early illustrations of Inspiration Point.	Original Inspiration Point
1.8 mi. N 42° 11.080´ W 74° 2.764´ Elev. 2,210 ft.	You are now on part of the carriage road system of the Hotel Kaaterskill. Some of these are now used as horse trails.	Junction with carriage road (marked as a horse trail). Left will lead you back to Scutt Road. Turn right and walk a few hundred feet to a marked junction.

GPS and Map Data	Description	Directions and Comments
1.9 mi. N 42° 11.129´ W 74° 2.706´ Elev. 2,200 ft. **Location V**	Junction, straight ahead leads to Palenville Overlook or to White Road parking area by way of old Kaaterskill Road. To the left follows the last stretch of the Harding Road to the Hotel Kaaterskill site.	Turn left and ascend.
2.3 mi. N 42° 11.292´ W 74° 3.016´ Elev. 2,430 ft. **Location K**	Confusing junction (see Hike 2). The first trail to left (red) is the most direct route to Scutt Road. Straight ahead leads to the Hotel Kaaterskill site. Trail to right (blue) leads to Boulder Rock and Pine Orchard.	Stop here and get your bearings. Look over the map and decide how you want to proceed.
	For the most direct route back to the starting point of the hike, take the red trail to Scutt Road. At the end of the red trail, turn left and follow the blue trail back to the dam above Kaaterskill Falls. See Hike 6 for details and mileage. To go on to North Lake, take the blue trail. Refer to Hike 2: Pine Orchard to Hotel Kaaterskill. You are now at the end of that hike (also indicated as Location K in that chart). Do that hike in reverse to return to North Lake.	

PART III

Along the Eastern Escarpment

VIEW FROM PIAZZA OF LAUREL HOUSE.

VIEW FROM PIAZZA OF MOUNTAIN HOUSE.

One of the most striking results of the primarily flat, sedimentary rock layers underlying the Catskill escarpment is the wide shelf formed where one of those layers is exposed along the front of the escarpment a few hundred feet below the level of the Mountain House. If you followed Hike 1 and climbed Mountain Turnpike, you walked the Long Level, a section of that road that passes over part of the ledge. Mountain Turnpike then leaves that ledge to climb the last stretch to North Lake. We will now return to the ledge and describe three of its most interesting sites: Moses Rock, Palenville Overlook, and Point of Rocks (Indian Head). Our path will follow an old road, cross an old railway grade, pass through a quiet forest, and reach the site of a remote boardinghouse with a magnificent view.

Modern visitors to the Catskills approaching from the Hudson Valley are most familiar with these famous outlooks as the dramatic rock cliffs high above the north side of the Rip Van Winkle Trail at the opening to Kaaterskill Clove. Anyone who rides through the clove can't help but wonder what the view must be like from the top.

The more eastern rock ledge today is called Palenville Overlook [N 42° 10.878′ – W 74° 2.178′ – 1,771 ft.], but was also referred to as High Rock and as Grand View Rocks. The more westerly is called Point of Rocks [N 42° 10.864′ – W 74° 2.429′] or Indian Head[33] (because the cliff face appears as a profile when viewed from the clove rim). The cliffs are on a horse trail and aren't generally visited by hikers, even though they can be reached easily on foot.

Climbing Up Palenville Overlook. *This engraving of risk-takers at Palenville Overlook explains why not all of our Victorian predecessors lived to become our ancestors. A.E.P. Searing's* The Land of Rip Van Winkle, *1884.*

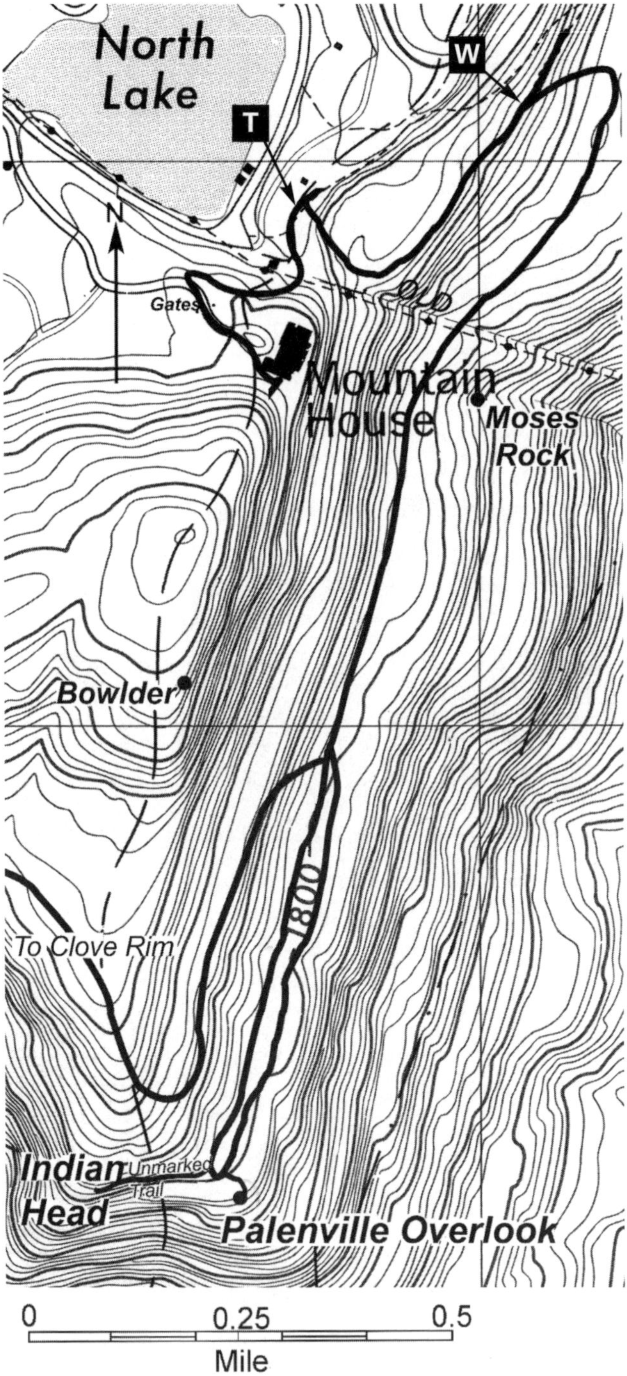
North Lake
T
W
Gates
OLD
Mountain House
Moses Rock
Bowlder
1800
To Clove Rim
Indian Head
Unmarked Trail
Palenville Overlook
0
0.25
0.5
Mile

Hike 6:

Palenville Overlook and Point of Rocks

Distance: 4.0 miles round-trip
Type of Trail: Carriage roads (parts of which will be muddy) and a short, unmarked trail
Difficulty: Moderate to difficult
Elevation Gain: 380 feet
Comments: Remember—you lose elevation at first, so the return trip is more difficult and will take longer.

This is the easiest route to Palenville Overlook. The total walk is a little less than four miles and mostly along a level, wooded old road. The initial steep descent of over 300 feet awaits you as a climb on the return trip. Highlights include the not-to-be-missed view from Palenville Overlook and the less-often-seen view from Point of Rocks (Indian Head). You will also cross the bed of the Otis Elevating Railway. The path may be muddy or even slightly flooded in places.

Go to the top of Mountain Turnpike near the North Lake picnic grounds (see Hike 1) and start downhill. After 0.3 mile take the side trail that goes steeply down to the right. At the bottom of the hill the trail turns abruptly south. This is the "Old Wood Road on Side of Mountain" shown on Van Loan's map. Follow this wood road 1.3 miles, passing the Otis Elevating Railway grade to the clearing near Palenville Overlook. The wooded trail is almost flat, for it sits atop the previously mentioned prominent rock stratum. The thin soil on the impermeable rock can become extremely muddy.

The Old Wood Road is virtually level from the Otis Railway to the clearing near Palenville Overlook. At one point the trail branches into two sections. At this fork, bear to the right. (The left branch will also get you to Palenville Overlook, but it drops slightly downhill and comes out east of the picnic tables.) Just beyond the fork in the trail, a horse trail to the right connects with the trails on the clove rim at Location V. You may want to follow this trail after you visit Palenville Overlook. Stay to the left here and continue on the level trail.

You will soon come to a clearing with a picnic table and fireplace. In season there are quite a few blueberries here. Don't eat lunch here. The best picnic spot is just a minute away. To the left is the top of the old quarry road. Follow it and look to the right. You should soon see the overlook. The ledge

Sunrise from South Mountain. *Harry Fenn, 1870, engraving in* Picturesque America. *The ledge depicted is probably Palenville Overlook.*

is off the old road to the right and down a hill. You will be no more than thirty feet lower in elevation than the picnic area. As you approach the ledge, you will pass a stone foundation. Here is a spectacular view of the valley and lower clove. The drop in front of you is precipitous. The first bridge in the clove is over 1,100 feet below, but only 0.3 mile away. It is not an exaggeration to say that you are looking directly down on the roofs of the buildings of Palenville. The view up the clove is spectacular too. No wonder an enterprising family threw caution to the rather strong wind and attempted to establish a boardinghouse here.

Shortly after the Civil War, Elizabeth Adkins (possibly spelled Atkins) and her brother, Thomas Dodd, built a house for about thirty guests on these cliffs. It was constructed for $10,000. The road up to it from Palenville (which may have followed a quarry road) was built for another $3,000. Most of that road still exists, but is difficult to follow. From here to the valley, it goes past two bluestone quarries and ends up at the White Road parking area. The boardinghouse was never successful and apparently operated for only a few years. It was said that guests found the house too windy. (The building had to be moored against the strong winds.)

Elizabeth's father, William, and his youngest son, William Jr., were living there in 1873. In perhaps the best "When I was a boy I had to … " story ever told: the twelve-year-old had to walk to school in Palenville each day and climb back up the steep road at night, sometimes leading an old blind horse! On one fateful day in May of 1873, the boy's father died, and as if that wasn't enough, the blind horse wandered away and walked off the cliff.[34]

All that is left of the house is a stone wall, which may have been part of the foundation. In recent years visitors to the spot have been dismantling the wall and using the stones to build chairs overlooking the clove.

Return to the picnic area. From there walk to Point of Rocks **[N 42° 10.864′ – W 74° 2.429′ – 1,793 ft.]** or Indian Head. The trail is unmarked and at nearly the same level as the picnic area. Walk in a westerly direction, staying at the bottom of the steep hill along an unmarked but well-traveled footpath. You should soon come to another dramatic ledge with views of the clove.

Modern hikers often ignore Point of Rocks. The marked trail does not lead there, and the satisfaction of seeing the view at Palenville Overlook makes seeking further views seem unnecessary. Point of Rocks, however, is very close and provides a very different perspective—wilder and more remote. Harry Fenn drew the view for Bryant's classic *Picturesque America.*

Glimpse of Catskill Clove from Indian Head. *Harry Fenn, 1870, engraving in* Picturesque America. *Indian Head has views into the Gulf, westward through the clove, and into the Hudson Valley.*

You may want to compare the view today with Fenn's *Glimpse of Catskill Clove from Indian Head* and with the description in Bryant's book:

> A delightful walk brings you at last to Indian Head. This name is given to a bold promontory which juts out over the Clove until it overhangs the bed of the tumbling, tossing Kauterskill. From this rock the mountain falls eighteen hundred or two thousand feet. Half a dozen tall pines, growing out of the cliff, divided into two groups on either hand, form a sort of dark, rustic frame for the exquisite picture. The Clove at this place is very narrow, and, along the bottom, the Kauterskill goes tumbling and foaming over the stones. Along the base of the cliff, on the left or southern side of the glen, winds the little road that leads from the village at its mouth up to the table-land beyond the famous falls. On both sides, the mountains tower high above your heads, heavily wooded to the summits with chestnut and pine, through the rich green of which, here and there, you can see the rugged face of a huge precipice,

Cloud view in the Kaaterskill Clove from near Hotel Kaaterskill, overlooking the Hudson valley in the distance. *The view seems to be from Point of Rocks looking east. From "Kaaterskill Mountains," an advertising brochure circa 1893. Courtesy of Justine and Hillard Hommel.*

> scarred and broken by the frosts, and spotted with dark lichen and moss. As we gazed down into the Clove a heavily-laden stage came lumbering into view, looking, as it does in Mr. Fenn's sketch, like a mere speck upon the winding road. We watched it creeping along, often half hidden by the trees, until it passed over the little rustic bridge that spans a brawling cataract, and vanished behind the dark shoulder of the mountain. It was a perfect day. About the great head of High Peak the clouds had thrown a scarf of white, the shadow of which darkened his mighty shoulders and the gorge beneath. The colors were constantly changing with the moving clouds, and the sunlight played and danced upon the walls of rock and the masses of deepest green, while the sound of the Kauterskill came floating up to us from its stony bed, where it dashed along, now sparkling in the sunlight and then plunging over mossy rocks into the shade. The wonderful effect of this play of light and shade is perfectly shown by the accompanying picture.

On your return to North Lake, you may want to try and find Moses Rock (see Bushwhack to Moses Rock).

Alternate Approaches to Palenville Overlook and Point of Rocks

In addition to the walk from North Lake, there are four other traditional ways to reach these cliffs—one from the clove rim, two from Palenville, and one from Boulder Rock. These descriptions start from points along other hikes. If you want to try any of these routes, you will need to refer to those hike descriptions.

On Hike 4 we walked along the clove rim and met the horse trail that parallels it at what I've labeled Location V [N 42° 11.129′ – W 74° 2.706′ – elev. 2,200 ft.] This is the junction of the Escarpment Trail with the Harding Road. From that junction, walk east a short distance and pass the intersection with the road to Hotel Kaaterskill on the left. Continue until the Harding Road makes a sharp right and the more wooded horse trail continues straight ahead. The broader branch to the right descends to Palenville along the old Harding Road, which we climb on Hike 9. Take the more wooded path straight ahead and cross a little stream. The stream is at the head of the Gulf. This wooded horse trail has become popular with mountain bikers. It goes through hemlock woods and mountain laurel until it descends to the road along the escarpment. Turn right. You are now following the route from North Lake described below.

From Palenville, you can start at White Road and climb the Harding Road as in Hike 9 until you meet the horse trail near the clove rim. You will then be able to turn right and follow the trail described in the paragraph above. A second route from Palenville, along old quarry roads, was used by the proprietors of the overlook's Dodd House. Today that route crosses private property and is not available to the general public.

There was also an approach from Boulder Rock, which I mention only for historic interest. I don't suggest that you try it. Nineteenth-century hikers descended through Fat Man's Delight or by the staircase at "The Bowlder" and followed a rough but popular trail to the overlook. An illustration from a period souvenir booklet shows how open the area was and depicts one of only two images I've seen depicting the Dodd House. Today you could set a compass heading or use a GPS unit to bushwhack to the ledges, but remember: even in Mountain House days this was a difficult trail. Today it is overgrown with bramble, and you are sure to get scratched up and be amazed at how small twigs can find their way into every portion of your pack and clothing. It was in attempting to retrace this route that I discovered the true meaning of bushwhacking: bushes do the whacking; hikers get whacked.

GPS and Map Data	Description	Directions and Comments
0.0 mi. N 42° 11.839´ W 74° 2.071´ Elev. 2,150 ft. **Location T**	The old stage road begins at the southern end of the chain link fence at the North Lake beach picnic grounds.	North Lake picnic area at top of Mountain Turnpike. Follow the turnpike and old stage-coach road downhill.
0.3 mi. N 42° 11.917´ W 74° 1.800´ Elev. 1,980 ft. **Location W**	See Hike 1 for a description of the trail from Mountain House Road to the Mountain House site.	The road branches. Take the steep downhill to the right. The left fork will take you to Palenville.
0.4 mi. N 42° 11.945´ W 74° 1.706´ Elev. 1,870 ft.	Van Loan and Rusk show a path descending to Moses Rock from this point. We choose an easier way because the excavation for the Otis Elevating Railway blocks the path	The road levels out and takes a sharp right turn.
0.7 mi. N 42° 11.729´ W 74° 1.851´ Elev. 1,859 ft.	An excursion to Moses Rock is best made starting from this point. To reach Moses Rock [N 42° 11.655´ – W 74° 1.815´ – elev. 1,733 ft.] continue another twenty or thirty paces beyond the Otis crossing, then go off trail to the left and follow the small brook, descending about 150 feet. After exploring Moses Rock, return to this point and continue toward Palenville Overlook.	Road crosses the old railway grade of the Otis Elevating Railway.
1.4 mi. N 42° 11.320´ W 74° 2.043´ Elev. 1,800 ft.	Old maps call this the Old Wood Road on the side of the mountain. It follows a wide, flat ledge, and tends to hold water. Its thin layer of soil rests on top of an underlying rock stratum.	At a fork in the path bear right and in a few paces come to: Junction with horse trail to the clove rim and Harding Road at location V. The horse trail can give you access to the clove rim trail, Scutt Road, and the trails on South Mountain. For now stay to the left and continue at this level on to Palenville Overlook.

GPS and Map Data	Description	Directions and Comments
1.7 mi. N 42° 10.919′ W 74° 2.244′ Elev. 1,800 ft.	This path is part of an old, unmarked road that was used to access bluestone quarries and the boardinghouse here. The road is easy to lose, goes over private property, and is not recommended.	Fireplace and picnic table at Palenville Overlook. Take the footpath to the left and downhill. It soon branches to the right and descends to a commanding view of the clove and valley.
1.8 mi. N 42° 10.878′ W 74° 2.178′ Elev. 1,771 ft.	A striking overlook where someone recently has dismantled part of the old foundation of the Dodd House to build a group of stone chairs overlooking the clove. The Dodd House, or Grand View Rocks House, was built shortly after the Civil War. It was short-lived. High winds may have prevented the success of this hotel. It is said that the house was moved and now is located on Scutt Road. Other oral sources say that the building materials were used for cottages on Bogart Road in Palenville. As you return to North Lake, your path follows the most likely route of the move. You be the judge.	Palenville Overlook. After taking in the view, return to the fireplace and picnic table.
1.7 mi. (again)	You may wish to explore the area here. There is another good overlook at this elevation just through the brush to the south.	An unmarked foot trail to the west will lead you to Point of Rocks.
1.9 mi. N 42° 10.864′ W 74° 2.429′ Elev. 1,793 ft.	Spectacular view of Kaaterskill Clove. Moore's Bridge can be seen deep in the clove. Point of Rocks is at the southeastern rim of a geologically interesting gorge named the Gulf, which may be the result of the sudden release of a glacial lake on South Mountain. For an account of the cascade that shaped the Gulf, see "The Great Cascade" by Robert Titus in the fall 2001 issue of *Kaatskill Life.*	Point of Rocks (Indian Head)

Bushwhack to Moses Rock

Bushwhack from North Lake. Read the full description below before you attempt this walk. It is not for everyone. This is one of two excursions for dyed-in-the-wool Catskill Mountain enthusiasts, the other being the hike to The Cellar on North Mountain. The hike to Moses Rock is only a little more than 1.5 miles round-trip, but it is nevertheless one of the more difficult hikes in this book and should not be attempted alone. The original approach to Moses Rock was along an old road and was destroyed by a deep cut in the ledge when the Otis Elevating Railway was built. The approach described here involves a steep scramble downhill, and you must climb back up that hill after your visit to the rock. This hike is recommended only for those who have the keenest interest in the area.

Distance: 1.75 miles round-trip
Type of Trail: Carriage roads and bushwhack
Difficulty: Moderate to difficult
Elevation Gain: 420 feet
Comments: Go with a companion; you will be off the beaten path and may not see other hikers. Please try to minimize impact on the area.

> And the Lord said unto Moses, Go on before the people, and take with thee … thy rod wherewith you smotest the river, take in thy hand and go. And thou shalt smite the rock, and there shall come water out of it, and the people may drink.
>
> —Exodus 17: 5–6, (King James Version.)

One sight of the large rock on a deeply wooded ledge a few hundred feet below the Mountain House will convince anyone that this passage from Exodus inspired the name Moses Rock. The contrast between the ledges near Palenville Overlook and Moses Rock is vast. Where those sunlit ledges give open and exciting views of the clove, Moses Rock has the quiet serenity of a wooded glen.

Now nearly forgotten, it was a popular stop in the nineteenth century. In many ways Moses Rock—like Druid Rocks and Fairy Spring—typifies locations popular to nineteenth-century vacationers, for whom the quest for the spiritual blended with the quest for the romantic. Spiritual feelings found expression in phrases like Cole's "sweet foretaste of heaven," and place names like Moses Rock and Jacob's Ladder. Mystical references to a land of gnomes, fairies, elves, and druids called to mind a romantic world much like Shakespeare's *A Midsummer Night's Dream* or, to us, Tolkein's Middle Earth.

No recent guide discusses Moses Rock. Even Roland Van Zandt, author of *The Catskill Mountain House,* confuses it with another site. Yet it appears on several maps, and serious Mountain House buffs will want to visit it, perhaps in combination with a walk to Palenville Overlook and Point of Rocks—the two spectacular ledges above the mouth of Kaaterskill Clove that are described in Hike 6. In the nineteenth century, Moses Rock was along an old road to Palenville. The road, which was north of the Rip Van Winkle Trail (now Route 23A) but south of Mountain Turnpike, was used to ascend the mountain as early as 1753.[35]

Van Loan gives directions to Moses Rock from the Mountain House. Those directions no longer work; the old road is obscured by the Otis Elevating Railway grade. Some modern trail maps will mislead you; they show the rock on the north side of the Otis. To find the rock, start at the southern end of the chain-link fence in the North Lake beach picnic area, just south of the handicapped-accessible viewing platform set to be completed in the summer of 2005. This is the top of Mountain Turnpike. Descend to the spot where a right-hand path leads to the snowmobile trail **[N 42° 11.917′ – W 74° 1.800′ – elev. 1,980 ft.]** Go down that right-hand path to the foot of the hill, where the road makes a sharp right turn. Van Loan's directions suggest that you should leave the horse and snowmobile trail at this point. Don't. Today the Otis Elevating Railway grade will block the route of the old road. Instead, continue on the snowmobile trail until you reach the Otis cut. About twenty yards beyond the cut, turn left and leave the trail. You should find a small brook (Alf Evers calls it Silver Brook; Beers's 1867 *Atlas* shows it as a tributary of Fountain Kill). Follow its course down the escarpment. After descending about 150 feet, you will come to Moses Rock, apparently unchanged since first described 250 years ago. It is directly on the brook.

Until a trail that provides easy access and minimizes damage to the area is created, hikers should limit their use of the area. After a hundred years of relative obscurity, Moses Rock remains pristine and is best reserved as a location for visitors with a serious interest in Catskill Mountain history.

Moses Rock gives a serene sense of the primitive forest. The rock is a nearly free-standing block of cross-bedded sandstone about twenty feet high, eighty feet long, and ten feet wide. The south end is close enough to the ledge above so that you can easily walk out on its top. The top is covered with ferns, moss, and forest undergrowth, and the side is covered with lichen. The

GPS and Map Data	Description	Directions and Comments
0.0 mi. N 42° 11.839′ W 74° 2.071′ Elev. 2,150 ft. **Location T**		North Lake picnic area at top of Mountain Turnpike. Follow the turnpike and old stage-coach road downhill.
0.3 mi. N 42° 11.917′ W 74° 1.800′ Elev. 1,980 ft. **Location W**	See Hike 1 for a description of the trail from Mountain House Road to the Mountain House site.	The road branches. Take the steep downhill to the right. The left fork will take you to Palenville.
0.4 mi. N 42° 11.945′ W 74° 1.706′	Van Loan and Rusk show a path descending to Moses Rock from this point. We choose an easier way because the excavation for the Otis Elevating Railway blocks the path.	The road levels out and takes a sharp right turn.
0.7 mi. N 42° 11.729′ W 74° 1.851′ Elev. 1,859 ft.		Road crosses the old railway grade of the Otis Elevating Railway.
0.8 mi. N 42° 11.655′ W 74° 1.815′ Elev. 1,733 ft.	Moses Rock. Return to the Old Wood Road or try to find the bluestone quarry shown on Van Loan's map.	Continue another twenty or thirty paces beyond the Otis crossing, then go off trail to the left and follow the small brook, descending about 150 feet. After exploring Moses Rock, you will return to this point and backtrack to North Lake, or continue toward Palenville Overlook as in Hike 6.
	According to the old maps, one of many bluestone quarries in the area is nearby. Sidewalks of New York City and many other eastern cities still have Catskills bluestone taken from these quarries. Other quarries are near Palenville Overlook and near Sphinx Rock on Prospect Mountain.	

small stream, tumbling down the face of the escarpment, gathers on the ledge above and enters the sloped space between the ledge and the rock. Before the stream reaches the north end of the giant rock, it enters a crevice and emerges on the other side. From below it looks indeed as if the staff of Moses has split the rock so that water will flow. But this is a not a spring; it is surface water and not safe to drink. The area below is cool and wet. The impression is that the area has reverted to its pre–Mountain House state.

In the Woods. *Thomas Nast, "Sketches among the Catskills," 1866. Bushes do the whacking to these dignified nineteenth-century hikers.*

PART IV

North Mountain Trails

SOUTH AND NORTH MOUNTAIN FROM PALENVILLE.

SOUTH (KAATERSKILL) LAKE.

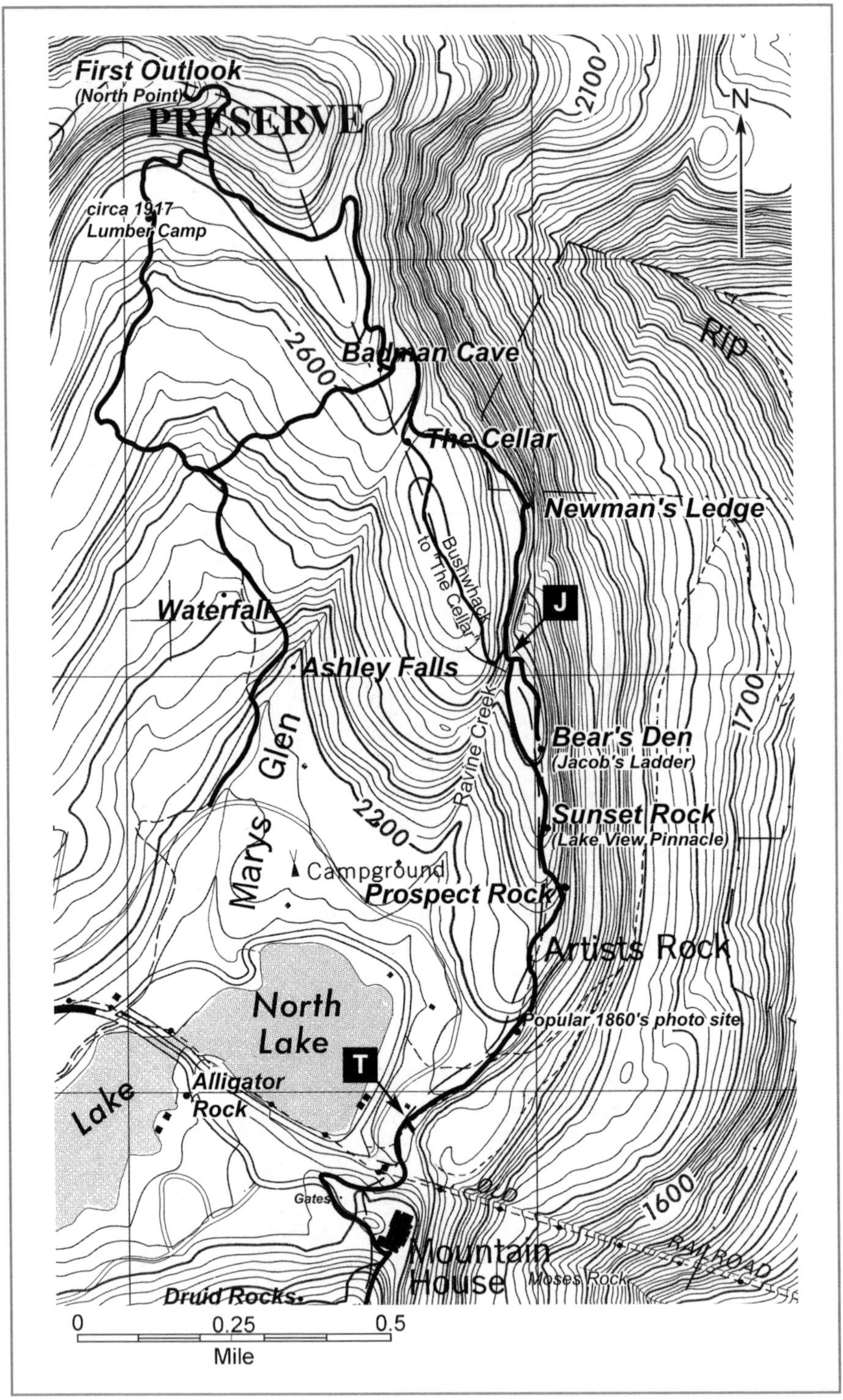
First Outlook
(North Point)
PRESERVE
circa 1917
Lumber Camp
2100
N
Rip
2600
Badman Cave
The Cellar
Newman's Ledge
Bushwhack to The Cellar
J
Waterfall
Ashley Falls
Ravine Creek
1700
Bear's Den
(Jacob's Ladder)
Marys Glen
Sunset Rock
(Lake View Pinnacle)
2200
Campground
Prospect Rock
Artists Rock
North Lake
Popular 1860's photo site
T
Lake
Alligator Rock
Gates
OLD
1600
RAILROAD
Mountain House
Moses Rock
Druid Rocks
0
0.25
0.5
Mile

Hike 7:

North Lake to Overlooks on North Mountain

Distance: 6.0 miles, approximately, round-trip
Type of Trail: Marked footpath
Difficulty: Moderate to difficult, with a tough scramble to the top of North Mountain
Elevation Gain: 870 feet, North Lake beach parking area to North Point
Comments: For a shorter hike, you can turn back after Bear's Den, reducing the trip to less than two miles and ending with the most important view in the Catskills.

This is the most popular hike among modern campers at North Lake and the one on which local residents most like to take houseguests. It is one of the longest hikes in this guide, but the rewards are great, even for those who are more interested in the views than the history. It is possible to cut the hike short and still enjoy most of the best scenery.

Highlights include extensive views of the Hudson Valley (bring a camera and binoculars!), the best views of the eastern escarpment, classic sites that inspired Hudson River School painters, a diverse variety of plants (including one of the few instances of arctic species in the Catskills), and some good, vigorous climbing through interesting terrain.

You will need only one car parked at the North Lake beach parking area, although it is also possible to return by the Mary's Glen trail.

Artist's Rock, Sunset Rock, Jacob's Ladder, Bear's Den, the Cellar, North Point—all are historically famous sites on North Mountain, but none are marked today at the locations known to Mountain House visitors of the nineteenth century. Some of those names—Bear's Den, Jacob's Ladder, the Cellar—are mostly forgotten. Others—Sunset Rock and Artist's Rock—are now given to locations different from the original sites. And some places named today—North Point, Badman Cave—are names that were not used in Mountain House days. Only Newman's Ledge bears the same name now as it did when it was named for Rev. Newman Hall, one of the leading figures of the Congregational church in the nineteenth century. The ledge was named during or after Newman's stay at the Mountain House on his 1867 visit from England.[36] We will explore North Mountain and find all of these original sites and straighten out the misnaming that has occurred over the past one hundred years—all, that is, except Artist's Rock. The only thing I'm sure of about Artist's Rock is that it is not at the site that has that name today.

Some of the site name changes were probably made intentionally and for valid reasons. In the case of Red Hill, the badly eroded trail was relocated for environmental reasons. With Sunset Rock, the regrowth of forest in front obscured the once-open view of the lakes and Pine Orchard. A similar, superior view is available from the top of nearby Bear's Den, which now is labeled Sunset Rock. In this heavily used area, cutting trees to maintain two similar views would not be wise forest management. Despite the trail's heavy use, this is still one of the nicest walks in the Catskills. Many people come again and again and never seem to tire of this classic walk. You will probably want to walk it in different seasons and, like the painters who made the views famous, see it under different atmospheric conditions.

Let's take the walk that is possibly the most popular in the region—from North Lake to North Point—and in the process identify each site along the way with the name used by Mountain House guests. We'll start where Rusk and Van Loan begin their descriptions, at the top of the Mountain Turnpike [**N 42° 11.839′ – W 74° 2.071′ – elev. 2,150 ft.**], Location T on the charts. This is now at the southeastern edge of the North Lake picnic grounds where the chain-link fence ends. If you stand here facing north, the Mountain Turnpike is on your right. Directly ahead of you, along the chain-link fence, is the blue escarpment trail. A third trail that went along the shore of North Lake to Mary's Glen would have been ahead to the left. Both Van Loan and Rusk tell us that we have a view of the valley as we walk along this area, but the area has many more trees now than it did in the 1800s. The forest has grown back after the many fires that damaged this area.[37]

As we walk along we will identify those places that can be clearly matched with the old sites and speculate about the position of any that are questionable. The first spot is a small concrete marker [**N 42° 11.885′ – W 74° 1.994′ – elev. 2,160 ft.**] It is a boundary marker between what was Catskill Mountain House property and the property purchased by New York State, probably in 1929–30.[38] The initials "CMH" and "NYS" are scratched into the top surface. The division between the two sets of initials presumably is the boundary.[39]

Both of the old guides tell us that the first main lookout is at Artist's Rock. It was this outlook that was supposed to be a favorite of Thomas Cole, who could see his house in Catskill from the ledge. The ledge labeled Artist's Rock today is north of the original Artist's Rock, and was originally called Prospect Rock. We'll describe it soon, but first we will consider possible locations of the

This detail from Van Loan's 1883 trail map shows the location of many sites near the Mountain House. Notice the small building (Dodd's) on Palenville Overlook at the mouth of the clove. Moses Rock is shown below the Mountain House. Artist's Rock is clearly seen to be at the top of the first climb and quite a way south of Prospect Rock. Sunset Rock is also shown; it is lower in elevation and some distance south of Bear's Den. Rip Van Winkle Ledge, now most easily accessible from Winter Clove resort, is on the north side of Sleepy (or Rip Van Winkle) Hollow. Courtesy of Justine and Hillard Hommel.

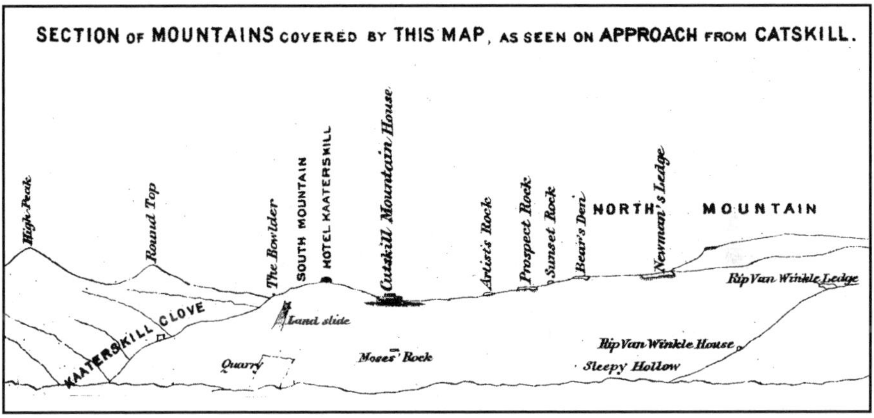

original Artist's Rock. It may have been anywhere from the area of the CMH/NYS marker to just south of Prospect Rock. I have yet to put all the clues together. (Maybe an interested reader can positively identify the location!)

Here are the clues that I have gathered. Artist's Rock had a good view of the Mountain House ledge. Rusk says that there was a boulder on the "brow of the mountain" here, but Van Loan doesn't mention the boulder. Rusk and Van Loan seem to disagree on the distance between Artist's Rock and Prospect Rock. Rusk says that it is a few yards after climbing some steps in the rocky way; Van Loan says that it is a few hundred feet, but the crude stone steps are part of that distance. Neither mentions any real climb before Artist's Rock, but both maps seem to show it on top of the first hill north of the level of the lakes. That location is also implied by a profile of the front of the escarpment inset into Van Loan's map. We need more information. A postcard of Artist's Rock shows a gazebo, but I haven't been able to correlate the photo with any spot along the trail nor verify that the photo depicts the same Artist's Rock that we are seeking.

The ledge just beyond the CMH/NYS marker and before the first hill is the location of a number of early stereoviews sometimes identified as

Artists Rock *(possibly the Artist's Rock on North Mountain). I have not been able to find this location, but it certainly is not the ledge labeled as Artists Rock today. Postcard, postmarked July 31, 1905.*

views from North Mountain. I've included one from around 1870 and identified the location [N 42° 11.943′ – W 74° 1.886′ – elev. 2,180 ft.] by comparing the shape of the rock ledge with the ledge as it appears today. The photo shows all the characteristics of Artist's Rock: a man looks out at the valley view; the Mountain House and South Mountain are in clear view to the south. But the most convincing evidence that this may be Artist's Rock is its striking similarity to an 1850s B. B. G. Stone sketch in the Greene County Historical Society's collection. Stone entitled his sketch "Artist's Rock."

The next location to consider is near the bottom of the first steep hill on the trail [N 42° 11.981′ – W 74° 1.860′ – elev. 2,190 ft.] Take a short walk to the right. Near the ledge is our second candidate. Here is a large boulder that Ed West believed to be Artist's Rock. Ed may well have been right, since a view of the Mountain House would have been possible from here and since Rusk says that Artist's Rock is "a bowlder on the brow of the mountain."

Return to the blue trail and climb the hill. The third, and I believe most likely location of Artist's Rock, is at the top of this hill [N 42° 11.999′ – W 74° 1.848′ – elev. 2,240 ft.] Here, to the right, is a ledge that seems to fit the descriptions: the view of the Mountain House would have been possible; this ledge is close to Prospect Rock; and the increased elevation sets it apart from the other possible sites we have already passed. In any case, Artist's Rock could not be much farther north because we soon lose any opportunity to see the Mountain House. Just a "few stone steps" above this last and very likely possibility, and you are on a flat expanse of glacially polished rock.

A little farther north and you reach Prospect Rock [N 42° 12.123′ – W 74° 1.773′ – elev. 2,280 ft.] Since no view of the Mountain House is possible from here and since this is clearly the spot that was called Prospect Rock, the current sign proclaiming this as Artist's Rock is inconsistent with

This ledge—with every crack, crevice, and shelf—can be found just north of the picnic area at North Lake, but the view is now obscured by new growth. The now-empty ledge at Pine Orchard cannot be seen from this point today. E.&H.T. Anthony stereoview, circa 1870.

the older guides. This and Newman's Ledge, 0.6 mile to the north, are the two major east-facing cliffs along our walk on North Mountain. The views from these two ledges are similar and extensive. Below you is Sleepy Hollow; we walked through it on our hike along Mountain Turnpike. The small round mountain below is Cairo Round Top. Notice that the shape of that hill has been "streamlined" by the southward-moving glacier. The steeper slope faces north and a gentler slope trails to the south. Friar Tuck resort is due east.

In the distance to the north is the office complex in downtown Albany; the Hudson River stretches north to south. Along the river you may be able to spot the Rip Van Winkle Bridge in Catskill; on the hill just beyond the bridge, you might see Olana, Frederic Church's Persian-style mansion designed by Church and his friend, Central Park architect Calvert Vaux.[40]

On the Red Path. *C.S. Reinhart, engraving in "Their Pilgrimage," 1884. Little mention is made of trail markings in the early guidebooks. The Red Path may refer to markers or to a feature of the path, such as is the case with Red Hill.*

At Saugerties an arm of land extends into the river, and on it is the Saugerties Lighthouse.[41] Farther to the south the Kingston–Rhinecliff Bridge can be seen, and the Hudson can be followed far below Kingston.

We leave Prospect Rock and follow the state trail uphill. The original trail here is quite eroded, and the state has blocked off the direct path that was called Red Hill (because of the color of the soil). That obliterated path, of course, may not have been the original path either. Follow the state path in order to protect this delicate area.

Soon we reach North Mountain's original Sunset Rock [N 42° 12.216′ – W 74° 1.823′ – 2,380 ft.], later called "Lake View Pinnacle"[42] and now unnamed and ignored. The large boulder that was Sunset Rock to Rusk, Van Loan, and thousands of Mountain House visitors is at the right of the trail as you climb a small hill before the bottom of Bear's Den. Hikers seeking Sunset Rock now pass it by without a second glance and walk on to Bear's Den. The name change is complete, but let's take the time to look at this once-famous landmark.

In previous times this pinnacle provided a good view of the lakes. You can climb the rock easily by simply walking up the ramplike north side. At the top you will note several old names and dates carved into the rock, indicating its former popularity. The name "Lake View Pinnacle" painted on the rock was still faintly visible in the summer of 2004. We are told that four distinct echoes could be heard from the north of the rock.[43] Now the forest surrounding the rock has grown up, the view is limited, and it is doubtful that the echo described by Van Loan can still be produced. To protect this overused area it is probably best to leave the forest here uncut and the old view hidden. Take a look, make a mental note of the change, and walk on about 0.1 mile to the base [N 42° 12.299′ – W 74° 1.858′ – elev. 2,400 ft.] of a conglomerate ledge that contains crevices and was known as Bear's Den. The name was used to describe both the ledge itself and one particular crevice near Jacob's Ladder.

Of all the spots whose names have been confused over the years, Bear's Den is the one that is most ingrained in the minds of today's hikers. Today almost everyone calls this Sunset Rock—the name of the nearby site that we just passed. From below, within, and on top, this fractured ledge of conglomerate is one of the most interesting and familiar spots in the region—a must for anyone who comes to North Lake. It is popular on many levels. Children and more adventuresome adults find its crevices challenging; those seeking scenery find the view of the lakes and Hudson Valley breathtaking; amateur and professional geologists find evidence of glacial action and hints of the once-towering mountains to the east.

Hikers climbed Jacob's Ladder to the top of the Bear's Den, now called Sunset Rock. Postcard, 1906.

Hikers from 1863 and probably much earlier ascended the ledge by the crude wooden Jacob's Ladder[44] depicted on countless postcards. The ladder was removed sometime prior to 1953, apparently because of liability concerns. The easiest and safest route is to take the blue trail north to a junction [N 42° 12.461′ – W 74° 1.868′ – elev. 2,420 ft.] and double back 0.25 mile on a yellow trail to the top [N 42° 12.322′ – W 74° 1.857′]. Once on top you will find a beautiful and classic view of the lakes and Pine Orchard.

It is hard to overemphasize the importance of this view. This, and not the view from North Point, is the classic view from North Mountain. It was painted, drawn, or engraved by Thomas Cole (1843, 1844), Sanford Gifford, Jasper Cropsey (1855), Thomas Nast (1866), William Bartlett (1836), Currier and Ives, and others over many years. Each painting captured a different mood or nuance of atmospheric conditions. Each time you visit the site you will be rewarded with a familiar, yet fresh view.

Once you've taken in the view, look at the site itself. Glacial erratics are located throughout the region. One on top of Bear's Den so impressed Van Loan that he commented on it and on the rock it lies upon: "Fifty feet north of the 'Bear's Den' is a bowlder of very fine white conglomerate, different from any other in this region. Imbedded in the conglomerate rock, which here forms the path, are pebbles of various sizes and colors that show glacial action. Many of them are rubbed and polished." The boulder is easy to find and is obviously a glacial erratic. Determining the distance it was transported is better left to geologists, but the pebbles are smaller than those in the ledge itself.

The conglomerate of the ledge indicates that the sediment that formed it was carried here by rapidly flowing water, perhaps a flood from streams that issued out of the Acadian Mountains. Those mountains rose high over the eastern horizon some 360 million years ago. Their core remains on the New York–Massachusetts border as the Taconics.

Walk north along the yellow trail to the junction with the blue trail. To your right the eastern edge of Bear's Den gives the first, good northerly views along the escarpment. From here the walk to North Point is still two miles ahead and 600 feet higher in elevation. There is still a lot to see, but if you choose you may turn left here and return to North Lake knowing that you have seen some of the best of the Catskills. To continue, walk to the right and almost immediately begin to climb a hill.

Halfway up the hill the trail turns abruptly to the right [N 42° 12.454′ – W 74° 1.897′ – elev. 2,460 ft.]. This was once a secondary trail leading to Newman's Ledge. The original trail continued uphill and passed the Cellar on the way to North Point (I describe that bushwhack elsewhere). For now, continue on the marked trail. We soon reach Newman's Ledge[45] [N 42° 12.603′ – W 74° 1.839′ – elev. 2,464 ft.] Much that was said about the view from Prospect Rock could be repeated, but this view is even more dramatic. We are higher and farther north. Our increased elevation gives a view farther down the river, Rip's Ledge on the north side of Sleepy Hollow is now closer, and the streamlined appearance of Cairo Round Top is more pronounced. From this point the blue trail leaves the escarpment and there are no further views until we reach the outlooks at North Point.

On the way to those outlooks we pass two interesting bogs. The first [N 42° 12.759′ – W 74° 2.087′ – elev. 2,580 ft.] is 0.4 mile beyond

View from North Mountain. *A.E.P. Searing's* The Land of Rip Van Winkle, *1884. The View from Bear's Den at the height of the hotel era. Today we think of North Point and beyond as North Mountain, but in the Victorian era anything north of the lakes was referred to as North Mountain.*

View from North Mountain. *Thomas Nast, "Sketches among the Catskills," 1866. The view from Bear's Den is arguably the best in the Catskills.*

Newman's Ledge. It is at the head of the streambed that runs through the Cellar and feeds Ashley's Creek. We will pass the spot for now and continue another 0.4 mile to the bog near Badman Cave. These small bogs are beautiful and fragile environments. They are also of great value for research in forest history; the acidic soil preserves pollen and small plant fragments for thousands of years and provides a record of plant life in the region since the ice age. Michael Kudish estimates the age of the bog at Badman Cave to be 3,420 years old.[46] Under no circumstances should you enter the bog or remove flowers or other plants.

At Badman Cave [N 42° 12.831′ – W 74° 2.090′ – elev. 2,656 ft.] the yellow trail straight ahead will lead you to a junction of the Mary's Glen trail (red), and from there to the North Lake gatehouse. We turn right and proceed uphill past Badman Cave and on to North Point. In another 0.5 mile we meet still another junction [N 42° 13.109′ – W 74° 2.419′ – elev. 2,750 ft.], this time with the Mary's Glen trail itself. Turn right again and start the last short, steep climb to North Point. Rusk and Van Loan did not use the term North Point, and called this simply the First Outlook [N 42° 13.193′ – W 74° 2.465′ – elev. 3,020 ft.] This offers a more expansive view than that from Bear's Den and, if you walk toward the northeast, allows views of the northern escarpment [N 42° 13.224′ – W 74° 2.436′ – elev. 3,020 ft.]

The view from this first outlook toward the lakes reveals the influence of glacial action on North and South lakes. There is a distinctive difference between a hollow eroded by a glacier and one eroded by a stream. A stream tends to erode material from its bed at the bottom of the hollow, creating a V shape. A glacier, on the other hand, fills the hollow and erodes the sides as well as the bottom. This creates a U shape. The broad, flattened U shape of the hollow stretching below you to the lakes is a sign of glacial action. The ice scoured out the hollow and, together with ice pushing over the escarpment from the valley, helped to create the basins of North and South lakes. Glacial scouring can be seen on the bedrock along the shore of the North Lake. (Lakes of this type should not be confused with kettle lakes, which form in glacial outwash when large blocks of ice are buried by sediment. The ice later melts and the sediment collapses, leaving a kettle hole. When such a hole fills with water, it becomes a kettle lake.)

A second outlook is somewhat farther ahead. The most ambitious hikers completed the walk "around the crest of North Mountain" and returned by a relatively trail-less trek, being advised to follow the water pipe back to the Mountain House. We will retrace our steps and return to the junction with the red Mary's Glen trail.

The Mary's Glen trail provides a wooded walk through an area that was extensively logged prior to 1920 before the land was sold to the state. Kudish[47] and Mulholland[48] tell us that a camp from the logging operation was located nearby, and that the trail follows for a short distance the cable railroad that was used to haul logs. Mulholland gives the camp's position as 0.25 mile from the junction with the trail to North Point. The recent book *Kaaterskill Clove*[49] by Greene County Historian Raymond Beecher discusses this lumbering operation. Beecher writes of the Mountain House owners' reasons for selling off the lumber, and their efforts to minimize the environmental impact of the logging. Little remains of the camp, but I have found a few rusted pipes, the site of a campfire, a lump of coal, and—most importantly—noted that the trail here is built up by a substantial but crudely constructed ramp [N 42° 12.992′ – W 74° 2.543′ – elev. 2,600 ft.]

The trail from the parking area on the North Lake beach access road to North Point is described in Hike 8.

View from North Mountain with Hotel Kaaterskill in the Distance. *Note that the Catskill Mountain House is conspicuously missing from this illustration in a Hotel Kaaterskill advertising brochure, "Kaaterskill Mountains," circa 1893. Courtesy of Justine and Hillard Hommel.*

GPS and Map Data	Description	Directions and Comments
0.0 mi. N 42° 11.839′ W 74° 2.071′ Elev. 2,150 ft. **Location T**	Start at North Lake beach picnic area at the top of the Mountain Turnpike. This was the site of the junction of several trails and the old stage road of Hike 1.	Walk north along the edge of the escarpment. A chain-link fence starts here and continues at the edge of the picnic area.
0.08 mi. N 42° 11.885′ W 74° 1.994′ Elev. 2,160 ft.		Mountain House marker—a small, concrete marker with "NYS" and "CMH" marking the former boundary between Mountain House and state land.
0.2 mi. N 42° 11.943′ W 74° 1.886′ Elev. 2,180 ft.	In the days of the Mountain House, this area had fewer trees. Early photos show views south from this ledge.	Walk along the ledge. Views are obscured by trees below the ledge.This is the first possible location of Artist's Rock.
0.25 mi. N 42° 11.981′ W 74° 1.860′ Elev. 2,190 ft.	Before the climb, and to the right, there is a large boulder with a bronze memorial plaque to a man named Clyde Knauert (1936–1971). Ed West, one of the most knowledgeable people on the Catskills, believed the rock with the plaque to be Artist's Rock.	Trail begins to climb a short, steep hill with a view on the right.
N 42° 11.999′ W 74° 1.848′ Elev. 2,240 ft.	At the top of the hill is another location that could be Artist's Rock. It certainly provides the correct view and is the right distance from the Mountain House.	Artist's Rock? Trail leads back away from the ledge and continues north to an open expanse of bedrock with glacial striations.
0.5 mi. N 42° 12.123′ W 74° 1.773′ Elev. 2,280 ft.	New York State now calls this Artist's Rock, but the designation is recent. Rusk and Van Loan both call this Prospect Rock and they indicate that this ledge is north of Artist's Rock. The view of the Hudson Valley from here is extensive. The cliff below to the left is Rip Van Winkle Ledge on the north side of Sleepy Hollow. You also can see the office towers in Albany and the Kingston–Rhinecliff Bridge on the Hudson. Unlike at Artist's Rock, no view of the ledge at Pine Orchard is possible; therefore, despite the sign to the contrary, this is not the original Artist's Rock.	We pass over the glacially scoured surface and come out on a large open ledge properly called Prospect Rock.

GPS and Map Data	Description	Directions and Comments
0.53 mi. N 42° 12.150′ W 74° 1.810′ Elev. 2,289 ft.	(Alternate climb required to protect fragile hillside.)	Red Hill. Follow the blue trail uphill.
0.65 mi. N 42° 12.216′ W 74° 1.823′ Elev. 2,380 ft.	In trail guides up to the 1950s, the state called this Lake View Pinnacle. Ed West seems to call it Sunrise Rock.(*Kaaterskill,* p. 98). It is a single large boulder to the right of the trail, accessible from the north side. The potential view from this rock is no longer available because of regrowth. Rusk and Van Loan's descriptions convince me that this, not the large ledge ahead, is Sunset Rock.	Original Sunset Rock on North Mountain. Climb a hill and pass a large rock to the right of the trail. This is the original Sunset Rock.
0.77 mi. N 42° 12.299′ W 74° 1.858′ Elev. 2,400 ft.	Hikers in good health with proper shoes and clothing may want to climb through the crevices to the top of Bear's Den. Otherwise, follow the blue trail north to the junction and backtrack to the top of Bear's Den. The site of Jacob's Ladder, a log ladder that assisted hikers to the top of Bear's Den, is off trail to the east at the GPS reading of [N 42° 12.318′ – W 74° 1.823′]. Without the ladder, there is no easy way up at Jacob's Ladder.	Base of Bear's Den. Conglomerate outcrop on blue trail. Continue on blue trail, but see notes in center column.
0.85 mi. N 42° 12.461′ W 74° 1.868′ Elev. 2,420 ft. **Location J**	To continue to North Mountain, stay on the blue trail, turn right, and proceed uphill.	Junction spur trail to the top of Bear's Den (the sign says Sunset Rock, but I prefer the original designation). Take the yellow trail to Bear's Den and return here after your visit.

GPS and Map Data	Description	Directions and Comments
N 42° 12.322′ W 74° 1.857′ Elev. 2,430 ft.	Bear's Den, because of its magnificent view and the wealth of paintings done at this spot, is the single most important site on North Mountain. The state calls this Sunset Rock, and gives the name Lake View Pinnacle to the original Sunset Rock. Bear's Den proper is a crevice just to the west of Jacob's Ladder. The entire ledge at the top of the ladder was referred to as the top of Bear's Den by Van Loan, Rusk, and the 1863 *Guide to Rambles*—where the only named spot on North Mountain is Bear's Den.	No mileage is given because you may elect to reach the top of Bear's Den by any of a number of ways. A couple of relatively simple climbs are along the blue trail as it passes to the west of the conglomerate outcrop. Return to Location J and proceed on the blue trail until it makes an abrupt right turn about halfway up the hill.
0.88 mi. N 42° 12.454′ W 74° 1.897′ Elev. 2,460 ft.	From this point, only the most enthusiastic history buffs will want to leave the state trail and try to retrace the Mountain House path to North Mountain. See the Bushwhack to The Cellar.	Former junction trail to Newman's Ledge is to the right and is now the main trail. Obliterated trail uphill was the original path. Continue right on blue trail.
1.2 mi. N 42° 12.603′ W 74° 1.839′ Elev. 2,464 ft.	Extensive views of the valley. From here to the outlooks on North Mountain we follow current naming conventions. This stretch of trail was not in use by Mountain House guests.	Newman's Ledge
1.6 mi. N 42° 12.759′ W 74° 2.087′ Elev. 2,580 ft.	Please don't disturb the bog. A bog is a very delicate environment and very useful to the study of forest history because it preserves layers of plant pollen that can be used to determine earlier plant types. The Cellar is about 400 feet to the south. The easiest approach is to climb the steep hill immediately ahead and turn left through the hemlock forest. The depression known as the Cellar is on the left.	Bog near the Cellar. Continue on blue trail.

GPS and Map Data	Description	Directions and Comments
2.0 mi. N 42° 12.831′ W 74° 2.090′ Elev. 2,656 ft.	Yellow trail (straight ahead) is a shortcut to Mary's Glen and the North–South Lake Public Campground. Turn right and climb uphill on the blue trail.	Badman Cave. Stay on blue trail and proceed uphill.
2.6 mi. N 42° 13.109′ W 74° 2.419′ Elev. 2,750 ft.	The next section of the hike has the steepest climb. The views from the outlooks are spectacular and worth the effort..	Trail junction. Mary's Glen is left, 1.1 miles along the red trail. Turn right and proceed uphill.
2.85 mi. N 42° 13.193′ W 74° 2.465′ Elev. 3,020 ft.	We now refer to this area as North Point. Rusk or Van Loan did not use that term. This is a more expansive view than that from Bear's Den, and allows views of the northern escarpment. The most ambitious nineteenth-century hikers would follow the trail "around the crest of North Mountain." The descriptions are vague and few, if any, illustrations exist of sites along the trail. It is therefore very difficult to identify the route of that hike.	First outlook
N 42° 13.224′ W 74° 2.436′ Elev. 3,020 ft.	We can see the northern escarpment as well as much of the Hudson Valley.	View to the north. Return by the way you came, or through Mary's Glen (see Hike 8)

Hike 8:

Through Mary's Glen to Ashley Creek and on to North Point

Distance: 6.0 miles, approximately, round-trip
Type of Trail: Marked footpath
Difficulty: Moderate to difficult, with a tough scramble to the top of North Mountain
Elevation Gain: 840 feet, Mary's Glen trailhead to North Point
Comments: You may want to return by way of the blue escarpment trail. If so, consider leaving a car at the North Lake beach parking lot.

The first part of this hike, from the trailhead parking to Ashley Falls, was described by Van Loan as "a delightful and shady walk," and he recommended it "to those who wish to avoid climbing." We will describe the entire path to North Point. One spot rarely mentioned in modern guides is the location of a lumber camp and the bed of a small cable railroad used to haul logs in the years before New York State purchased the land.

This a nice wooded walk that can be very easy if you choose to go only as far as Ashley Falls. It is a demanding hike if you go on to North Point. You also can make a loop and take the yellow spur trail to Badman Cave, and then back to the campground by the eastern escarpment. Be sure to check the map for distances if you try any variation on the hike as described below.

From the Mary's Glen trailhead on the north side of the road from the campground gate to North Lake beach, it is only about 0.25 mile to Ashley Falls [N 42° 12.421′ – W 74° 2.302′ – elev. 2,240 ft.], a small, pretty waterfall over one of the ledges of North Mountain. Take the short yellow trail to the base of the falls. Nineteenth-century hikers crossed the stream below the falls and climbed the ledge. From the top of the ledge, they crossed the stream again and followed a "well defined path" southwest along the top of Hawley's Ledge back to the lakes. Instead, you will need to return to the red trail before climbing the hill to continue on to North Point.

Once up the hill, the woods are rather thick and the trail is not very easy to follow. You will soon cross the stream just above the falls. At this spot the state has placed a marker for Mary's Glen [N 42° 12.434′ – W 74° 2.329′ – elev. 2,310 ft.] (The romantics among us will want to look for the love poem carved into a large flat rock in the streambed.) From across the stream, the trail turns north.

In about 0.1 mile, you may hear the sound of a waterfall off to the left. The fall is small and probably dry in mid to late summer. If it is running, you'll discover a pretty little waterfall [N 42° 12.523′ – W 74° 2.394′ – elev. 2,375 ft.] that is worth the short excursion.

This entire trail passes through a glacially scoured hollow. Look at the contour map and notice the half-bowl shape of the ledges of North Mountain. This hollow was once filled with ice. The ice scoured out the hollow and deposited the countless rocks that line the path and the surrounding woods.

Another 0.25 mile brings you to a ledge [N 42° 12.676′ – W 74° 2.413′ – elev. 2,420 ft.] and a yellow trail to the right that leads to Badman Cave. Continue to the left and climb the ledge, where there is another junction with the yellow trail that leads to the North Lake road just outside the main gatehouse. Day hikers can park a car at the Scutt Road parking area and take that trail to this point and on to North Lake without entering the campground.

Stay on the red trail, and in another 0.5 mile you will reach the site of a lumber camp [N 42° 12.992′ – W 74° 2.543′ – elev. 2,600 ft.] Most signs of the camp are gone, but you will be walking along the path of a short cable railroad that was used to move logs. You will recognize the spot by a crude ramp that climbs a ledge. On the right side the ledge forms a rock shelter. Just before this land was sold to the state, the Mountain House owners sold logging rights to this area. Nature is taking over again, and in the eighty or ninety years since the logging, she has reclaimed the area. You will walk through an open, young forest here. Off to your right are thick hemlock and spruce woods.

In less than 0.25 mile, you climb another small ledge and come to the junction with the blue trail [N 42° 13.109′ – W 74° 2.419′ – elev. 2,737 ft.] that leads left up a steep climb to the top of North Point, or straight ahead back to North Lake by way of the eastern escarpment. See Hike 7 for a description of North Point and the blue trail from the lakes.

GPS and Map Data	Description	Directions and Comments
	Mary's Glen trailhead day-use parking area on road to North Lake Beach.	Park at Mary's Glen day-use parking area.
0.0 mi. N 42° 12.247′ W 74° 2.427′ Elev. 2,180 ft.		Walk across the bridge to the trailhead and turn right onto Mary's Glen trail (red).
0.26 mi. N 42° 12.409′ W 74° 2.339′ Elev. 2,200 ft.	Junction of yellow trail to Ashley Falls.	Follow yellow trail to Ashley Falls, then return to red trail.
0.29 mi. N 42° 12.421′ W 74° 2.302′ Elev. 2,240 ft.	Ashley Falls. In the days of the Mountain House, hikers were told to cross the creek above the falls and follow the path past the charcoal pit and back to the Mountain House, a distance of 0.75 mile. Finding any part of this path is left for a future exploration.	Back on the red trail, continue north toward North Point.
0.33 mi. N 42° 12.434′ W 74° 2.329′ Elev. 2,310 ft.	The state labels this spot as Mary's Glen. A small boardinghouse at the foot of Scutt Road was called Glen Mary. Both terms-—Mary's Glen and Glen Mary—were used in Mountain House days.	Cross stream above falls and follow the red trail markers.
0.47 mi. N 42° 12.523′ W 74° 2.394′ Elev. 2,375 ft.	A small, seasonal waterfall is off the trail to the west.	Continue on red trail.
0.67 mi. N 42° 12.676′ W 74° 2.413′ Elev. 2,420 ft.	The yellow trail is a shortcut to Badman Cave and the blue escarpment trail.	Yellow trail joins with red. Continue uphill. At the top of the small ledge, the yellow and red trails separate. The yellow trail leads to North Lake Road near the gatehouse. Continue on the red.

GPS and Map Data	Description	Directions and Comments
1.17 mi. N 42° 12.992′ W 74° 2.543′ Elev. 2,600 ft.	Trail climbs ledge on man-made ramp. This is the site of a small cable rail system at a lumber camp in the 1910s. Don't expect anything elaborate. Nature has covered virtually all traces. I passed over this path many times without noticing it. All that remains are a few rusted pipes in the woods and an occasional chunk of coal.	Rock shelter on right of trail.
1.4 mi. N 42° 13.109′ W 74° 2.419′ Elev. 2,737 ft.	This is the location of mile 2.6 on Hike 7.	Junction with blue trail. Turn left and begin the steep uphill to North Point.
1.55 mi. N 42° 13.193′ W 74° 2.465′ Elev. 3,020 ft.	First lookout North Point	Top of ledge with views toward Pine Orchard and the lakes
1.60 mi. N 42° 13.224′ W 74° 2.436′ Elev. 3,020 ft.	Lookout to the North	Views to the north

Bushwhack to the Cellar

Distance: 2.5 miles round-trip from North Lake beach
Type of Trail: Marked footpath and bushwhack
Difficulty: Moderate
Elevation Gain: 440 feet
Comments: Read the described hike before you start; there are easier options you may want to consider.

One North Mountain landmark from Van Loan's map is not on the current trail. I decided to try and locate the Cellar using Van Loan's map and description. It is, Van Loan tells us, "a natural cavity about one hundred feet square." His map is clear, but the trail has been moved, so I followed Van Loan's trail description. The way is overgrown, and the Cellar [N 42° 12.697′ – W 74° 2.076′ – elev. 2,575 ft.] is difficult to find. It is even more difficult to recognize. This is an excursion for purists who have to take the original routes.

The Cellar is at the head of Ashley's Creek, but more of a narrow passage than a square cavity. The walls on both sides are steep, creating the cool, moist, primitive atmosphere so revered by our nineteenth-century predecessors. The forests on the opposite sides of the passage are strikingly different. On the west is a mature hemlock and spruce woods, in Rusk's words "as beautiful a piece of wood as is often met with." On the east is stunted pitch pine with blueberry undergrowth.

The narrow passageway is, according to Robert Titus, the outlet of a glacial lake. A full description can be found in the latest edition of his book, *The Catskills in the Ice Age.*

Some will want to use the table below to bushwhack along the path described by Van Loan, but a simpler approach is to take the Escarpment Trail north from Newman's Ledge. The trail proceeds north, then turns left and ascends a short but steep hill. At the top of the hill, a striking ledge, about twenty feet high, juts out above and to the left of the trail. Immediately after the ledge is a small bog on the left [N 42° 12.759′ – W 74° 2.087′ – elev. 2,580 ft.], and beyond the bog another steep uphill. (Bogs of this type are fragile environments and are of great value for research in forest history. Under no circumstances should you enter the bog.) This bog is at the head of the streambed that runs through The Cellar and feeds Ashley's Creek.

GPS and Map Data	Description	Directions and Comments
0.0 mi. N 42° 11.839′ W 74° 2.071′ Elev. 2,150 ft. **Location T**	From the top of Mountain Turnpike at the picnic area, follow the blue trail north as for Hike 7 to the hill beyond the junction to Bear's Den.	Mountain Turnpike
0.85 mi. N 42° 12.461′ W 74° 1.868′ Elev. 2,420 ft. **Location J**		At intersection of blue trail and the spur to Bear's Den (the state's misnamed Sunset Rock).
N 42° 12.454′ W 74° 1.897′ Elev. 2,460 ft.	The trail uphill is rough. On top are relatively open woods. You will need a GPS unit, a compass, and a good sense of direction.	Newman's Ledge trail is to the right. The original trail passing the Cellar is obscured, but went uphill. Leave the blue trail and climb to the top of the hill. Find the highest part of the hill and turn right. The Cellar is about 0.3 miles at about 10° west of magnetic north.
1.1 mi. N 42° 12.697′ W 74° 2.076′ Elev. 2,575 ft.	The Cellar is a narrow gap at the head of Ashley's Creek. The bog that feeds it is to the north, and the blue trail is just beyond.	The Cellar. Climb out on the west side and walk north to find the blue trail

Climb the second hill. The blue trail continues to Badman Cave. A bushwhack left of the trail for 400 to 500 feet will take you to the top of the Cellar. You will have to return by the same route, since the terrain through the Cellar and on the opposite side is rough.

Last on North Mountain. *Thomas Nast, "Sketches among the Catskills," 1866.*

PART V

Hikes in Kaaterskill Clove

BUTTER MILK FALLS. KAATERSKILL CLOVE VIEWS. HALFWAY TREE.

Hike 9:

The Road That Couldn't Be Built

Distance: 4.5 miles round-trip
Type of Trail: Carriage road
Difficulty: Moderate to difficult
Elevation Gain: 1,260 feet
Comments: Check the maps and decide before you go which option you may want to take on your return. With a little planning, you can place a second car for a convenient return trip.

The story of the Harding Road to Hotel Kaaterskill is one of backwoods ingenuity winning out over college training. Built by local men in a single year after engineers declared it impossible, the road now provides a picturesque approach to the clove rim by foot, horse, or mountain bike. The road passes through the Gulf, a gorge cut deep into the north wall of Kaaterskill Clove. At the road's deepest incursion a small, sheltered stream is all that remains of the torrent that must have carved this gorge. Other features include glimpses of Kaaterskill Clove, a wide variety of valley and mountain plants, naturally carved rock ledges, and construction cuts made by the men who built this road over one hundred years ago.

Take Route 23A to Palenville and turn north on White Road just west of Gloria Dei Episcopal Church, which was built just before Rusk's and Van Loan's guides were published. You may also start at the small parking area on Route 23A near the entrance to the clove, but parking is limited there. The walk is best when combined with a walk along the clove rim (see Hike 4) or other options on South Mountain. You may want to leave a car at the Scutt Road parking area near North Lake or at the North Lake beach parking area in order to make this a one-way hike. Plan before you leave.

George Harding's road to Hotel Kaaterskill was built in the winter of 1880–81 while he was building the hotel on the top of South Mountain. It is known by many names, including Kaaterskill Park Turnpike. It is sometimes called "The Road That Couldn't Be Built" because of the story of its difficult construction. Just a few years later, rail service on the Ulster and Delaware reached South Lake. Because of this, the road didn't receive the attention of travelers, artists, and writers that created the legacy of the Mountain Turnpike to Pine Orchard. If this beautiful approach to South Mountain had the advantage of the same sixty years of history enjoyed by the

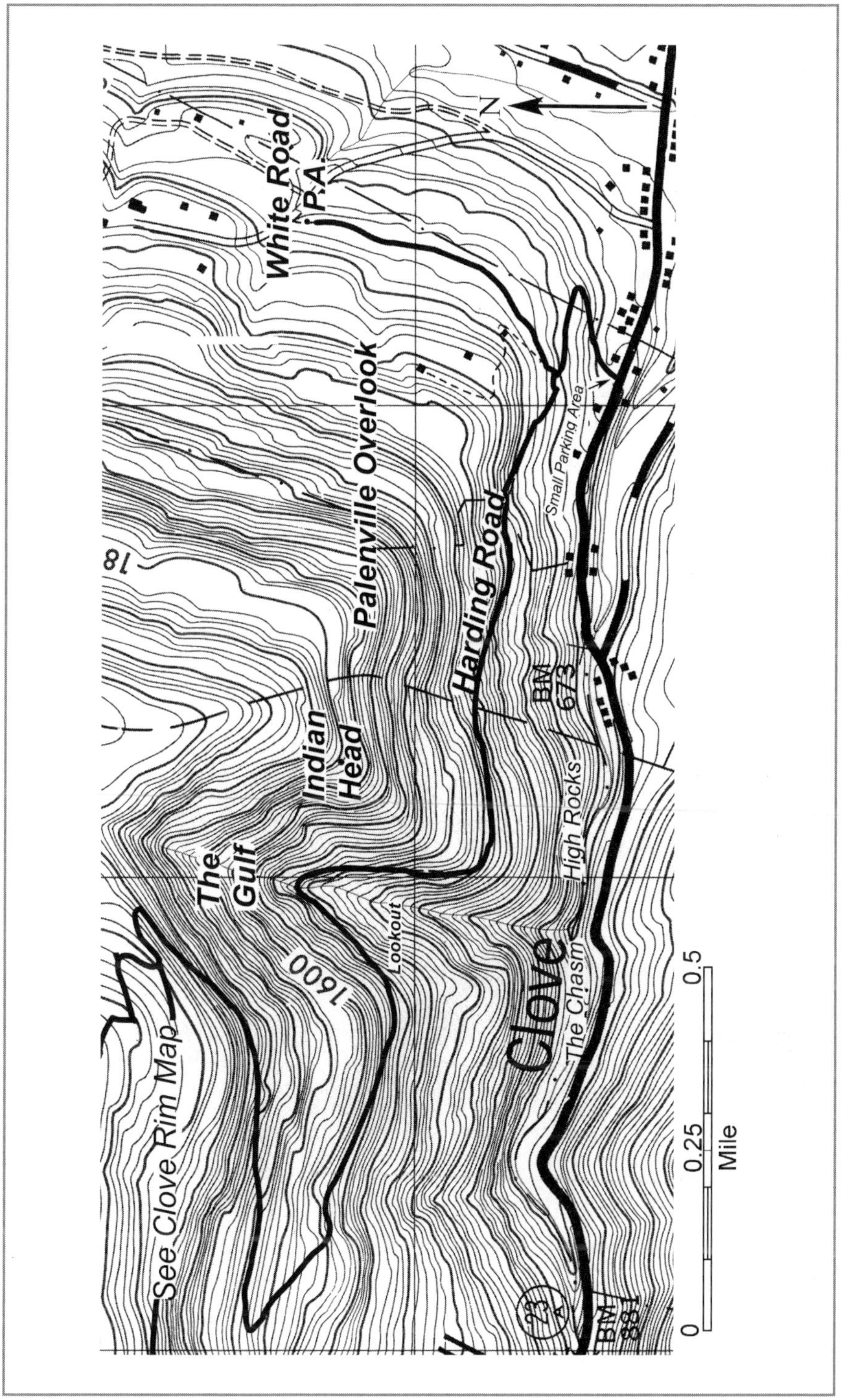
White Road
P.A
Palenville Overlook
Harding Road
Small Parking Area
BM 673
Indian Head
The Gulf
High Rocks
Lookout
1600
Clove
The Chasm
See Clove Rim Map
23A
0
0.25
0.5
Mile

Mountain Turnpike, it too would have been the subject of paintings and awe-filled descriptions that immortalized the older approach.

A comparison of the two roads is inevitable. Both pass through a gorge, provide glimpses of the terrain below, cross wild picturesque streams, tell of the difficulties of early mountain travel, and give a sense of the sublime. It is even possible to draw point-by-point parallels in the description of the two roads. The most striking difference is that the Mountain Turnpike looks down into the Hudson Valley, whereas Harding Road looks down into Kaaterskill Clove. Harding's road leads to the footpath along the north rim of the clove, giving the hiker an opportunity to experience the clove from many different perspectives in a single moderate walk. To take advantage of this opportunity and to avoid the need to retrace your path back down the mountain, it is wise to leave a car at the Scutt Road parking area or at North Lake.

Now part of the Sleepy Hollow Horse Trail system, Harding Road is also popular with hikers and mountain bike riders. The road takes a steep and winding route on the north side of the clove, passing through the Gulf. It has been said that Harding engaged experts (either railroad engineers or a surveyor from Philadelphia, depending on the account that you read) who pronounced the route impossible. Not one to be dissuaded, Harding found

View on the Horse Shoe Curve on the Road to Palenville, Passing around Tremper's Clove, under Indian Head, the Hudson valley in the Distance. *Views of Harding's road to the Hotel Kaaterskill are rare. This one, from the west of the horseshoe curve is from a Hotel Kaaterskill advertising brochure, "Kaaterskill Mountains," circa 1893. Courtesy of Justine and Hillard Hommel.*

two local men, Edward Dibble and Collins Hyser,[50] who climbed to the ledges on the south side of the clove and traced out a potential route by sight. The road was completed "at enormous expense"[51] in the winter and spring of 1881. Harding's publicity trumpeted the new road, as can be seen in this paragraph from a souvenir publication that is full of hyperbole:

> We believe that the feeling of every one who has gone up and around the mountain side, from the beautiful valley of the Catskill below, along the firm, smooth road beginning at the mountain's base, is, before his arrival at the broad plateau upon which the HOTEL KAATERSKILL is situated, that of overpowering astonishment at the magnitude of the work executed under circumstances so difficult and in a period so brief. The site chosen was three thousand feet above the sea-level; it was without any artificial path or approach. The season was winter, the snow was lying three feet deep from the mountain's summit to its base, the thermometer indicated a temperature of ten degrees below zero, and the winds were blowing at a rate which they seldom or never attain in the lowlands. As all the material for the hotel had to be hauled by horses to the selected site, from the steamboat landing or railroad station on the banks of the Hudson below, a road had to be built, and the skill and experience of some of the most noted railroad engineers of the country were called into requisition to supply plans for its construction. They were all found either impracticable or too costly, and the plan of a native mountain engineer was finally adopted. The choice could not have been a better one, as the result proves, for among the most famous of the mountain roads of Switzerland, including those built by the first Napoleon, there is none finer in any single particular than that over which the visitor is rapidly driven up the face of the Kaaterskill. That road being finished, others were at once constructed, and there are now completed, or in course of completion, twenty miles of the most perfect driving-roads in the country, which open up to the guests of the Hotel the most attractive features of the Catskill Mountains.[52]

Begin the ascent at the White Road parking area [**N 42° 10.920′ – W 74° 1.569′ – elev. 860 ft.**] and proceed past a stone quarry until the road comes to a T [**N 42° 10.657′ – W 74° 1.797′ – elev. 825 ft.**] Turn to the left and proceed a short distance downhill to the Harding Road itself [**N 42° 10.643′ – W 74° 1.817′**]. There, turn right and begin the climb through the clove. The road to the left leads to Route 23A. At the foot of this road is a small, marked parking area that is an alternate starting point for this walk. We soon pass another unmarked trail, leading off to the left. There are still other branches off our road, suggesting that the ravine that we will pass through had much use, perhaps providing hemlock for the tannery in the clove. Indeed, both Rusk and Van Loan indicate that there were wood roads into this ravine from the mouth of the clove and from the area of Moore's Bridge.

Signs of the construction methods used for this road are numerous and interesting. Notice the many supporting stone walls, some quite high and many feet long, all along the climb. Notice also the numerous stone culverts. A few of these have filled in, and where this has happened, the road below the culvert is often badly eroded.

The first view of the clove is located in the area of the sign-in box [**N 42° 10.747′ – W 74° 2.575′ – elev. 1,193 ft.**] From there we can see into the clove and upward to Kaaterskill High Peak on the opposite side. Directly ahead we can look across the Gulf and upward to the steep side of South Mountain near the top of our walk. Before we get there, the road will take us deep into this ravine and then deep into the clove before it turns back to the east. High above us to the northeast, but out of view, is the ledge known as Point of Rocks (Indian Head). Below us is the lower portion of Kaaterskill Clove.

This is where the road turns into a ravine. Far below us is the small stream that starts near Fairy Spring and enters the clove just near the deep chasm east of Moore's Bridge.

There are two ravines on the north side of Kaaterskill Clove—Lake Creek Ravine (which contains Kaaterskill Falls) and this ravine, known as the Gulf (which the Hotel Kaaterskill brochures called Tremper's Clove). The Gulf, according to Robert Titus, was created when escaping waters from a glacial lake cascaded violently down the side of the clove.[53] As you pass by the relatively small stream, try to imagine the torrent that carved out this large scar on the side of Kaaterskill Clove. Nowhere is this more evident than at the deepest incursion of the road into the ravine [**N 42° 10.958′ – W 74° 2.601′ – elev. 1,289 ft.**] There the road makes a hairpin turn, crossing the stream near the abutment of an old bridge, reminiscent of the Rip Van Winkle House site on Mountain Turnpike—dark, lush, and green with moss and hardwood forest. The small stream tumbles through a deep scar far too big for its thin flow to have cut.

The road now takes us back out into the main part of Kaaterskill Clove, climbing gently uphill past dripping rocks on the right. As the road turns back into the clove, we are at a location reminiscent of Little Pine Orchard on Mountain Turnpike. The road is eroded because of a blocked culvert that we will soon pass. The path bypasses the original road to avoid the eroded section, which is often flooded. Just across the small stream and downhill is a small ledge [N 42° 10.890′ – W 74° 3.138′] from which you can get a view (only partially obscured by small trees) to the east into the clove. About 250 feet to the west of that ledge and at the same level is a flat area similar to the area around Sphinx Rock on Prospect Mountain, complete with large boulders at the base of the ledge. The area is wooded and the view is obscured, but had the road been in use throughout the nineteenth century, that view would have been revered and would have become a well-known feature of the Kaaterskill region.

Return to the road and follow it uphill past the blocked culvert. Continue to the point where the road turns abruptly back to the east [N 42° 11.010′ – W 74° 3.274′ – elev. 1,760 ft.] There, under the ledges of the clove rim, is what was known as the Amphitheater. Uphill and not far to the east is Inspiration Point; almost due south is Moore's Bridge. From this point on to the next junction, the trail climbs slowly and steadily. Near the end of this section is yet another indication of nineteenth-century road construction techniques. A ledge on the left of the trail has a bed of shale that has been extensively undermined. I suspect that the shale was used to surface the road.

From there, it is only a short distance to the junction with the horse trail to Palenville Overlook, where you have several options.

Continuing to the left less than 0.2 mile, you will reach the junction with Ledge Drive that I've called Location V [N 42° 11.129′ – W 74° 2.706′]. The Harding Road leads uphill to the right to the Hotel Kaaterskill site and on to the Mountain House site and North Lake. You may want to pass this junction and leave the carriage road in about 500 feet to take the clove rim trail (see Hike 4). This will take you above the clove, make your walk an exploration of the whole north side of Kaaterskill Clove, and give you some of the very best views in all of the Catskills.Those who are up for a longer walk and who have left a car at the base of Mountain Turnpike may want to continue from the junction with the horse trail and go to Palenville Overlook. From there, it is possible to follow the Old Wood Road to Mountain Turnpike and descend to the parking area near Bogart Road (see Hike 6 and Hike 1).

GPS and Map Data	Description	Directions and Comments
0.0 mi. N 42° 10.920′ W 74° 1.569′ Elev. 860 ft.	White Road parking area, Palenville	White Road is the right-hand turn just past Gloria Dei Episcopal Church on Route 23A west as you approach Kaaterskill Clove in Palenville. The parking area is less than 0.5 mile uphill on the left. Park here and follow the horse trail.
0.1 mi. N 42° 10.838′ W 74° 1.618′ Elev. 860 ft.		Note the stone quarry on the left.
0.2 mi. N 42° 10.656′ W 74° 1.797′ Elev. 825 ft.	Junction. Turn left, downhill. The path to the right follows the old road to Palenville Overlook. It passes an old homestead and a bluestone quarry, but it is not marked; may pass over private property, and there are turnoffs that can be confusing.	At junction turn left and descend a short distance.
N 42° 10.643′ W 74° 1.817′ Elev. 815 ft.	As you climb Harding Road, note the stone walls supporting the road on the left, as well as the stone culverts. Talus or slag on the right is probably from another quarry. At an elevation of about 1,100 feet, the road levels off.	Junction. Turn right onto Harding Road and begin ascent.
0.8 mi. N 42° 10.747′ W 74° 2.575′ Elev. 1,193 ft.	Just beyond the trail register box, the trail turns to the right. We are turning into The Gulf, a ravine in the north side of Kaaterskill Clove. Note the eroded surfaces of the rocks.	Registration booth
1.1 mi. N 42° 10.958′ W 74° 2.601′ Elev. 1,289 ft.	This spot is reminiscent of Sleepy Hollow at the site of Rip's House.	Hairpin turn at deepest penetration into the Gulf.

GPS and Map Data	Description	Directions and Comments
1.2 mi. N 42° 10.907′ W 74° 3.126′	A small grassy area with a small stream that flows in spring. The trail ascends gradually here, followed by a steep ascent to the next turn.	Sharp right turn into the Amphitheater. A short downhill climb from here leads to two interesting areas.
N 42° 10.890′ W 74° 3.138′	Outlook toward the lower clove. Use care since there is a downhill slope leading to a small ledge. The ledge provides a mostly open view eastward into the clove. About 250 feet to the west is a small flat area.	Before the turn, ahead and downhill, is an excursion to a small ledge with a view.
1.6 mi. N 42° 11.010′ W 74° 3.274′ Elev. 1,760 ft.	We are at the western-most reach of the road. This is deep in the Amphitheater below Inspiration Point.	Sharp turn back to the east along a level stretch of the old road.
N 42° 11.165′ W 74° 2.533′ (interpolated position)	Red shale has been removed from under the ledge at the side of the trail. It may have been used to surface part of the road.	Ledge at side of trail.
2.2 mi. N 42° 11.203′ W 74° 2.529′ Elev. 2,120 ft.	You've reached the top. From here you can go to Palenville Overlook, follow the carriage road or rim trail to Scutt Road, or continue on to the Hotel Kaaterskill site.	Trails at clove rim. Refer to Hike 4 and Hike 5. Location V is just ahead to the left. The horse trail to Palenville Overlook is to the right.

Hike 10:

The Clove, from Fawn's Leap to Kaaterskill Falls

Caution: This is a bushwhack—read the full description before you start this hike. Do not attempt this hike alone; you may need a hand up in some locations. Don't attempt this hike in cold weather when there will be danger of ice, or when the stream flow may be high during spring melt or after a heavy rain. Be sure to file a "flight plan" because you will be off trail; other hikers may not pass by for days if you need assistance.

Distance: 4.0 miles one-way
Type of Trail: Bushwhack, with a portion on marked footpath
Difficulty: Difficult
Elevation Gain: 1,000 feet
Comments: Expect to get wet. Don't go alone. Don't go after a heavy rain or thaw, or when conditions may be icy. Parking can be difficult. Leave one car at the parking area above Bastion Falls and shuttle your party to the nearest legal parking area to Fawn's Leap. Highlights include beautiful waterfalls, foundations of an abandoned community, the site of an old tannery, a wild streambed, Bastion Falls, Delmura Falls, the classic site of stream capture, and Kaaterskill Falls from below. Van Loan and Rusk describe parts of this as a ride, because it was the route of the original clove road.

The hike through Kaaterskill Clove begins at Fawn's Leap, the scenic waterfall located at the edge of Route 23A in a part of the clove famous for its many landmarks. But before we start walking, let's drive west along Route 23A from Palenville and enter the clove. We drive over the first bridge[54] and pass the last of the buildings in the community of Palenville. After a short but scenic mile, we reach Moore's Bridge near Fawn's Leap.

Route 23A, the road through the clove, was built by a private corporation and operated as Hunter Turnpike, complete with tollgates, in the 1820s.[55] Between the first two bridges, the modern road follows the path of the old turnpike. It twists and rises along a ledge. The steep side of Kaaterskill High Peak rises to your left. This is a good place on a hot summer day to turn off the air-conditioning in your car. Heavier cool air descends through the forest and gives you a hint of the mountain climate ahead.

The streambed is far below to your right and has many beautiful glens and small cascades. Artist's Grotto and La Belle Falls are near the first bridge,

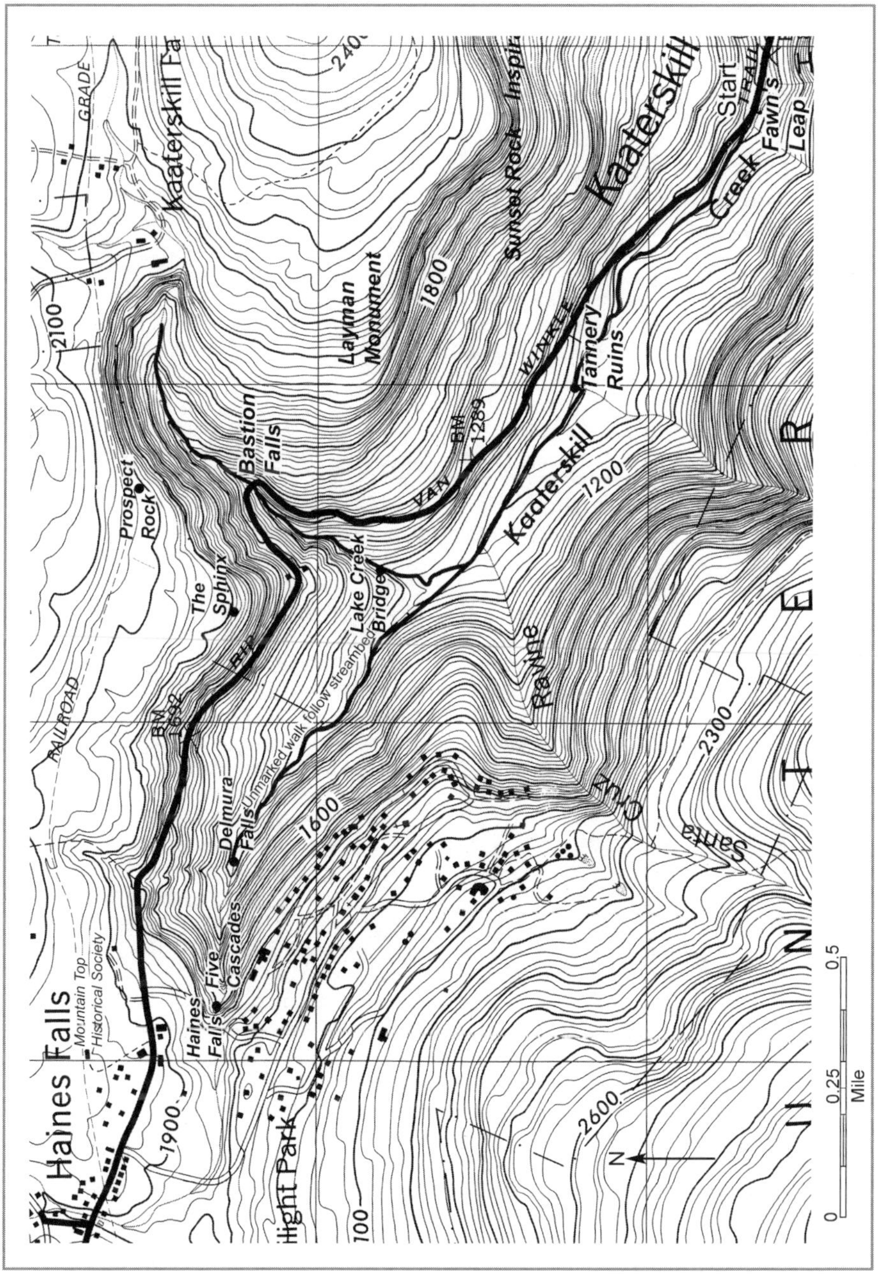

Artist Rock and Palenville Overlook. *Here, from the Rip Van Winkle Trail (Route 23A), is the familiar view of Indian Head on the left and Palenville Overlook on the right. (This is the only reference I've seen that calls Indian Head "Artist Rock.") Note the tiny bump depicting the Dodd House on Palenville Overlook.*

known as Intemann Bridge.[56] The tollbooth for this part of the turnpike was located near the parking area that is now used to access the popular swimming holes on the stream. Here the creek has cut deeply through the sedimentary layers, creating a high wall of rocks and a deep and narrow stream bed called the Chasm. Palenville Overlook and Point of Rocks (Indian Head) towering above to the right are depicted in an illustration from A.E.P. Searing's *The Land of Rip Van Winkle.* A small stream that enters the clove through a gorge on the north wall called The Gulf[57] divides the cliff wall.

Continuing along the road we come to the second bridge, still called Moore's Bridge by local residents [**N 42° 10.625′ – W 74° 3.290′ – elev. 880 ft.**] In a slower-paced age without the hazards of stopping on a major highway, tourists took time to look at the many landmarks here. The sheer wall of rock on the south is covered with ice each winter. When the ice melts, Profile Rock, a formation that looks like a man in a fur cap, is as striking today as when first discovered over one hundred years ago. The ledge itself is called Church's Ledge and is supposed to be the site of the well-known Asher Durand painting, *Kindred Spirits.*[58] Below the bridge is Dog Falls. Early maps and guides show a road starting on the west side of the bridge and going to the Gulf. It is difficult to imagine a road here. Perhaps the floods of 1996, which caused the extensive erosion still apparent downstream from the bridge, destroyed the roadbed.

Just beyond Moore's Bridge on the right side of the road is a small area where people park cars to view Fawn's Leap. Both Rusk and Van Loan discuss the legend of this name. Parking is very limited anywhere near here, so it may be necessary to park a considerable distance away and make your way along the highway—possibly the most nerve-racking part of your walk. Carefully cross the road, climb over the guardrail, and you are at the top of Fawn's Leap [**N 42° 10.645′ – W 74° 3.454′ – elev. 890 ft.**] A stereoview of the falls from below shows a small part of the building that once stood on the ledge next to the falls. The ravine that enters below the falls is Hillyer Ravine. The one that enters above the falls is Wildcat Ravine.

Follow the main stream up the clove. Starting in 1915 the portion of the road between Fawn's Leap and Haines Falls was relocated to reduce the grade for automobile traffic. The new road became known as the Rip Van Winkle Trail in 1922,[59] and New York State paved the road in 1928.[60] You may choose to follow the streambed, picking your way over and around small and large boulders—a process one hiker described as "spending the day climbing over Buicks." It may also be necessary to wade through the stream for short sections. Alternately you may follow the old, overgrown road on the right (north) side of the stream. The road is being used today as a pathway for power lines. Most people will want to hike a combination of the two. Expect to get wet! It may be safer to walk knee-deep through parts of the stream rather than try to stay dry by jumping from rock to rock.

Just west of Fawn's Leap, Route 23A turns to the right and leaves the stream and the original path of the Clove Road. This is the approximate area of Brockett's, a nineteenth-century rest stop frequented by Hudson River School artists. I suspect that the site was destroyed by the construction of the new road.

There is a foundation [N 42° 10.905′ – W 74° 3.883′ – elev. 1,050 ft.] uphill from the old road and quite near the current highway. Farther along on the old road itself are the ruins of a tannery [N 42° 10.932′ – W 74° 4.024′ – elev. 1,050 ft.], built in 1817 and closed in 1866[61] at the end of the Civil War.

Years before tourists sought out the wonders of the clove, industry was established here. Tanning operations throughout the area cut hemlock trees and used the bark to tan hides, many of which were brought here from South America. The effect on the land was a concern then, as it would be today. Searing's highly fictionalized travelogue, *The Land of Rip Van Winkle,* has her characters pass by this tannery, which was already in ruins even when she wrote in 1884. "Sir," her character exclaims, "we are a most unthrifty, wasteful people! Thus, from year to year, we recklessly devastate our forests, lay bare the sources of our streams, and so are gradually changing the climate itself!"[62]

Extensive foundations from the tannery survive, including what seems to be a sluice for a waterwheel. The area deserves interpretation by someone with knowledge of mills and tanneries.

Immediately across Kaaterskill Creek from the tannery foundations, Buttermilk Ravine enters the clove. A nice waterfall[63] is in sight, and other falls are said to be further up the ravine. Here the road starts to drift away from the stream.[64] We will stay on the streambed. We soon come to Santa Cruz Ravine [N 42° 11.117′ – W 74° 4.400′ – elev. 1,120 ft.], and just beyond, the confluence of Lake Creek entering Kaaterskill Creek from the north. There may have been a sawmill near here.[65] We will return to this spot and follow Lake Creek to Bastion Falls after we explore a little more of Kaaterskill Clove. For now, follow the left stream and continue up the clove. Rusk calls the first major waterfall Delmura Falls [N 42° 11.518′ – W 74° 5.041′ – elev. 1,400 ft.], a name that I've heard nowhere else, but one that fits the wall-like ledge the water flows over (*del muro* is Spanish for "of the wall").

Beyond this point are several other waterfalls, called the Five Cascades, and finally Haines Falls itself. But we must stop at Delmura and return to

Bridge in Catskill Clove. *Harry Fenn, 1870, engraving in* Picturesque America. *This is Moore's Bridge near Church's Ledge.*

Lake Creek, because it is difficult to climb these falls and we may enter private property belonging to Twilight Park.

From the point where Lake Creek joins the Kaaterskill, we walk the streambed until we find the location of Lake Creek Bridge [**N 42° 11.240′ – W 74° 4.436′ – elev. 1,220 ft.**] The bridge on the old road crossing Lake Creek is gone; however, the abutment remains. That abutment is clearly marked by a man-made ramp leading from the east side of the creek.

This was the starting point of the original path from the old road to Bastion Falls, Kaaterskill Falls, and the Laurel House. That path is no longer traceable, but was far more difficult than today's Kaaterskill Falls path. The construction of the "new" road in the 1920s and the extremely steep sides of the streambed have combined to obliterate much of the trail. Unfortunately, the wild beauty of the spot is marred by the sounds of trucks as they climb the steep road and shift into lower gears to negotiate the hairpin turn at Bastion Falls, above you but out of sight.

This deep in the clove, Lake Creek cuts sharply into the sediment. Massive boulders—many as large as a car, and some as large as a room—line the stream's sides and bottom creating innumerable small waterfalls. The size of the boulders and their smoothly eroded shapes tell a tale of rapid water flow. Large boulders that protrude above the stream are more angular, not having been subjected to the erosive power of the sediment-laden stream. Here the least difficult path is to scramble upstream over the boulders. I did this in late July when the stream was just a trickle. I wouldn't want to try this route after a heavy rain or during a spring thaw. Those boulders tell of violent floods, but on this day they were beautiful to observe.

Profile Rock can still be seen from Moore's Bridge. Postcard, circa 1905.

This portion of the scramble ends, and a marked trail begins at Bastion Falls [**N 42° 11.471′ – W 74° 4.255′ – elev. 1,480 ft.**], where Route 23A crosses the streambed. At this point you will need to use your best judgment. Depending on the amount of water flow in the stream, you may choose to walk under the bridge and climb to the road from the upstream side, or scurry up the steep bank to the right of the bridge. It is also possible to turn around and climb out of the gorge further downstream. The northeast bank is the less difficult climb, but watch out for debris from cars.

The remainder of the hike to Kaaterskill Falls is on a marked trail. Allegra Goodman's novel *Kaaterskill Falls,* Thomas Locker's illustrated book *To Climb a Waterfall,* the hobby of geocaching, the increased popularity of ice climbing, and the renewed interest in the Hudson River School have all added to the popularity of this historic waterfall that is just 0.25 mile from the road. As a result this trail gets extensive use year-round and can be very crowded on weekends.

Fawn's Leap is just beyond Moore's Bridge. Note the foot of a building on the ledge at the top right of the picture. A J. Loeffler stereoview, circa 1870.

Buttermilk Falls on the Kaaterskill Creek opposite the old tannery ruins. From R. Lionel DeLisser, Picturesque Catskills, Greene County, *1894.*

The series of waterfalls and rapids at the start of the trail is well-known to motorists who travel Route 23A from Palenville to Haines Falls, although many don't know its name. Before the highway was rerouted in the 1920s, these waterfalls were known only to hikers who walked from Lake Creek Bridge to Kaaterskill Falls. At that time the cascade seems to have been considered to be two separate entities. Based on stereoviews of the period, the name Bastion Falls was reserved for the first drop that is now visible from the hairpin turn on Route 23A. The series of smaller drops culminating in the portion now channeled under the bridge at the hairpin turn may have been unnamed, or may have been called Terrace Falls.[66]

The abrupt change in the direction of the stream here has caught the attention of geologists for over a hundred years. The explanation is "stream capture," or the more romantic term, "stream piracy." It is believed that the original course of Lake Creek was westward and that it was, in fact, the headwaters of Schoharie Creek, which still flows into the Mohawk River. Glacial erosion in the Hudson Valley carved the steep front of the escarpment, causing streams flowing east to have a much steeper gradient than those flowing west. One of those east-flowing creeks, the Kaaterskill, rapidly widened and cut into the streambed of the Schoharie west of Kaaterskill Falls, cutting off the headwaters, and diverting them eastward.[67]

Another notable feature of this stretch of Lake Creek is that it contains one of the lowest-elevation stands of old-growth forest in the Catskills. Michael Kudish (who calls this Spruce Creek)[68] mentions a 300-year-old hemlock that escaped the tanners.[69]

The highlight of this walk, however, is the magnificent Kaaterskill Falls. Rusk quotes William Cullen Bryant's and James Fenimore Cooper's descriptions of the waterfall. Those descriptions can be read in the reprint from Rusk's guide in the back of this book.

One of the most dramatic features of the two-tiered waterfall is the large cavern near the bottom of the upper falls. A pathway through this cavern was once accessible via a stairway from the top. Thomas Cole and Winslow Homer both produced images of this cavern that are icons of Catskill Mountain illustration. Today it is dangerous, and there is no approved way to reach it.

Perhaps the best time to see the falls is after the first green of spring when the early spring torrent has subsided but streams are still flowing. Choose a day midweek to avoid crowds. The scene you will see today is the same as that visited in 1874 by Harry Fenn and his fellow travelers writing and sketching for *Picturesque America:*

The most famous beauty of the region is the Fall of the Kauterskill. On the high table-land of the South and North Mountains lie two lakes. ... A little brook, making its way from these lakes, westward along the shoulder of the mountain, soon reaches the edge of a very steep declivity, over which it leaps into a deep pool in the centre of a great amphitheatre of rock.

Gathering its strength again, the torrent makes a second leap over huge bowlders, which have fallen from the ledges above and lie scattered down the glen, dashing itself into foam in its headlong fury. Tumbling from one ledge to another, it reaches, at length, the bottom of the glen, when, meeting the stream that flows from Haines's Fall, the mingled waters hurry down the stony pathway through the Clove, and out into the valley, until, swollen to a wide stream, they glide placidly into the Hudson at the village of Catskill. There is nothing more beautiful in American scenery than this water-fall as it leaps from the lofty height and dashes into spray in the hollow basin below. The strata of which the mountain is formed lie piled upon one another horizontally, and through them the water has cut its way smoothly like a knife. Some distance above the margin of the pool, in which the fallen waters boil as in a caldron, there is a stratum of soft stone, which has broken up and crumbled in the dampness. Wearing away several yards deep into the cliffs, it has left a pathway all around the Fall, from which you have a fine view,

Old Tannery in Kaaterskill Clove. *From R. Lionel DeLisser,* Picturesque Catskills, Greene County, *1894.*

Bastion Falls and the rapids below it are at the hairpin turn on the Rip Van Winkle Trail (Route 23A). At this point the road has left the main portion of Kaaterskill Clove and has entered Lake Creek Ravine. American Views stereoview, circa 1860s.

[This is no longer a safe pathway. *R.A.G.*]* and often, when the stream above is swollen, through a veil of glittering drops dripping from the rocks above. Exquisite as is the effect of the whole Fall, when seen from the rocks at the foot of its second leap, this last point of view is even more striking. Standing on the narrow pathway, you look through the great white veil of falling waters, leaping out over your head and sending up clouds of spray that float off down the gorge. Sometimes, when the sun is shining brightly, a dancing rainbow will keep pace with you as you creep around the semicircle beneath the rock. Here, too, you get an enchanting glimpse of the edges of the Clove, down which the stream goes headlong, and can mark the wild figures of the pines that cling to the verge of the cliffs, and seem, with their black spears, to pierce the sky.[70]

---

* The pathway described is no longer safe. It should not be attempted. See the illustration from 1884.

Catskill Falls. *Harry Fenn, 1870, engraving in* Picturesque America.
A classic view of Kaaterskill Falls

Winter, too, is a great time to visit the falls. The winter of 2002–03 had an unusually long and deep cold spell, causing the falls to freeze from bottom to top. The phenomenon is rare, but well documented. Near the end of the cold spell, I went to the top of the falls to see what Thomas Cole described when he visited the frozen waterfall on February 27, 1843. His description of the scene on that day long ago is far better than any I could give:

> To visit the scene in winter, is a privilege permitted to but few; and to visit it this winter, when the spectacle is more than usually magnificent, and, as the hunters say, 'more complete than has been known for thirty years,' is, indeed, worthy of a long pilgrimage. What a contrast to its appearance in summer! No leafy woods, no blossoms glittering in the sun, rejoice upon the steeps around.
>
> Hoary Winter
> O'er forests wide has laid his hand,
> And they are bare—
> They move and moan, a spectral band
> Struck by despair.
>
> There are overhanging rocks and the dark-browed cavern, but where the spangled cataract fell stands a gigantic tower of ice, reaching from the basin of the waterfall to the very summit of the crags. From the jutting rocks that form the canopy of which I have spoken, hang festoons of glittering icicles. Not a drop of water, not a gush of spray is to be seen. No sound of many waters strikes the ear, not even as of a gurgling rivulet or trickling rill. All is silent and motionless as death; and did not the curious eye perceive,

The Ascent to Kaaterskill Falls.
C.S. Reinhart, engraving in "Their Pilgrimage," 1884.

The many Victorian images of tourists exploring Kaaterskill Falls give a false sense that the area is safe and easy to negotiate. This view shows some of the many accoutrements that made the area relatively safe. Those features are now gone, so be careful and stay on the marked trail. Note the flat rock leaning against the streambed. On the left of the rock there is a stairway leading down from the observation railing to the footbridge. Parts of some of those stairs still exist and can be seen from the end of the state trail. From an 1884 picture folder published by Wittemann Bros. Courtesy of Larry Tompkins.

Under the Catskill Falls. *Harry Fenn, 1870, engraving in* Picturesque America. *The cavern under Kaaterskill Falls.*

through two window-like spaces of clear ice, the falling water, one might believe that all was bound in icy fetters.But there falls the cataract, not bound but shielded, as a thing too delicate for the frosts of winter to blow upon.[71]

First Leap of the Falls. *Harry Fenn, 1870, engraving in* Picturesque America. *Note the lowering basket.*

One hundred sixty years later, February 1, 2003, brought almost the same scene, except that on this day three ice climbers were scaling the column. When I told one climber of Cole's description, he remarked that when clinging to the frozen waterfall, there is no silence. It sounds like a roaring rocket.

Just how high is Kaaterskill Falls? It is often said to be the highest waterfall in New York State—higher than Niagara. Is it? Niagara's American Falls is said to be 176 feet high; however, all but the first 70 feet of that falls cascades over the rocks at its base. The Horseshoe Falls at Niagara is 167 feet.

Taller falls than Niagara in New York include Taughannoc Falls in the Finger Lakes region, with a single drop of 215 feet. Inspiration Falls in Letchworth Park, also in the Finger Lakes, is 315 feet high, but with a very low volume of water.

A survey of the many descriptions of Kaaterskill Falls shows several estimates. The earliest are vague guesses of 300 and even 400 feet. These exaggerations probably reflect the awe of mountain wanderers who happened on the spectacular waterfall. By the late 1820s the estimate of 175 feet for the first fall and 85 feet for the second had been established. This estimate is still used in the brochure given out at the North–South Lake Public Campground. Van Loan in the 1870s and "a visitor" in 1863 give the heights as 180 feet and 80 feet. This seems to be the most common estimate throughout the late 1800s. Only Rusk, who seems to pride himself on accurate measurements (a kindred spirit, I'm afraid), uses 160 feet as the height of the first fall and 80 feet as the second.

I suspect that the most accurate, albeit disappointing, measurement was made in 1992. In a letter dated August 28 of that year to Justine Hommel of the Mountain Top Historical Society, James West, then superintendent of the Bureau of Real Property of New York State Department of Environmental Conservation, states:

> On August 27, 1992 [New York State] Department [of Environmental Conservation] surveyors measured the height of Kaaterskill Falls using a Topcon Electronic Distance Meter. They determined the height of the upper falls to be 166.6 feet and the height of the lower falls to be 64.1 feet for a total of 230.7 feet.

That is 30 feet less than the most popular estimates, but the traditional, apparently erroneous 260-foot height will likely be quoted for years to come. Regardless of its true height, few other spots can challenge Kaaterskill Falls as "the best piece of work that I've met with in the woods."[72]

The Stairs to the Falls. *Thomas Nast, "Sketches among the Catskills," 1866.*

GPS and Map Data	Description	Directions and Comments
0.0 mi. N 42° 10.645′ W 74° 3.454′ Elev. 890 ft.	Explore the area around Fawn's Leap. The ravine that enters below the falls is Hillyer Ravine. The one that enters above the falls is Wildcat Ravine. It is said that there are waterfalls up each of the ravines. I haven't visited them as of this writing and do not recommend that you explore those areas.	Fawn's Leap at side of Route 23A.
0.5 mi. N 42° 10.905′ W 74° 3.883′ Elev. 1,050 ft.	Uphill from streambed and near Route 23A. You will have to descend back to the old road or the streambed. A well-known nineteenth-century stop, Brockett's, was nearby. I suspect that area may have been destroyed when the new road was built.	Foundation, perhaps part of East Hunter.
0.6 mi. N 42° 10.932′ W 74° 4.024′ Elev. 1,050 ft.	Extensive foundations are visible, including what seems to be a sluice, perhaps for a waterwheel. The area deserves exploration and interpretation by someone with knowledge of mills and tanneries. Please do not disturb the foundations, which were in ruins when Van Loan described them in the 1870s. Immediately across Kaaterskill Creek, Buttermilk Ravine enters the clove. A nice waterfall is in sight. Other falls are said to be up the ravine.	East Hunter Tannery
0.8 mi. N 42° 11.046′ W 74° 4.235′ Elev. 1,105 ft.		Foundations

GPS and Map Data	Description	Directions and Comments
1.0 mi. N 42° 11.116′ W 74° 4.400′ Elev. 1,120 ft.	This is a bail-out point. The easiest way out is back the way you came. Uphill to the right will take you up a steep climb to Bastion Falls and Route 23A. We will come back here and make that climb after we explore further into the clove.	Santa Cruz Ravine enters the clove from the south. Just upstream, Lake Creek enters from the north. The main streambed (to the left of Lake Creek) continues through Kaaterskill Clove. Follow the main stream bed.
1.7 mi. N 42° 11.518′ W 74° 5.041′ Elev. 1,400 ft.	Mentioned by Rusk, but not by Van Loan, Kaaterskill Creek tumbles over this wall of stone across its path. We will stop here and return to Lake Creek.	Delmura Falls. Visit the spot, then return downstream to Lake Creek.
2.4 mi. N 42° 11.116′ W 74° 4.400′ Elev. 1,120 ft.		Back to Lake Creek. Turn north up creek bed.
2.50 mi. N 42° 11.240′ W 74° 4.436′ Elev. 1,220 ft.	Explore the area on the east side of the creek, where you will find a built-up ramp to the bridge. I haven't yet explored beyond the west side of the bridge.	Lake Creek Bridge
	A very steep climb out of the clove toward Bastion Falls. This steep terrain and the very large boulders in the streambed indicate a young and very active stream. You don't want to be here when the stream is flowing rapidly.	Continue uphill following the streambed of Lake Creek.
2.8 mi. N 42° 11.171′ W 74° 4.255′ Elev. 1,480 ft.	I have crossed under the bridge in dry seasons. In slightly wetter seasons I've climbed out on the right-hand side. Once out, take the state trail to Kaaterskill Falls. If you have had it, and you left a car at the parking area, you might want to save Kaaterskill Falls for another day. GPS reads consistently too high in elevation, so I have taken elevation from a contour map.	Bastion Falls. Find your way to the road. (See suggestions in the center column.)

GPS and Map Data	Description	Directions and Comments
3.3 mi. N 42° 11.598′ W 74° 3.870′ Elev. 1,760 ft.	"The best piece of work I've met with in the woods," says Leather-stocking in James Fenimore Cooper's *The Pioneers.* From this location you have a good view of the falls. Look at the top surface of this rock for another carving of S. Root's name. Caution is the word here. Don't try to climb to the top of the falls or to the ledge in the cavern under the falls. The trail is eroded and dangerous. Remember that the elegant ladies in long skirts shown under the falls in many old illustrations arrived there by a staircase from above.	Kaaterskill Falls
3.8 mi. N 42° 11.471′ W 74° 4.255′ Elev. 1,480 ft.		Return to Bastion Falls.
4.0 mi. N 42° 11.394′ W 74° 4.444′ Elev. 1,550 ft.	The parking area is locally called Molly Smith's, for a souvenir shop and snack bar that was here in the 1950s. A historic marker for Frank Layman has been placed here recently. It directs your attention to the Layman's Monument that is part of the clove rim hike.	Follow the road uphill to the parking area above the hair-pin turn on Route 23A.

Afterword

To paraphrase George Lucas, books are not released, they escape, and that is certainly the case with this one. There are many things that could have been included in this book had time and space permitted. Some things came to light too close to the publication deadline to be explored, some locations worthy of exploration are now in private hands or require crossing private lands, and the need to limit the scope of the book forced the exclusion of still other important areas.

Chief among these important places are Prospect Mountain near the Laurel House, and the lower sections of Kaaterskill Clove that include the many waterfalls in Palenville. The lower clove was once an important retreat for artists and visitors. Today it is full of popular swimming holes accessed by what local rangers refer to as "herd paths"—unofficial and unmaintained access routes of dubious safety. That safety issue and the nature of current use caused me to skip over this important area.

Prospect Mountain is another issue. A path across this mountain, which lies west of South Mountain between the Laurel House and the hamlet of Haines Falls, was among the earliest trails in the region. It became the route of the two railways that served the hotels. Three important locations once accessible from that path deserve special mention. One, the Sphinx—

The Sphinx guards access to the top of Kaaterskill Clove from its perch above the Molly Smith parking area. Postcard, circa 1920.

View from Prospect Rock—Kaaterskill Falls. *A.E.P. Searing's* The Land of Rip Van Winkle, *1884. Today, no publicly accessible trail leads to Prospect Rock, which is more of a steep hillside than a ledge.*

This 1883 map from an edition of the Hotel Kaaterskill's souvenir publication, "Haunts of Rip Van Winkle," shows many of the traditional features of the region, but also includes information not seen on other maps. The locations of the stables and the hotel's laundry are depicted. Several paths developed by the hotel that are shown on this map and mentioned in the text are not depicted on the older maps. The text also gives names to many of the carriage roads near the hotel. Courtesy of the Greene County Historical Society.

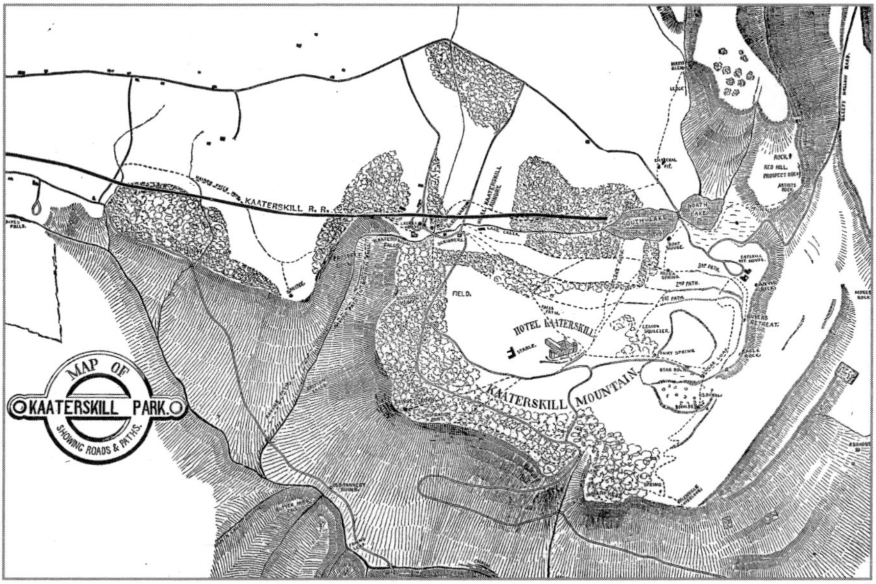

well-known to postcard collectors—stands guard over the upper clove above Molly Smith's parking area. As best as I can determine, it is on state land. Access to it, however, is either via an extremely difficult climb or a relatively easy approach that requires crossing private property. Very near the Sphinx is a clearing that takes in the upper portion of Kaaterskill Falls, a beautiful view of the clove, and the peaks of Round Top and High Peak. No other spot allows all three to be seen at the same time. The third location is a viewpoint named (like the ledge on North Mountain) Prospect Rock. This Prospect Rock is perhaps the best place from which to see both the upper and lower portions of Kaaterskill Falls in a single view, but it, too, is virtually inaccessible except by crossing private land.

Opening these areas would be a real benefit to visitors and to the mountaintop community. Recently there has been renewed interest in a rail trail between the hamlet of Haines Falls and Laurel House Road that would follow the rail corridor and run close to the trail that was discussed by both Van Loan and Rusk. Reopening that trail would provide a link between the local community and the beautiful facilities at North–South Lake.

At least one other set of trails dates back to the Mountain House days and connects with the Mountain House trail network. Winter Clove resort near Cairo has historic trails that were known to both Rusk and Van Loan. Today their trail system reaches to North Point.

The map of the Kaaterskill Park that is included in this book shows trails developed by the Hotel Kaaterskill that have not been explored in over seventy-five years. Can those trails, with their stairways and other improvements, still be found? I look forward to the challenge.

Good-By. *Thomas Nast, "Sketches among the Catskills," 1866.*

APPENDIX

In Their Own Words: Historic Guides to the Kaaterskill Region

View at More Bridge.
From Rusk's An Illustrated Guide to the Catskill Mountains.

Selections from

Catskill Mountain Guide With Bird's-Eye View Maps and Choice Illustrations

By Walton Van Loan
Catskill, NY

A composite of the 1879 and 1882 Editions
With notes from later editions.

WHERE TO WALK.

STARTING FROM THE MOUNTAIN HOUSE.

Circuit of South Mountain	One hour.
Direct path to South Mountain	Half an hour.
Path to Kaaterskill* Falls, south of Lake	Two hours.
Path to Kaaterskill Falls, north of Lake	Two and a half hours.
Palenville Overlook, over South Mountain	Three hours.
To Sunset Rock, South Mountain	Three hours.
To Moses' Rock, direct route	One hour.
To Boat House on South Lake	Half an hour.
To Lovers' Retreat, South Mountain	Fifteen minutes.
Artist's Rock, Prospect Rock, North Mountain	One hour.
Sunset Rock, Bear's Den, North Mountain	One and a half hours.
Newman's Ledge, North Mountain	Two and a half hours.
Around the Crest, North Mountain	Five hours.
Mary's Glen, North Mountain	Two hours.

*Kau-ters-kill.

WHERE TO WALK.

CIRCUIT OF SOUTH MOUNTAIN.

TAKE the direct path, following the painted guide-mark (round white, crossed by a red bar) until you climb the second ledge, where, by taking the right-hand path, along which the painted guide-mark (square white, with red dot) will lead you past many bowlders—covered with gray lichen—whose tops are carpeted with moss and ferns. You will soon come to the "Druid Rocks"—several detached rocks of conglomerate, one of which resembles a gigantic toad or rabbit, according to the position from which you observe it. For some distance, after passing these, you follow near the ledge of which they once formed a part; the path then leads you up this ledge and after going a short distance sweeps in a half-circle to the left and brings you to the next higher ledge, where, near each other, are the "Lemon Squeezer" and "Fairy Spring." Water dripping from this ledge has formed a small basin, and at times the border of it is covered with a green moss. The "Lemon Squeezer" is a very narrow fissure in the ledge known by some as the "Elfin Pass."

Just beyond "Fairy Spring" *turn to the left,* and come out on top of South Mountain, as the path leading to the right is very difficult for strangers to follow any distance without a guide. [The 1897 version states: The path leading to the right, and the road a little beyond, leads to the Hotel Kaaterskill, which is in full sight. *R.A.G.*]

Follow the path to the most prominent rock (on which a star is painted) and then the path to the bowlder, not far distant, is easily found.

Return by way of the eastern face of South Mountain and descend through the "Pudding Stone Hall," which will bring you a moment afterwards to the second ledge, where you branched off to make the "Circuit of South Mountain." "Eagle Rock" and "The Sphinx" are portions of the front ledge on the South Mountain. To see the latter to advantage it is well to descend the ledge by a foot-path to the North of it.

Author's note: The 1897 version adds the following paragraph:

TO HOTEL KAATERSKILL.

Take either path to top of South Mountain, and from Star Rock, half a mile from Mountain House, take marked path or road the other half mile. A walk double the distance is via the Lake Road to Kaaterskill Station, thence by road or marked path, for a distance of three-fourths of a mile, after crossing the bridge at the railroad station.

On the south side of the road, near the lake, is a large bowlder that resembles an alligator, with its jaws wide open.

DIRECT PATH TO SOUTH MOUNTAIN.

Follow the path that enters the mountain at the South-west corner of the Mountain House and look for the painted guide-mark (round white, crossed by a red bar) which leads you first up quite a small ledge and next up a second and much higher ledge, (at the top of this ledge the path divides), the direct path still ascends, and passing through "Pudding Stone Hall" the third ledge is ascended and the top of South Mountain reached. To the bowlder and back along the path marked out is but a short walk. High Peak and Round Top loom up grandly as seen from the top of South Mountain, while the Highlands at West Point and Mountains in New Jersey are visible on the Southern horizon.

Author's note: The 1891 edition describes a new path that may be along the modern state trail. The first climb of the modern trail was slightly modified in the fall of 2003 by creating a zigzag to lessen the slope and to bypass the eroded hillside.

NEW PATH TO SOUTH MOUNTAIN.

Just as you enter the woods by the usual route, turn to the left, as the sign board indicates, and the new path follows under the eastern ledge of South Mountain; passing a rustic Summer House on the way, and as far beyond, you reach the top of the mountain near eagle rock, and only a short distance from Star Rock and the Bowlder.

PATH TO KAATERSKILL FALLS—SOUTH OF LAKE.

The shortest and shadiest path to the Kaaterskill Falls, begins back of the Mountain House barns, and is very distinct all the way.

There are two fine springs on the left as you go. Soon after passing Scribner's house and saw-mill you reach Glen Mary, near the Laurel House, and cross Lake Creek on a rustic bridge, which is but a short distance from the Kaaterskill Falls.

The above path *on the South side* of the Lake had better be avoided for a day or two after a rain, as some portions of it are badly drained.

PATH TO KAATERSKILL FALLS—NORTH OF LAKE.

Follow the main road or water-pipe beyond the two lakes, then take the path at the left, opposite the charcoal-pit—follow at the side of the stone fence—and the path through the woods is very direct to the Scribner Road. Cross over and enter the opposite lot on the right-hand side of the house. The path will lead you across Spruce Creek at the Laurel House laundry, near the Kaaterskill Falls.

On the South-side of the road, near the lakes, is a large bowlder that resembles an alligator with its jaws wide open.

The waters from the two lakes and from Spruce Creek combine, a short distance from the grand amphitheatre of rock, and plunges over the projecting seventy feet of massive roofing to the natural cavern beneath, a clear fall of one-hundred and eighty feet. It then passes a few yards over a smooth flat rock and takes another plunge of eighty feet.

Parties can descend by safe steps to the bottom of the two falls, two-hundred and sixty feet. A well-trodden and safe path leads behind the first fall and comes out on the opposite side of the amphitheatre. You can then cross back at the top of the second fall. The Bastion Falls are on this stream and can be reached by a path that follows the stream and comes out on the Clove road.

SUNSET ROCK ON SOUTH MOUNTAIN.

Start from Scribner's or Mary's Glen, near the Laurel House, and take the path marked out on the map. No visitor to the mountains should miss going to the Sunset Rock, as the view of the Clove is magnificent, and the grandeur of High Peak, seen from its base in the Kaaterskill, two-thousand feet below you, to its summit, four-thousand feet, is wonderful in its mass of unbroken foliage.

The view west takes in Haines' Falls, the Hunter Valley and distant mountains.

A remarkable echo is produced here by the firing of a gun.

Authors note: An addition in the 1897 version states: A path has been laid out below the ledge, passing under Inspiration Point and coming out at the road at the head of "The Gulf."

PALENVILLE OVERLOOK, OR HIGH ROCK.

Take the direct path up and over South Mountain to the "Bowlder," near which, to the left, is a fissure in the ledge forming a narrow passage-way down through the ledge. The path is quite plain for some distance, but over the stony portion you will find it indicated by piles of stone.

The "Overlook" or "High Rock," is 1728 feet above the bed of the creek below, and is almost perpendicular.

The usual way back (to the Mountain House) is to follow the old wood-road on the east side of the mountain. Just before the rise in this road toward the "Long Level," the path at the right leads to "Moses' Rock."

MOSES' ROCK—DIRECT PATH.

Go down the mountain road and take the path beginning on the "Long Level" *Pass by* the old wood-road (leading to the Palenville Overlook) and descend the path to the rock, which is about one-hundred feet in length and twenty feet high. The face of the Rock is covered with moss, and at a point three feet from the ground water issues through a crevice in its side. A path from here leads to the foot of the mountain, directly below the Mountain House.

TO BOAT-HOUSE ON SOUTH LAKE.

Follow the main road west, and where it turns to the right, by an open space, take the path directly ahead among the trees.

TO BOATS ON NORTH LAKE.

Cross the mountain road where it turns to go down the mountain, by the carpenter's shop, and follow the wood-road down the bank to the lake.

LOVER'S RETREAT—SOUTH MOUNTAIN.

A few hundred feet South of the Mountain House and along the path near the edge of the ledge, a large hemlock and pine are so near each other that their roots above ground intermingle, forming *seats for two.* The path beyond here will lead to South Mountain, but the direct path is preferable.

ARTIST'S ROCK AND PROSPECT ROCK—NORTH MOUNTAIN.

Go down the Mountain road to the general entrance of North Mountain, at the top of the second hill (where the road turns to the right and descends) and take the right-hand path. The first outlook is from a smooth ledge along the path, and a little beyond, Artist's Rock is situated. Here you have a fine view of the Mountain House and its projecting ledge. After leaving this point the path ascends some rude stone steps, and a few hundred feet beyond comes out on Prospect Rock. A more extended view both North and South can be had here than at the Mountain House. In the North the Adirondacks are visible on a clear day, and the city of Albany can be seen with a good opera glass. The southern view takes in the Highlands at West Point.

This spot was the favorite of Thomas Cole, the artist, whose studio in Catskill, in which he painted the "Voyage of Life," can be distinguished by those knowing its location.

SUNSET ROCK AND BEAR'S DEN—NORTH MOUNTAIN.

Passing "Artist's Rock" and "Prospect Rock," as above directed, the path ascends "Red Hill," and a short distance further passes to the left of a large rock. This is "Sunset Rock." Walk to the highest part of it, and facing the west, call out in a loud voice, and an echo will be heard coming as it were from the distant side of North Mountain. The path now leaves the front ledge, and passing rather to the left, brings you to "Jacob's Ladder."

One opening into the "Bear's Den" can be seen near the foot of the ladder, but a more interesting examination of the numerous caverns or fissures in the rock can be seen after ascending the ladder and going a short distance to the left, along the top of the ledge. From the top of the "Bear's Den" the view takes in both lakes, the Mountain House, South Mountain, High Peak and Round Top, the grand basin formed by the curve of North Mountain and the distant valley of the Hudson, backed by the more distant mountains of New Jersey, Connecticut, Massachusetts, and Vermont. By many this is thought to be the grandest combination of mountain scenery to be met with here or elsewhere.

Fifty feet north of the "Bear's Den" is a bowlder of very fine white conglomerate, different from any other in this region. Imbedded in the conglomerate rock, which here forms the path, are pebbles of various sizes and colors that show glacial action. Many of them are rubbed and polished.

NEWMAN'S LEDGE—NORTH MOUNTAIN.

Continuing on from Bear's Den the path follows the front ledge a short distance and then winds among the bushes and trees of the next slope of North Mountain.

Turning to the left and ascending nearly to the top of the hill, the path to "Newman's Ledge" turns to the right (the path to crest of North Mountain continuing on up to the top).

A very impressive view is here obtained of Sleepy Hollow ravine, Cairo Round Top, the distant valley, and the windings of the mountain stage road. The perpendicular face of the ledge is ninety-nine feet, and is the most prominent one seen while ascending the mountain from the valley.

This ledge is named after the Rev. Newman Hall, of London, and is the termination of the path along the front ledge of North Mountain.

AROUND THE CREST OF NORTH MOUNTAIN.

Arriving at the intersection of the path to "Newman's Ledge," after leaving the "Bear's Den," continue on to the top of the slope, and turning to the north, pass to the east of the cellar (a natural cavity about one hundred feet square), and follow as near as possible the highest crest or ridge of the mountain.

When at the second outlook, notice particularly the direction of the Mountain House, and on the descent, keep as near as possible in that direction, as the foliage will prevent the house being again seen. By following this advice you will come out in the spring lot (shown on map), or, at all events, strike the water-pipe that crosses the spring lot, and affords a ready guide back to the Mountain House.

Around the crest is a long and difficult path, and strangers would do well to be accompanied by some one that is familiar with the route.

MARY'S GLEN—NORTH MOUNTAIN.

Go down the mountain road to the general entrance of North Mountain. Take the left hand path—a wood-road—part of the way along the eastern shore of North Lake; cross Ravine Creek, and just before reaching "Glen Mary," cross Ashley's Creek on a log placed there for the purpose. From here the sound of the fall can generally be heard, distant about two hundred feet up the creek.

Arriving at the falls, cross the stream, and ascend the bank so as to cross back again on the top of the falls, where a well defined path will bring you out on the main road by the charcoal pit, three quarters of a mile from the Mountain House. This delightful and shady walk is recommended to those who wish to avoid climbing, and is a favorite walk with the ladies.

WHERE TO RIDE.

IN THE VICINITY OF THE MOUNTAIN HOUSE.

Around the Clove, 14 miles, stopping at Haines' Falls	All day.
Around the Clove, Haines' Falls, Kaaterskill Falls	Three hours.
To Kaaterskill Falls, 2 ½ miles	Three hours.
To Haines' Falls, 4 miles	Four hours.
To Star Rock, Tannersville, 8 miles	Three hours.
To Tannersville, 6 miles	Six hours.
To Hunter Village, 11 miles	All day.
To Stony Clove, 12 miles	All day.
To Plattekill* Clove, 10 miles	All day.
To High Peak, walk from Haines' Falls	Five hours.

*Plau-ter-kill.

Around the Clove, 14 miles, stopping at Haines' Falls

Go down the mountain road, and after reaching the foot of the second hill you are on the "Long Level." The Mountain House appears like a Grecian Temple perched on the overhanging rocks almost above you. As the house is lost from site, you pass a wood-road leading down the mountain side at your right to "Moses Rock." The next wood-road is on the left, at the top of "Featherbed Hill," used by those undertaking to reach "Rip Van Winkle Ledge" by this difficult but very attractive route. At the foot of the hill, as the road turns to the right on "Short Level," a path is seen entering the woods on the left, which is a cut-off of half-a-mile.

The steep and half-circle curve at the end of "Short Level" is called "Cape Horn."

A little below this on the right is an open space named "Little Pine Orchard."

The steep portion of the road that comes next is "Dead Ox Hill," named in consequence of the sudden death of an ox that was overcome by exertion on drawing up too heavy a load. The path or cut-off spoken of above, comes out on the left of the foot of this hill. This is not far from the Rip Van Winkle House, and the flat rock marked "Sleepy Hollow"* that has a reputation of being the identical rock on which old Rip slumbered for twenty years.

The bridge, crossed half-way down Sleepy Hollow Ravine, is called "Black Snake Bridge."

After passing over the level and shady road beyond the toll-gate, at the foot of the mountain, and descending a steep hill near "Pelham's Four Corners," the Mountain House can be seen, for the first time since leaving the "Long Level."

Turn to the right at "Pelham's Four Corners" and follow the road along the base of the mountain. Occasionally the Mountain House will be in sight. When opposite, and nearest to the Mountain House (at Bogart's), a gate opens into an old mountain road that leads up the mountain to Moses' Rock and is used as a path to the Mountain House.

The Pine grove on the left, not far beyond, is known as "Boardman's Grove," named after the Rev. Dr. Boardman, of Philadelphia.

At the intersection of this road with the Clove road, near the Palenville Post Office, turn to the right. This is near the entrance of the celebrated Kaaterskill Clove. On the right you will see the "High Rock" or "Palenville Overlook," 1728 feet above the bed of the stream below, and on the left the shoulder or slope of "High Peak." Crossing the bridge at the real entrance of the Clove, you pass the studio of the Artist

*Irving's *Legend of Sleepy Hollow* is located at Tarrytown.

Hall, with its old fashioned chimney outside of the house and then stop at Burger's Hotel to water your horses.

The "Palenville Overlook" is almost above you, and the house on the "High Rock" comes to the very edge of the precipice. The prominent ledge below it has an old quarry at its base, and during the past year a party of treasure-seekers have been digging here under the direction of some money-making fortune teller.

The peculiar water-worn cavities in the bed-rock of the stream, for a few rods below the bridge, near the woolen factory, are well worth examination.

The "Artist's Grotto" and "La Belle Falls" are points of interest within ten minutes walk of Burger's. The path to them is at the toll-gate. Just beyond the toll gate a landslide is passed, the clearing made by it giving a fine view across the gorge, and exhibiting a perpendicular wall of red shale, resembling a series of square blocks with their edges toward you.

A second slide is soon passed. Across the Kaaterskill from this a stream comes out of a wild looking ravine known as "The Gulf."

Old wood-roads lead to this ravine from the bridge near Burger's and from the bridge at "Profile Rock." The road now curves to the left and takes you past the rustic cottage of E. T. Mason, to whom we are all indebted for removing the shanty at "Fawn's Leap," and with it the tax of twenty-five cents formerly charged each visitor at the beautiful falls.

You next pass in sight of "The Chasm," a precipice similar to the one opposite the first landslide, and also on the other side of the creek.

At and near the bridge that re-crosses the Kaaterskill is "Church's Ledge." On the left side of it is a projecting rock resembling a man's face, the head covered with a fur hat. The "Profile Rock" is seen to best advantage after crossing the bridge, and walking a few yards on the old wood-road to the right of it.

The rapids and falls near this bridge are much admired. By the continued action of pebbles, several circular holes have been worn in the bed rock, their sides smooth and straight. Hillyer's Ravine is at the western end of Church's Ledge. A few rods further on, and Fawn's Leap will be found, a beautiful fall hemmed in by high and rocky walls.

An old legend is, that a doe made the leap of the chasm over the fall, and that her fawn, in attempting to follow, fell into the deep pool, and swam round the pool for two days, the doe remaining near and watching it. It will repay the time taken to leave your conveyance and examine the beauty of the fall and its surroundings.

"Wild Cat Ravine" empties a small stream into the Kaaterskill Creek, just above or west of Fawn's Leap.

You next pass the ruins of the first boarding house in the Clove (Brockett's), and just beyond the remains of a settlement near the Old Tannery ruins. It was quite a hamlet when the mountains here were covered with hemlock.

Opposite this location can be seen "Buttermilk Falls," other falls being up the same ravine.

Looking high up to the right of the Clove Road you see the beautiful curve of South Mountain. In the autumn, when the leaves have fallen, the exposed numerous and regular ledges resemble the ruins of an immense amphitheatre.

Not far from the left side of the curve is the "Sunset Rock" of South Mountain.

The road now begins to rise, and you soon reach the Lake Creek bridge. A path leads from here up the stream to the Kaaterskill Falls, distant one mile passing Bastion Falls on the way.

A path to the left of the bridge leads down to the creek, and follows the same to Haines' Falls, passing on the way the foot of the great land slide, "Triton Cave,"

"Shelving Rock," and "The Five Cascades." From this bridge can be seen, on the opposite side of the Clove, Santa Cruz Ravine, being the nearest one to Haines' Falls.

All who have compassion for the horses will walk up the very steep portion of the road from this point to the top of the Clove.

Half-way from the bridge to the top of the Clove is "Dripping Rock," a large moss-covered rock that is always moist and dripping with water that oozes through its many crevices. A little beyond, a large bowlder infringes on the road, and after one more steep pull the top of the Clove is reached. The road turning to your right is very rough and seldom used. Continuing on the direct road just above and at the very top of the mountain we find ourselves on the brink of the Great Land Slide.

The road here has been repeatedly washed away down into the abyss to the depth of six hundred feet, intersecting the Kaaterskill just below the Cascades.

Opposite, High Peak looks down from over two thousand feet above.

Parties who wish a hard climb occasionally scramble down the Landslide and up Haines' Ravine. From Shelving Rock and past the Cascades, the ascent is one long to be remembered. The hand of man is not visible here except in the rustic stairs winding up through the immense precipices.

Some of the steps are really part of the mountain being cut in the rocks by the strong arm of the mountaineer; but it will be found far easier to descend the stairs at Haines' Falls, and, continuing down the Cascades, return the same way. It is but a short distance from the Slide to the Haines' Falls House.

This very popular resort has just been enlarged so as to double its former capacity. New parlors and one hundred and sixty feet of new piazza now front the Cauterskill Clove and a splendid view through it. Over the plains and the Hudson may be seen the Berkshires of Massachusetts and Mount Riga in Connecticut.

The paths for Buttermilk, Wild Cat, and Viola Falls start here.

Mr. C. W. Haines, the proprietor, has recently had a Western Union Telegraph Office, with a direct New York wire, put in the house for the convenience of his guests.

Past the house, and but a few rods in the rear, is a platform in the grove. Here we alight and leave the horses to enjoy the shade after their hard pull up the mountain. But a few steps distant we see the gate.

On entering the gate a payment of 25 cents is made, *once* for the whole season.

Take the road down to the shady path, leading to the right, and to the top of the falls. Looking from the projecting rocks the scene is wild and grand. The water leaps and dashes through the gorge 475 feet in less than one-fourth of a mile.

A broad sheet of water at the main fall descends 150 feet, and at the Spray Fall 160 feet.

Half-way down the stairs is Crystal Spring, an appropriate name on account of the purity and coolness of the water.

From the foot of the stairway a fine view of the fall is had, even when the ordinary stream is running, but while there, a large body of water is allowed to plunge over the rocks above, and the scene is then wild and exciting. The dashing waters encircle the many irregular bowlders in the stream, and rush wildly to the cascades below.

THE FIVE CASCADES.

Walk down the stream a few yards, and *cross it at the top* of the first cascade, where a steep but safe stairs leads to its base.

Cross the stream and descend the second cascade, following the distinct path on below the fifth cascade to Shelving Rock, overhanging Naiad's Bath.

The view here is grand beyond description. Looking up the gorge are the five cascades, from 30 to 90 feet each in height, and you see the top of Spray Falls above them, 400 feet from your position.

A visitor, having spent five years in Europe and California, declares this view from Shelving Rock to be the most beautiful scene of the kind he has ever witnessed.

This charming spot was visited years ago by Cole, Durand, Kensett, Cassilear, and others, when ropes and ladders had to be used in descending and ascending the ledges at the cascades.

The paths are now good, and none should fail to visit this favorite resort of the artists.

From Haines' Falls to the Mountain House there is a footpath, shady most of the way, as follows:

To Kaaterskill Falls, via Sphinx Rock and Prospect Rock ....One and a half miles.
From the Kaaterskill Falls to the Mountain House ....One and a half miles.
Haines' Falls to the Mountain House by road..Four miles.
Haines' Falls to Palenville, entrance of Clove ....Three miles.
Haines' Falls to Catskill ....Thirteen miles.

Having digressed to describe the points of interest at and near Haines' Falls, we now continue the trip "Around the Clove."

Half a mile beyond Haines' Falls you now cross a bridge at the saw-mill near the house of Miles Haines. Take the road to the right, passing the large mill pond, after which the road is almost due east to the road branching off to the Kaaterskill Falls and Laurel House, passing on the way the Clifton House and several smaller boarding houses, also passing the rough cross-road called "Featherbed Lane." A short distance from the Laurel House road, at the foot of a hill, you cross a second bridge at Spruce Creek, the upper waters of which are carried through a pipe to a fine spring on the side of North Mountain, and thence direct to the Mountain House, furnishing an abundant supply of pure and cool water.

From Spruce Creek bridge the road takes a south-easterly course and is shady all the rest of the way, passing in site of the water-pipe near the charcoal pit, crossing between the two lakes, and passing the "Alligator Rock" on the right hand, between the lake and the Mountain House.

It takes from four to five hours to make the circuit of the mountain above described, allowing a short time at Haines' Falls, and leaving Kaaterskill Falls, at the Laurel House, for a separate visit.

A party out however, for a day's ride, could examine with more leisure the beauties on the way, and include a walk below the double falls of the Kaaterskill, at the Laurel House, and also a visit to the "Sunset Rock" on South Mountain.

"Prospect Rock," on Prospect Mountain, half a mile from the Laurel House, affords a splendid view of the Kaaterskill Falls. In Cooper's "Pioneers," Leather Stocking is made to say of the falls: "To my judgement, lad, it's the best piece of work that I've met in the woods."

On the extreme edge of Prospect Mountain, overlooking the Clove, is the "Sphinx," a large bowlder standing upright, the top arching inwards and the outer part of its base within one yard of the precipice. This is midway between the Laurel House and Haines' Falls, a little off the direct path, but at the end of a plain and easy path. A charming view of the Clove, High Peak, Haines Falls, and the Hunter Valley can be had from the "Sphinx."

TO KAATERSKILL FALLS—FROM MOUNTAIN HOUSE.

Take the direct road west of the Mountain House, passing between the two lakes, and the *second* road leading to the left is the Laurel House and Kaaterskill Falls road.

TO HAINES' FALLS—FROM MOUNTAIN HOUSE.

Take the direct road west, passing the lakes and all cross-roads, turning to the left at the large mill-pond near Miles Haines', which is about half a mile from the falls.

TO HIGH PEAK—WALK FROM HAINES' FALLS.

The path to High Peak crosses the top of Haines' Falls, passes over an open field, enters the woods, and following along the side of the mountain, passes the upper part of Santa Cruz Ravine, near the falls of the same name, and then branches off to the right. It will be necessary to have a guide in taking a trip to High Peak. The view from High Peak covers a larger area than from any other spot in the Catskills.

TO "STAR ROCK," TANNERSVILLE—FROM THE MOUNTAIN HOUSE.

Take the direct road west to the intersection of the Clove at the mill-pond near Miles Haines'. Turn to the right on the Tannersville and Hunter turnpike, in front of Miles Haines'.

Arriving at Tannersville, turn to the right at the corner of Roggen's Hotel, and go up the road nearly two miles to the first one leading to the right, and a short distance on the latter road a path on the left will lead you to the top of the knoll, from which can be seen a fine view of Stony Clove, Plattekill Clove, Eastkill Clove, and the surrounding mountains.

TO HUNTER VILLAGE—FROM THE MOUNTAIN HOUSE.

Take the same route as to Tannersville, and five miles beyond is the pleasant village of Hunter, located on the Schoharie Creek, the waters of which traverse two hundred miles before emptying into the Mohawk.

TO STONY CLOVE.

The road turns to the left, between Tannersville and Hunter. In the Clove the mountains tower up almost perpendicular two thousand feet.

The gorge is very narrow. Hunter Mountain on the west is 4053 feet high. Ice can be found in crevices of the rocks, on either side of the road, in the hottest part of the summer. Brook trout can be found in the stream passing through it. Refreshments can be obtained at Amos Connelly's, one and a half miles from the top of the Clove.

PLATTEKILL CLOVE.

Take the direct road west nearly to Tannersville. The road to the Clove branches off to the left. There are several falls in the stream passing through it.

This wild mountain pass was used by the French and Indians in their attacks upon the early settlers of the valley of the Hudson.

ADDITIONAL RIDES AND WALKS.

Many other Rides and Walks will suggest themselves to lovers of mountain rambling who may have followed one or more of those already described, but the above list includes all that should *certainly be gone over* to see the wonders and beauties of this section of the Catskill Mountains.

Selections from

An Illustrated Guide to the Catskill Mountains with Maps and Plans

by Samuel E. Rusk

PALENVILLE OVERLOOK.

WALK FROM PALENVILLE.

Palenville Overlook is the high point of South Mountain on the right of the entrance to Cauterskill Clove and overlooks Palenville. A small house marks the spot. The distance from the post-office is two miles, and the roads and paths which wind up the rugged steep to it are shown on the map.

Its elevation above Palenville is some fifteen hundred feet, and the side of the mountain is so nearly perpendicular that the chief view of the houses below is of their roofs. The views of the Hudson valley is [*sic*] similar to the one from the Mountain House, but less extended.

There is a path from here over South Mountain to the Mountain House—a walk of a mile and one-fourth; and also another path along the side of the mountain which intersects the road below the Mountain House.

CAUTERSKILL CLOVE.

No visitor to the Catskills should depart without having seen the many attractions of the justly celebrated **Cauterskill Clove.** It is a fact to be especially noticed that the greater number of the water-falls in the whole range of the Catskill Mountains are centered around this Clove. The roads from Catskill and Saugerties converge at the entrance, which is at the upper end of Palenville. It is three miles, or a little more, from here to the top of the mountain, and ten miles to Hunter—this road constituting the Hunter Turnpike.

By the bridge, at the entrance of the Clove, is the quaint studio of the artist [George H.] Hall. Opposite is the Palenville Hotel at whose watering tub horses are watered when driving through the Clove. On the south side rises the long and steep slope of High Peak; while to the north an almost perpendicular wall reaches the height of seventeen hundred feet above the road, at which point is the Palenville Overlook.

Just above the toll-gate, an eighth of a mile along, is a path leading down the steep bank to the creek, where are located the **Artists' Grotto** and **La Belle Falls.** It will take but a few minutes to reach these interesting places.

A few rods on from the toll-gate a land slide extends from the road down to the creek, and on the opposite bank is a high, perpendicular wall of red sandstone. The passage between them is the **Red Chasm.** The projecting point of the top of the mountain above it is the **Point of Rocks.** Just west of this Point is a wild gorge, extending down the side of South Mountain, and partially dividing it, which is known as **The Gulf.** An old road or path, starting from the bridge at the entrance of the Clove, leads along up the side of the mountain and has several diverging branches which reach The Gulf at different elevations.

Soon the road passes the cozy summer cottage of E. T. Mason. A short distance more reaches the top of a hill at a turn in the road, to the right of which the creek flows through a defile in the rocky barrier called **Deep Chasm.**

The objects of special interest to be next seen are at **More Bridge** [Moore's Bridge],—a trifle more than a mile on the way,—which spans the Cauterskill. **Church's Ledge** rises close by the road and bridge, and part of its irregular side, seen from a point across the Bridge and a few feet to the right of the road, resolves itself into the features of **Profile Rock. More Falls** are just below the bridge, and above, the water has worn queerish channels and circular cavities into the red sandstone bed of the creek.

At the west end of Church's Ledge is a gorge known at **Hillyer's Ravine.** Half way up the steep, visible side of the mountain it expands into a wide basin. Above are precipitous cliffs, down which dash the waters of a small stream forming Viola Falls. (See description elsewhere of Viola Falls, Wild Cat Falls, Buttermilk Falls, and Santa Cruz Falls, which are here only mentioned.)

From More Bridge the road follows for a ways close on the north bank of the Cauterskill, whose waters a few rods along come pitching down between the cleft rocks into a dark shaded pool below. This chasm is called **Fawn's Leap**; tradition saying that a young deer, being pursued by a hunter and his dog, leaped across the gulf and escaped, while the dog fell into the water beneath and was drowned. The spot is so close to the road that but a few minutes will be consumed in stopping to view it.

A small stream enters the Cauterskill above Fawn's Leap, up which are located Wild Cat Falls of a hundred feet in height.

The curved side of South Mountain up to the right, with its many ledges rising one above another forms **The Amphitheater**, best seen in the autumn when the foliage is less dense. At its western extremity the projecting part of the mountain forms Sunset Rock.

At the base, the road passes along a flat where was once quite a hamlet; but now only the **Old Tannery Ruins** and a few piles of stone on either side mark the sites of the numerous buildings that existed when the mountains furnished plenty of hemlock bark for tanning purposes. Behind the Tannery Ruins is Buttermilk Ravine with a pleasing Cascade visible from the road, while the upper part of the Ravine contains the Buttermilk Falls proper. In crossing the flat, Santa Cruz Ravine may be seen on the left, descending the side of the mountain in an easterly direction.

The road takes a short turn at the end of the flat and gradually ascends to **Lake Creek Bridge.** From here, up, is the really steep part of the mountain road, a mile long, and people usually walk this portion to lighten the horses' burden.

A path leads up Lake Creek through the Kaaterskill Ravine to the Kaaterskill Falls and Laurel House, one mile distant, passing Bastion Falls on the way. To the left of the Bridge and opposite this path is another path leading down to the Cauterskill and thence up through the ravine to Haines' Falls, a mile and an eighth distant, passing by Naiads' Bath, Shelving Rock, and The Five Cascades.

Dripping Rock is a moss-covered ledge by the side of the road half way up the mountain from Lake Creek Bridge over which flows a small stream of excellent potable water. During the remainder of the ascent the increasing exhilerating [*sic*] effect of the pure mountain atmosphere is especially noticeable. A portion of Haines' Falls may be seen from a ways below Dripping Rock.

Near the top of the mountain is a road to the right, called **Feather-bed Lane**, connecting with the Mountain House road. It is steep and rough and not adapted to driving. A few yards more reaches the top of **The Great Land-slide**, which extends from the road down to the bed of the creek—a descent of nearly five hundred feet. The view from here down through the Cauterskill Clove and beyond to the Berkshire Hills of Massachusetts is much admired and is specially delightful near the sunset hour.

Having here reached the upper end of the Cauterskill Clove, it is but a short distance to the Haines' Falls House.

HAINES' FALLS REGION.

The name **Haines' Falls** has been used in three senses. First it was applied particularly to the Falls; afterward, also, to the house of Charles W. Haines, at the Falls; and, more recently, any of the numerous houses within a radius of about a mile are mentioned as being at Haines' Falls. In order to clearly designate which is meant, it has been thought best to use the name Haines' Falls for the Falls only; Haines' Falls House for the house there; and Haines' Falls Region for the locality in general.

The place is thirteen miles from Catskill, situated at the head of the long-time famous Cauterskill Clove, and, consequently at the front of the mountain range. The view through the Cauterskill Clove extends beyond the Hudson, into Massachusetts and Connecticut. The elevation above the Hudson of points where the houses are placed, varies from one thousand and nine hundred to two thousand and three hundred feet. On the south side the land rises quite abruptly to the summit of High Peak and Round Top, while to the north a more gradual ascent leads to the top of the North Mountain ridge. It is a region of much singular wildness and scenic beauty; and many years ago, before other people had made it their summer home, noted artists sought it out as a rich field of subjects for their canvas. The view of the Hudson valley, as seen from near Shady Grove House, is excellent.

With the exception of a few hotels that have been in existence for many years, this region was the first to provide summer boarding-houses among the Catskills. There are now many houses, with accommodations for from twenty to a hundred people each. While, during the past fifteen years, the accommodations have been increased forty-fold, there is, almost every year, added provision for the increasing influx of people.

In this region is the Cauterskill and Schoharie water-shed which sends the water east to the Hudson at Catskill, or, in the opposite direction; flowing by the circuitous route of the Schoharie and Mohawk Rivers to the Hudson above Troy, and following in its course some two hundred and fifty miles to Catskill, where it is then but a dozen miles from its source.

From most houses in the Haines' Falls Region **conveyances** run daily to Catskill to meet the Day Boats each way and the trains as late as half past three o'clock. For a later hour special arrangements can he made. The regular fare, including baggage, from Catskill is two dollars.

Conveyances may be had for local excursions.

The *Mails* between here and New York are sent and received daily or oftener—Catskill being the post-office.

The Western Union **Telegraph Office**, with direct wires is at the Haines' Falls House.

There is a Methodist Episcopal **Church**, in which services of other denominations as well as its own are held.

Haines' Falls.

WALKS ABOUT THE HAINES' FALLS REGION AND VICINITY
DISTANCES FROM THE HAINES' FALLS HOUSE

Catskill Mountain House, by path via Laurel House	3
by road	4
Clum Hill	$2\frac{3}{4}$
Fawn's Leap and Profile Rock, in Cauterskill Clove	2
Haines' Falls	1–16
Haines' Falls Ravine,—through it to Lake Creek Bridge	$1\frac{7}{8}$
High Peak	4
Kaaterskill Falls and Laurel House, by path via Prospect Rock	$1\frac{1}{2}$
Kaaterskill Falls and Laurel House, including Bastion Falls, via the turnpike to Lake Creek Bridge; thence up the Kaaterskill Ravine	2
Kaaterskill Falls and Laurel House, by road	$2\frac{1}{2}$
Old Indian Fort, between High Peak and Round Top	$4\frac{1}{2}$
Overlook Mountain House, by path around the summit of High Peak to Plaaterkill; thence by new road	11
Parker Hill	3
Plaaterkill, by path around the summit of High Peak	6
Prospect Rock	1
Rifted Rocks	$\frac{1}{4}$
Santa Cruz Falls	1
Tannersville	$2\frac{1}{2}$
The Five Cascades, Shelving Rock, Naiad's Bath, Triton Cave,—in Haines' Ravine	$\frac{1}{4}$
The Sphinx, or Noah's Ark	$\frac{7}{8}$
To Buttermilk Falls, $1\frac{3}{4}$; thence to Wild Cat Falls, $\frac{3}{8}$; thence to Viola Falls, $\frac{1}{4}$	$2\frac{3}{8}$

There are descriptions of nearly all of the above walks in these pages. Where the routes are by direct road, no descriptions are given. The map will show the location of these places and the way to them.

DRIVES IN THE VICINITY OF THE HAINES' FALLS REGION.
DISTANCES FROM THE HAINES' FALLS HOUSE, BY THE MOST USUAL ROUTES.

	MILES
Around South Mountain, via Mountain House, Sleepy Hollow, Palenville, and Cauterskill Clove,—round trip	14
Catskill Mountain House	4
Cauterskill Clove,—through it to Palenville	3½
Clum Hill	2¾
Hunter	7
Kaaterskill Falls and Laurel House	2½
Overlook Mountain House, by new road via Plaaterkill	14½
Parker Hill	4½
Plaaterkill	9½
Sleepy Hollow, where Rip Van Winkle slept!	6¾
Stony Clove	9
Tannersville	2½

TO HAINES' FALLS AND UNDER THEM.

At the east side of Haines' Falls House a road leads down to **Haines' Falls**, which are but a few rods distant from the house, on the Cauterskill Creek. Passing through a gate, a payment of twenty-five cents each is required. No charge is made for subsequent visits during the same season.

A short, well defined path, to the right, leads through a growth of laurels on the brink of a precipice to the top of the Falls. Here, from the outer extremity of a pendent rock at the side of the Falls, the view disclosed is extraordinarily wild. The main sheet of water pours over the projecting rock into the narrow, deep-cleft gorge, a hundred and fifty feet; while on the south side the waters of the beautiful **Spray Falls** make a sheer descent of a hundred and sixty feet.

Just before passing over the Falls, the water descends a fifteen foot ledge. Its long continued action has worn a number of circular holes into the solid rock at the foot of the ledge. The principal cavity is several feet deep. Many sketches and paintings have been made of the view from the top of this ledge down through the ravine.

Sometimes in winter a hollow icicle, an hundred feet in length, hangs from the top of the Falls; and the water which flows with muffled sound down through the interior forms underneath, a huge cone of glistening ice.

To go **under the Falls**, the path to the left of the gate should be followed. It is but a few steps to the first long flight of stairs. At their foot is a natural gateway, formed by two trees, one of which has grown so that the wall of rock is imbedded in its side. A few yards beyond this gate-way is **Crystal Spring**; of pure, ice-cold water, which emerges from underneath the massive ledge of rock that has just been descended. Several more flights of stairs are passed,—from which glimpses of the falling water may be had through the foliage,—before reaching the bottom of the Falls.

The accompanying illustration was made from the foot of the Falls, and it is from this point that the most comprehensive view is obtained of their wildness and sublimity. While visitors are down here, the ordinary stream of water is increased from the pond above, thereby adding to the beautiful spectacle. At such times it is advisable to be down the stream as far as the stairs, unless one does not mind being drenched by the cloud of spray. Farther down the gorge are **The Five Cascades**. (See description.) The bottom of the Cascades is less than a fourth of a mile from the top of the Falls; yet, in this short distance, the stream descends nearly five hundred feet.

The Falls and Cascades were the subjects of numerous paintings, many years ago, by such artists as Kensett, Cassilear, Cole and Durand. In those days ropes and ladders were daily used in descending and ascending; but now, good safe stairs render access comparatively easy for the artists, with their implements, as well as for others; and down here, Gifford and M'Entee [McEntee] have often been.

THE FIVE CASCADES, IN HAINES' RAVINE.

All of **The Five Cascades** are within a distance of an eighth of a mile below Haines' Falls. Crossing the creek at the foot of the stairs, the top of the first Cascade is just in sight. It is a fall of eighty feet. The stream should be followed down, on the right side, a little farther than this Cascade, where **Jacob's Ladder**—an extremely steep but substantial stair of some thirty steps—is to be descended. The first and second Cascades are near together, and the stream is recrossed between them. Another flight of stairs overhangs the side of the second Cascade, which is sixty feet high, and leads safely to its base. From here the path continues down the stream, on the left side, past the third and fourth Cascades, to

SHELVING ROCK AND NAIAD'S BATH.

The illustration here given of **Shelving Rock** conveys an excellent idea of its appearance. As may be seen, it projects far over the stream. The waters of the fifth Cascade tumble down underneath it, forming a beautiful pool, known as

Naiad's Bath,—

A lovely cave,
Dusky and sacred to the Nymphs, whom men
Call Naiads.—*Odissey*

The cut shows the fourth Cascade, in the background. The combined picture of the Rock, Bath, Cascades, and the immediate surroundings is so enchanting that, when once seen, it is likely to be long retained in the memory.

A gentleman, who has traveled many years in California and Europe, pronounces the view from Shelving Rock the most charming one of the kind that he has ever beheld. People make repeated visits to this spot and prolong them for hours.

The ravine is walled in by perpendicular ledges the greater share of its length. On the north side, just below Shelving Rock, is a strata of rock, in some places five feet thick, containing considerable copper and sulphur.

From Shelving Rock the walk may be continued down

THROUGH HAINES' RAVINE TO LAKE CREEK BRIDGE.

One hundred yards below Shelving Rock, by a path on the north side of the stream, will reach the foot of The Great Landslide. If further procedure down the Ravine is undesirable, the slide, itself, may be ascended to the road,—much more easily than its rugged appearance indicates. A hundred yards more and the water pours over a perpendicular wall of solid rock to the depth of twenty-five feet. This is Delmura Fall,—the name being derived from the Spanish, meaning the wall.

The creek itself may now be followed and many places seen which will well repay the needed exertion; or, the walk may be more easily accomplished by taking an old wood road close on the north bank, which leads to the Hunter Turnpike, at a point just above the Lake Creek Bridge and nearly opposite the path up the Kaaterskill Ravine.

HIGH PEAK.

WALK FROM THE HAINES' FALLS REGION.

From Haines' Falls it is four miles, in a southerly direction to the summit of **High Peak.** The elevation of this mountain is 3664 feet, and it is conceded that its summit commands the most extensive view of any place in the Catskills. Parts of the path to it are not clearly marked, and it will be expedient to have a guide in taking this trip the first time.

The path crosses the Cauterskill just above Haines' Falls and, after passing across a sloping field almost to the ledge of rocks at the upper side, turns to the left and enters the woods from near the south-eastern corner of the field. The ledge mentioned constitutes the Rifted Rocks, which are well worth visiting. (See description.) Before entering the woods, a glance to the east will reveal the Laurel House and Kaaterskill Falls, directly facing.

The route is now all the way through the dense forest. Following a wood road, of gradual ascent, along the side of the mountain for a mile, Santa Cruz Creek is reached. The beautiful Falls of the same name are but a little way down the stream and may be easily visited in this trip,—it being preferable to leave them for a stopping place in returning. (See description.)

Across Santa Cruz Creek the wood road turns to the right and becomes steeper. Other old roads diverge at various points, but the proper one to follow is most clearly defined. The first one to the left, and but a few rods from the Creek, is the path to Buttermilk, Wild Cat, and Viola Falls. (See description.) Two miles from Santa Cruz the road is left behind, and the journey is continued up the steep side of the Peak,—for a ways along or near the mossy bed of a tiny stream,—as indicated by the blazed trees. At the foot of an exceedingly steep pitch is **Comfort Spring**,—the source of the rivulet,—where it is customary to lunch, as water can scarcely ever be found nearer the top. Cole's last trip to the mountains was a visit to High Peak, and it was at this spring where he paused to take his noonday lunch.

Near the end of the ascent is a small, open space on a ledge of rock, which is called **Hurricane Ledge**. It affords an excellent view. To the north, over the long stretch of forest that has been passed through, the Cauterskill Clove lies some three thousand feet below. Up, beyond, the whole northern section of the mountain range may be seen, and between two of the peaks, Albany is discernible on a clear day. More to the east, quite a tract along and beyond the Hudson is visible.

The summit of High Peak is clothed with a growth of tall spruce and a thick carpet of green, velvety moss. The path does not lead directly to the pinnacle, but out along the eastern side, on the verge of a precipice. In the close foreground are the Cauterskill and Plaaterkill Cloves; then comes the Hudson valley—the river visible north to Albany and far to the south beyond, the Berkshire Hills, the Green Mountains and other parts of Massachusetts, Vermont, and parts of Connecticut with the Adirondacks in the north—all together forming a natural panorama such as man seldom beholds. The Upper Lake by the Catskill Mountain House appears far below, like a tiny mirror.

There, as thou stand'st,
The haunts of men below thee, and around
The mountain summits, thy expanding heart
Shall feel a kindred with that loftier world
To which thou art translated, and partake
The enlargement of thy vision. Thou shalt look
Upon the green and rolling forest tops,
And down into the secrets of the glens,
And streams, that with their bordering thickets strive
To hide their windings. Thou shalt gaze, at once,
Here on white villages, and tilth, and herds,
And swarming roads, and there on solitudes
That only hear the torrent, and the wind,
And eagle's shrieks. * * * * * *

But the scene
Is lovely round; a beautiful river there
Wanders amid the fresh and fertile meads,
The paradise he made unto himself,
Mining the soil for ages. On each side
The fields swell upward to the hills. —*Bryant.*

Shelving Rock and Naiad's Bath.

From a point a short way south of this outlook, and down a ledge, there is a less obstructed and more extended view in that direction. The Overlook Mountain House is plainly visible on Overlook Mountain.

Returning to the previous point of observation, a path may be found to the tip-top—a few yards distant. Here, by the help of a ladder to its lower branches, the tallest tree may be scaled by the venturesome. It is no easy feat; but one most estimable young lady of a party assured the writer that she had looked out upon the world from among its upper branches. It is quite an improvement on the views from below, as the other trees, in every direction, may be overlooked.

SANTA CRUZ FALLS.
WALK IN THE HAINES' FALLS REGION.

Santa Cruz Falls are one mile from Haines' Falls, on the way to High Peak. A description of the route to them may be found in the second and third paragraphs of the description of High Peak. It is said that a bottle of Santa Cruz rum supposed to have been left by some hunters, was found on the bank of the stream, from which circumstance this name was given. Having reached Santa Cruz Creek, it is but a few yards down the stream to the Falls. Either side of the Creek may be followed, but the best path is on the west bank.

The peculiar view disclosed, from the top of the Falls through the vista of the Cauterskill Clove, is remarkably fine.

* * full many a spot
Of hidden beauty have I chanced to espy
Among the mountains; never one like this;—*Wordsworth.*

The descending spurs of the mountains dovetail into each other through the Clove; beyond spreads the wide valley of the Hudson with the river stretching across it; while the Berkshire Hills rise in the background,—the highest peak in the centre being Mt. Riga, near the junction of Massachusetts, Connecticut and New York. This picture is

View from Santa Cruz Falls.

best seen in mid-afternoon, as the sun is then in a position to properly light it up. Durand and other artists have spent much time at this spot. There are two Falls, but a stone's throw apart, each some sixty feet in height. At the upper one the descending water is much broken by projecting points of rock; but at the second, it pours down in a broad, translucent sheet, and in the morning a rainbow is frequently formed in the mist at the base,—so near that the hand may be thrust among its colors.

The Falls may be descended on either side, with but comparatively little difficulty. The ledge of rock which forms the second Fall extends, in an arc, quite a distance to the right, so that the shorter route is on the left side of the stream. On down the ravine are numerous cascades.

RIFTED ROCKS.
WALK IN THE HAINES' FALLS REGION.

The Rifted Rocks are across the Cauterskill, beyond Haines' Falls, and in sight from the road. The path is via the top of the Falls—the same as in going to High Peak.

From a ledge of conglomerate, Nature has, at some period, cut off a slice about twenty feet wide by three hundred feet long and moved it out from the remaining part, so that there is a passage behind, varying in width from ten to twenty feet.

The strip is some fifteen feet high and broken crosswise into blocks from twenty to forty feet long. The entrance to the passage is at the west end only, as, near the other extremity, a sentinel of pudding-stone blocks the way.

BUTTERMILK FALLS, WILD CAT FALLS, VIOLA FALLS.
WALK FROM THE HAINES' FALLS REGION.

These three Falls are on separate streams that flow northerly from toward High Peak down in the Cauterskill Clove,—emptying into the Cauterskill Creek. Each one is about half a mile from the mouth of the stream on which it is located.

The first part of the path to them is the same as in going to High Peak, and the reader is referred to the article, "High Peak. Walk from the Haines' Falls Region." for a description.

Having crossed Santa Cruz Creek and turned up the hill a few paces,—the path leaves the High Peak path, at nearly a right angle to the left, and continues easterly three-fourths of a mile to **Buttermilk Falls.** The first Fall is some seventy feet high, and a second one, just below, has about the same height.

Three-eighths of a mile farther along the path reaches the top of **Wild Cat Falls**—a sheer descent from a projecting ledge of about a hundred feet.

It is but a fourth of a mile more, by the same path, to **Viola Falls**. This takes its name from the fact that some violets were found in bloom near it as late in the season as the second of November. There are no very high Falls here, but the succession of small ones is so great that the water descends probably half a thousand feet in an eighth of a mile. Hillyer's Ravine is the name of the gorge through which the stream descends.

There are views from the tops of the Falls mentioned, down into the Cauterskill Clove and out on the Hudson valley. On each of the streams are other smaller falls besides the one named. The public have heretofore known but little concerning these Falls; but in a region less diversified by magnificent water-falls than that surrounding the Cauterskill Clove, these would have been sought out as attractions of a high order. The streams are, however, small, and perhaps people will not yet care to make this excursion, excepting just after rains have augmented the flow of water.

WALK FROM THE HAINES' FALLS REGION TO THE LAUREL HOUSE.

BY PATH VIA PROSPECT ROCK.

This is the shortest route and the one usually chosen to walk from one of these places to the other. The distance is a mile and a half and the path is shady the greater part of the way.

From the Haines' Falls House, the route is down the road past the Great Land-slide; up the rough road—Feather-bed Lane—to the north across a little bridge; and up the steep hill in the field to the east. At the top of the hill, near a lone hemlock tree, the path divides (The lower one is the more direct way to reach the Sphinx. The Laurel House may be reached by this way, but it is a trifle farther and the path is not quite as good.) The upper one follows for a short distance, along a piece of woods; then crosses a field; passes through a grove and into a pasture. (In the edge of the pasture, on the south of the path, is a prominent bowlder, by which, a path leads down the hill to The Sphinx.) Across the pasture the path again divides; the lower one making a detour of a few steps to Prospect Rock and then uniting beyond with the upper one. (A description of the beauties seen from Prospect Rock may be found under the heading of "Prospect Rock. Walk from the Laurel House.") On, a fourth of a mile from Prospect Rock, the path emerges from the woods and crosses a field—passing in its way by a Fish Pond—to the road, a short distance above the Laurel House.

This short walk gives a great diversity of scenery, and is a favorite one.

THE SPHINX, OR NOAH'S ARK.

WALK FROM THE HAINES' FALLS REGION.

The Sphinx is on the brow of the mountain between Haines' Falls and Kaaterskill Falls, seven-eighths of a mile from the former place.

The route from the Haines' Falls House is down the road, a few yards past The Great Land-slide, to a rough road—Feather-bed Lane—on the left. Up the Lane a short distance a small bridge is crossed. Here the path leaves the Lane and ascends a steep hill in a partially cleared field on the right hand side. At the top of the hill, near an isolated hemlock tree, the path divides. (The upper one is the direct path to the Laurel House.) The one on the lower or right hand side is the most direct to the Sphinx, and, although part of it is not well defined, no one should have any difficulty in following it. Several trees and stones along the route are marked with spots of white paint. Beyond the hemlock tree the path—this part of it a wood road—soon enters the woods and at a fourth of a mile reaches a partially open space on the top of a ledge. This is Bellevue Point. It overlooks the upper part of the Cauterskill Clove, with a glimpse of the Five Cascades to the west and Hunter and Rusk Mountains in the far background.

Continuing about a fourth of a mile farther, another open space is reached. Turning to the right, the path winds down a small ledge, easily passed, to The Sphinx. It is a curiously shaped rock, being about twenty feet high, with a base of ten feet square and its upper side projecting so as to resemble the prow of a ship. **Noah's Ark** was its original and obviously more appropriate appellation, although of late the other name has been more freely used. (There is another Sphinx on South Mountain.) The Ark stands close on the brink of a precipice on the side of the Cauterskill Clove, commanding a fine view thereof; and of the sides of High Peak and Round Top base to summit.

The walk may be continued an eighth of a mile farther to

PROSPECT ROCK,

As follows: Proceeding northward from The Sphinx, through the clearing to the top of the hill, the upper path which diverges at the hemlock tree will be intersected. A few rods through the trees to the east is **Prospect Rock,** with its view so delightfully unique that none should fail to witness it. A description of this place may be found under the heading of "Prospect Rock. Walk from the Laurel House." Prospect Rock may be conveniently visited from the direct path between the Haines' Falls and Laurel House Regions—it being but a few yards off that path.

WALK OR DRIVE FROM THE HAINES' FALLS REGION TO CLUM HILL.

Clum Hill is two miles and three-fourths from the Haines' Falls House, and by the same road for either a walk or drive from this place. The route is west, by the turnpike, a mile and a half where a road branches to the south, in front of Maplewood. The remainder of the journey and the place are described under "Clum Hill. Drive in Tannersville." and "Clum Hill. Walk in Tannersville."

WALK FROM THE HAINES' FALLS REGION TO PARKER HILL.

The distance for a walk to **Parker Hill** is about three miles, and the route is as follows:

One mile west from the Haines' Falls House the turnpike should be left, and the road to the right followed for some three-fourths of a mile, where another road intersects it on the west;

Or,

There is a shorter way to reach this point of the journey: By entering a path close by the west side of the Shady Grove House, a few rods will lead past the barns and through a clump of fir trees into the fields beyond. Across these fields, diagonally to the north-west, three-fourths of a mile will reach the road mentioned in the first route. By this road, the walk is continued toward the north-west; passing two houses and, farther on, two isolated barns. A few yards beyond the second barn is the path up Parker Hill, on the right hand. The top of the Hill and its side toward the road were long since divested of their wood. For a description of the view obtained from this Hill, see "Parker Hill. Walk or drive from Tannersville."

Parties taking this walk usually return by road by the way of Tannersville—a circuit of seven and a half miles.

It is not advisable to take the path mentioned via the Shady Grove House, immediately after a rain, as part of it is then quite muddy.

WALK FROM THE HAINES' FALLS REGION TO PLAATERKILL.

BY PATH AROUND THE SUMMIT OF HIGH PEAK.

This, the shortest route, is six miles; by an old wood road mostly through the forest. The first three miles is by the same path as to High Peak, and, therefore, the reader is referred to the article, "High Peak. Walk from the Haines' Falls Region," for a description of the same. The remaining three miles of the old road is plain enough to be followed without difficulty, and leads to the head of the **Plaaterkill** Clove.

This route is, also, the shortest way from this place to the

OVERLOOK MOUNTAIN HOUSE,

And is continued from Plaaterkill,—making the total distance eleven miles.

LAUREL HOUSE REGION.

Besides the **Laurel House**, there are but two or three houses here. The Laurel House was named from the laurel—the *Kalmia latifolia* of botanists—which is profusely distributed through the forest immediately surrounding the house.

The location of the Laurel House is fifteen miles from Catskill, between the Catskill Mountain House and Haines' Falls—the last half mile leading thereto being a private road. Its elevation is 2038 feet. Standing just above the Kaaterskill Falls—which are Laurel House property—the view from the front of the house extends through the wide Kaaterskill Ravine, and embraces beyond, High Peak, Round Top, and other mountains, along the Schoharie valley.

A sea of fog sometimes fills the ravine below, but it is soon dispersed by the morning sun.

Earth's children cleave to Earth—her frail
  Decaying children dread decay.
Yon wreath of mist that leaves the vale,
  And lessens in the morning ray:
Look how, by mountain rivulet,
  It lingers as it upward creeps,
And clings to fern and copsewood set
  Along the green and dewey steeps;
Clings to the fragrant kalmia, clings
  To precipices fringed with grass,
Dark maples where the wood-thrush sings,
  And bowers of fragrant sassafras.
Yet all in vain—it passes still
  From hold to hold, it cannot stay,
And in the very beams that fill
  The world with glory, wastes away,
Till, parting from the mountain's brow,
  It vanishes from human eye,
And that which sprung of earth is now
  A portion of the glorious sky.—*Bryant.*

From a point on the Laurel House road, but a few yards from where it leaves the Mountain House road, is a magnificent view of the mountains, from High Peak west to Hunter Mountain and beyond.

Conveyances from these houses run daily to Catskill to meet the boats and trains, and the route therefrom leads up the mountain through Sleepy Hollow. Carriages and stages can be obtained for drives to the many delightful resorts in the vicinity.

The **Mails** are received once or more each day—Catskill being the post-office.

A Western Union **Telegraph Office**, with direct wire to New York, is located in the Laurel House.

There is **trout** fishing in the neighborhood.

WALKS ABOUT THE LAUREL HOUSE REGION AND VICINITY.

DISTANCES FROM THE LAUREL HOUSE.

		MILES.
Bastion Falls		1/4
Catskill Mountain House,	by path south of South Lake	1 1/2
" "	by path via Druid Rocks	1 1/2
" "	by path along north of South Lake	1 3/4
" "	by road	2 1/2
" "	by path via Sunset Rock	3
Council Bluff		3/4
Fawn's Leap and Profile Rock, in Cauterskill Clove, via Kaaterskill Ravine		2
Glen Mary		1/8
Haines' Falls,	by path via Prospect Rock	1 1/2
	by path via Kaaterskill Ravine and Haines' Ravine—including Bastion Falls, Shelving Rock and The Five Cascades	2 1/4
Haines' Falls, by road		2 1/2
High Peak		5 1/2
Kaaterskill Falls		0
Palenville, via Kaaterskill Ravine and Cauterskill Clove		3
Palenville Overlook, by path via Lemon Squeezer, Fairy Spring and Fat Man's Delight		2 3/4
Prospect Rock		1/2
Santa Cruz Falls		2 1/2
South lake—Catskill Lakes		3/4
Sunset Rock, South Mountain		1
The Outlook, on North Mountain		2 1/2
The Sphinx, or Noah's Ark		3/4

Laurel House, at Kaaterskill Falls.

Descriptions of nearly all of the above walks are given in these pages. Some of the routes are so direct that any description would be superfluous. The location of places may be seen on the map.

The Kaaterskill Falls.

DRIVES IN VICINITY OF THE LAUREL HOUSE.
DISTANCES FROM THE LAUREL HOUSE, BY THE MOST USUAL ROUTES.

	MILES
Around South Mountain, via Mountain House, Sleepy Hollow, Palenville, Cauterskill Clove, and Haines' Falls,—Round Trip	15
Catskill Mountain House	2 ½
Grand View, East Windham	21
Haines' Falls	2 ½
Hunter	9
Overlook Mountain House, by new road via Plaaterkill	16 ½
Parker Hill	6 ½
Plaaterkill	11 ½
Sleepy Hollow	4 ½
Stony Clove	11
Tannersville	4 ½
Windham	19

KAATERSKILL FALLS.

In the name **Kaaterskill Falls**, the original Dutch spelling of the word has always been retained; but it is now more frequently written Cauterskill, and, except when referring to these Falls or the ravine leading therefrom, the latter form is used throughout these pages.

It is but a few feet from the Laurel House to the top of the Falls. The **Spray House** stands on the very verge, and its platform, with timbers bolted to the rock, projects over the awful chasm. This is the point from which to view the Falls from above; and over this first Fall the water drops a hundred and sixty feet, broken into millions of foamy fragments ere it strikes below, and flowing along a few yards it again plunges to the depth of eighty feet.

Midst greens and shades the Cauterskill leaps,
From cliffs where the wood-flower clings;
All summer he moistens his verdant steps,
With the sweet light spray of the mountain springs;
And he shakes the woods on the mountain side,
When they drip with the rains of autumn tide.
But when in the forest bare and old,
The blast of December calls—
He builds in the starlight, clear and cold,
A palace of ice where his torrent falls;
With turret, and arch, and fretwork fair,
And pillars blue as the summer air.—*Bryant*

The Kaaterskill Falls were the subject of one of Bryant's beautiful poems,—the first portion of which is copied above,—and in Cooper's "PIONEERS," Leather-Stocking says of them:—"To my judgement, lad, it's the best piece of work that I've met with in the woods; * * * * I've sat on the shelving rock many a long hour, boy, and watched the bubbles as they shot by me, and thought how long it would be before that very water which seemed made for the wilderness would be under the bottom of a vessel, and tossing in the salt sea. It is a spot to make a man solemnize."

Gifford made a fine painting of the Ravine leading from the Falls, and Durand, M'Entee, Cole, Church, and other well known artists have made visits to this delightful spot.

It is from under the Falls where its grandeur becomes most striking. At a gate by the Spray House a payment of twenty-five cents is made—for once during the season—and a charming path followed a few yards through the forest to the head of the stairs. Rustic seats are placed along the way, and there are resting-places at various landings along down the many flights of stairs passed in reaching the bottom of the Falls.

In the immense amphitheater which curves behind the water of the first Fall is a level path on which one may safely pass entirely around behind the falling water [This area is so dangerous that I must specifically warn against trying this. See note. *R.A.G.*]* Midway along the path the flood comes pouring over the enormous arch of rock and as it descends, is eighty feet distant from the point of observation. After passing around by this path, the stream may be re-crossed a few yards below, at the top of the second Fall where the stairs continue down to the foot, and reach a seat placed so as to give an unobstructed view of both Falls. While parties are down here, the gate of a dam immediately above the Falls is opened, thus augmenting the usual flow of water and the scene is then truly marvellous.

It is but a fourth of a mile down the stream to

BASTION FALLS.

The path to it crosses at the foot of the second Fall, and instead of following the creek, which has a sharp turn at this point, it takes a more direct course along the wooded slope of the ravine, meeting the creek just above **Bastion Falls** and crossing it again by a foot-bridge of logs.

These Falls make a very pleasing picture, and a view of them will convey the idea that the name is derived from the bastions of rock which partially divide the stream as it breaks over the edge of the precipice.

The path continues down

THROUGH KAATERSKILL RAVINE TO LAKE CREEK BRIDGE.

It is three fourths of a mile from Bastion Falls and the shaded path is all the way on the right side, quite close to the stream.

This path through the Kaaterskill Ravine—always a pleasant one—is much used as a short route for walks from the Laurel House to Fawn's Leap, Palenville, and up Haines' Ravine.

GLEN MARY.

WALK IN THE LAUREL HOUSE REGION.

Glen Mary is an eighth of a mile from the Laurel House to the right of the Laundry. A rustic foot-bridge here crosses the Lake Creek, with its mossy rocks, just at the junction of Spruce Creek—the mingled waters passing over Kaaterskill Falls a few yards below.

---

*Rusk's statement of the safety of this trail was written when a maintained stairway was available. Some people have made the fatal mistake of attempting to go behind the falls above the trail Rusk describes. For your protection, and to avoid endangering your rescuers, *please avoid this area.*

SUNSET ROCK.—SOUTH MOUNTAIN.
WALK IN THE LAUREL HOUSE REGION.

Sunset Rock is a point on the side of South Mountain, overlooking the Cauterskill Clove. The distance from the Laurel House is one mile, by a good path through the forest. By the Laurel House Laundry the path crosses the creek to the right—below Glen Mary, which is visible,—and part of the way is a wood road. Half of a mile along, a path on the right leads to Council Bluff.

The view of the whole extent of Cauterskill Clove as disclosed from Sunset Rock is the best that can be found; and the vastness of High Peak,—seen from down in the Clove, where its sides are so irregularly cleft by the ravines leading from Buttermilk, Wild Cat, and Viola Falls, up over the dense forest to its summit,—is truly an imposing spectacle. To the west Haines' Falls appear in the foreground, with the Schoharie Valley and bordering mountains in the distance.

There is a path over South Mountain from Sunset Rock to the Mountain House,—a two mile walk.

COUNCIL BLUFF.
WALK IN THE LAUREL HOUSE REGION.

Council Bluff is three-fourths of a mile from the Laurel House. The path to it is described under the heading of "Sunset Rock. Walk in the Laurel House Region." The Bluff, which projects on the side of the Kaaterskill Ravine, affords a view down into the Cauterskill Clove and portions of Haines' Falls and Santa Cruz Falls.

WALK FROM THE LAUREL HOUSE TO THE HAINES' FALLS REGION.
BY PATH VIA PROSPECT ROCK.

This route is the shortest one between these places, and much used for a walk. From the road, an eighth of a mile above the Laurel House, a path crosses the field to the west (passing in its way by the head of a **Fish Pond**—private property of the Laurel House), and enters the woods. A fourth of a mile through the woods it divides—the right hand branch continuing direct, while the left hand one leads a few steps out of the way to Prospect Rock, and unites with the other in a pasture a little beyond. (From this point a path turns down the hill on the left to The Sphinx, and this way may be used to reach Haines' Falls, but it is a little farther.) The direct path is readily followed the remainder of the way, and the whole walk is very enjoyable.

PROSPECT ROCK.
WALK FROM THE LAUREL HOUSE.

Prospect Rock is half a mile distant from the Laurel House by an extremely pleasing path. Up the road a little beyond the Laurel House barns the path enters the field to the left, through a gate; crosses the upper end of the Fish Pond, and passes into the forest, through which it continues very clearly marked by being much trod. Carc must be taken to turn to the left by the first diverging path, as the main one leads to the Haines' Falls Region, and Prospect Rock is a few steps off from this.

Prospect Rock is the best possible place from which to see the Kaaterskill Falls from a short distance. It is about on a level with the top of the Falls, and a bold curve in the deep ravine places them directly facing. Both upper and lower Falls are visible from top to bottom and, also, the Laurel House, above.

'Twas here a youth of dreamy mood,
A hundred winters ago—
Had wandered over the mighty wood,
Where the panther's track was fresh on the snow;
And keen were the winds that came to stir
The long dark boughs of the hemlock fir.
[*The Cauterskill Falls, by Bryant.*]

It is but one-fourth of a mile farther to

THE SPHINX, OR NOAH'S ARK.

By a path, a little ways west from Prospect Rock, is a cleared space which slopes to the left and forms a V shaved piece; and **The Sphinx** is at its lower extremity. A description of it is under the heading of "The Sphinx, or Noah's Ark. Walk from the Haines' Falls Region."

WALK FROM THE LAUREL HOUSE TO HIGH PEAK.

The distance to **High Peak** by the shortest path is five miles and a half. A full description of the walk may be found under the headings of "Walk from the Laurel House to the Haines' Fall Region. By path via Prospect Rock," and "High Peak. Walk from the Haines' Falls Region." This trip may be made more easily by driving as far as Haines Falls, thus reducing the walking distance to four miles. Along the route, a mile from Haines' Falls, the path is very near

SANTA CRUZ FALLS,

And it will take but a few minutes to go to this charming spot.

WALK FROM THE LAUREL HOUSE TO CATSKILL MOUNTAIN HOUSE.

BY PATH ALONG NORTH SHORE OF SOUTH LAKE.

The distance by this route is a mile and three-fourths, and the way is mostly shady. At the Laundry the path crosses the creek straight ahead, and beyond a few trees crosses a field to Scribner's road, near a small house. Crossing the road a half mile will reach the lower end of South Lake, from which point the path continues quite near to the Lake, on the north-west side, and strikes the Mountain House road near the Charcoal Pit. The remainder of the walk is by the road.

BY PATH SOUTH OF SOUTH LAKE.

This walk of a mile and a half is the shortest route between these places, and is the one generally taken, although after rains it is somewhat muddy. Most of the way is through the woods. From the Laundry the path is to the right, across the foot-bridge at Glen Mary, to Scribner's. Beyond the house, the left hand path should be taken. It is clearly defined through the forest, and comes out by the Mountain House barns, passing Hygeia Spring on the way.

WALK FROM THE LAUREL HOUSE TO PALENVILLE OVERLOOK.
BY PATH VIA LEMON SQUEEZER, FAIRY SPRING, AND FAT MAN'S DELIGHT.

The shortest path from the Laurel House to **Palenville Overlook** is two miles and three-fourths. To the right of the Laundry, the route is across the foot-bridge at Glen Mary, to Scribner's. Beyond the house are three diverging paths, and the center one—an old wood road—should be followed. A mile through the woods it intersects a path from the Mountain House, near Druid Rocks. Turning to the right it ascends a small ledge and winds around to and underneath another ledge, soon passing the Lemon Squeezer and Fairy Spring. A few yards beyond, the path from Sunset Rock to the Mountain House is entered as it ascends the last ledge necessary to reach the summit of South Mountain. The path now crosses the narrow summit, passing by a bowlder known as Star Rock, to the front or eastern side of the mountain. Again turning to the right, a ledge is soon descended, to the left of which point is the U. S. Coast Survey Signal, and it is but a few rods more to the Bowlder. Passing down the ledge here, through the Fat Man's Delight, the descending, tortuous path is quite well marked—in some places by piles of stones—for the remaining three-fourths of a mile to Palenville Overlook. (For description of this place, see "Palenville Overlook. Walk from Palenville.")

CATSKILL MT. HOUSE REGION.

The Catskill Mountain House having existed for more than fifty years and being the largest house in the Catskills, it is quite generally known throughout this country as well as to many foreigners. A mile and a half intervenes between this house and the nearest one to it. It stands on the eastern side of the mountain range, on the edge of a high ledge of rock, overlooking the Hudson valley, and at an elevation of 2225 feet. It is plainly visible from a great distance to the east.

From the house a tract of many hundred square miles of the Hudson valley is spread to view; with sixty miles of the river visible, appearing as a mere bright thread stretched across the patchwork plain of field and wood. The Green Mountains and Berkshire Hills form the dim background, and the Highlands appear far to the right.

Directly south of the house, paths lead to the summit of South Mountain, which attains an altitude greater by 292 feet. The beautiful Catskill Lakes lie to the west a half mile and the road in that direction passes between them.

The route to the Mountain House is by the way of Catskill. Stages of the house meet the boats and cars at that place, which is twelve miles distant. In ascending the mountain the road winds up through Sleepy Hollow; and the rock may be seen where Rip Van Winkle is supposed to have slept after quaffing from "that wicked flagon!" (For description of this place, see "Sleepy Hollow.") The stage fare from Catskill, including hand baggage, is two dollars. Trunks are charged for extra.

Conveyances may be had for drives, the principal ones being to Kaaterskill Falls, Haines' Falls, Stony Clove, and around South Mountain through the Cauterskill Clove.

The **Mail** is carried regularly by the stages of the house to and from the Catskill post-office.

A Western Union **Telegraph Office** is in the house with a direct wire to New York.

WALKS ABOUT THE CATSKILL MOUNTAIN HOUSE REGION AND VICINITY.
DISTANCES FROM THE MOUNTAIN HOUSE.

	MILES
Artist's Rock, and Prospect Ledge	½
Catskill Lakes, (North Lake, South Lake), by road	½
Haines' Falls, by Path via Laurel House	3
" " by road	4
Hygeia Spring	⅜
Kaaterskill Falls, by path south of South Lake	1 ½
" " by path along north shore of South Lake	1 ¾
" " by road	2 ½
Lovers' Retreat	⅛
Mary's Glen	1
Moses' Rock	1 ¼
Newman's Ledge	1 ¾
Palenville Overlook, by path over South Mt., via Pudding-stone Hall and Fat Man's Delight	1 ¼
South Mountain.—top of it, by direct path	½
" " Circuit of the top, by path via Druid Rocks, Lemon Squeezer, Fairy Spring, and Pudding-stone Hall	1 ¼
Sunset Rock, on South Mt., by path over the Mt.	2
via Scribner's	2 ½
Sunset Rock, North of Mountain House,	⅞
Jacob's Ladder,	⅞
Bears' Den,	⅞
The Outlook, on North Mountain	2 ¾

DRIVES IN THE VICINITY OF THE CATSKILL MOUNTAIN HOUSE.
DISTANCES FROM THE MT. HOUSE, BY THE MOST USUAL ROUTE.

	MILES
Around South Mountain, via Sleepy hollow, Palenville, Cauterskill Clove, and Haines' Falls,—round trip	15
Haines' Falls	4
Hunter	10
Kaaterskill Falls and Laurel House	2 ½
Parker Hill	8
Plaaterkill	13
Sleepy Hollow	2
Stony Clove	12 ½
Tannersville	6

MARY'S GLEN.
WALK IN THE MT. HOUSE REGION.

The shady walk of a mile, without climbing, from the Mountain House to **Mary's Glen** is a desirable one. The way is down the mountain road to the top of the second small hill, where the left one of the two paths on the north should be followed. It leads past the eastern end of North Lake crossing a small stream near the Lake. Half a mile farther Ashley's Creek is crossed on a log for a foot-bridge. A pretty falls are some two hundred feet further up the stream. A path leads from the top of the falls to the road, by the charcoal pit west of the lake, and the return is usually by this way.

HYGEIA SPRING.

WALK IN THE MT. HOUSE REGION.

Hygeia Spring is three-eighths of a mile from Mountain House, on the path which passes east of the barns and enters the woods. It is a nice spring of cold water, walled up, and with conveniences for drinking.

MOSES' ROCK.

WALK IN THE MT. HOUSE REGION.

Moses' Rock is on the eastern side of the mountain, below the Mountain House. The way to it is down the mountain road about half a mile and then by a path on the right down the mountain three-fourths of a mile farther. (From the path a short distance from the road a path diverges and leads along the side of the mountain to Palenville Overlook.) The Rock is about one hundred feet long by twenty feet high, and water flows from an opening in its side a yard above the ground.

(This path continues down the mountain and is the shortest way to Palenville.)

SOUTH MOUNTAIN.

WALK IN THE MT. HOUSE REGION. BY DIRECT PATH TO THE TOP.

It is half a mile from the Mountain House to the summit of **South Mountain** by the shortest path. This walk is probably more frequently taken than any other here.

The path ascends among the trees from near the south-west corner of the Mountain House. A painted guide-mark along it consists of a round, white spot and a red bar crossing it. Passing up a small ledge and reaching the top of a second, higher one, paths diverge. The one to the summit is through **Pudding-stone Hall** and up a third ledge. This Hall is a narrow passage between the ledge and a huge block of pudding-stone broken and separated therefrom. The plain path winds along the eastern ledge of the summit and commands views much the same as those from the Mountain House but much increased in extent and variety.

I looked upon a plain of green,
   That some one called the Land of Prose,
Where many living things are seen,
   In movement or repose.
* * * * * * * * *
But most this fact my wonder bred,
   Though known by all the nobly wise,
It was the mountain streams that fed
   The fair green plain's amenities.—*Stirling*

The summit of South Mountain and much of its sides are nearly barren. Slightly back from the eastern edge is a bowlder on the very top, called **Star Rock**. The elevation here is 2,497 feet. At the edge of the mountain, east from this point, a part of the projecting ledge is called the Sphinx.

The path continues southerly to Palenville Overlook, which is a mile and a fourth from the Mountain House. Descending one ledge, a signal used by the U. S. Coast Survey stands on the left. A few yards further along the Bowlder appears on the edge of a high ledge. To the left of the Bowlder is the only near, convenient way down. A rent in the ledge, called the **Fat Man's Delight**, affords passage through, although the fat man may find difficulty in getting through the thirty feet of its length. From here the path is quite winding down through the shrubbery to Palenville Overlook. (For description, see "Palenville Overlook Walk from Palenville.")

CIRCUIT OF THE TOP.

Near the south-west Corner of the Mountain House the same path is taken as in going to the summit of the mountain. At the top of the second ledge it separates to the right and winds along below the third ledge, through the forest, nearly half a mile to **Druid Rocks.** These Rocks are some blocks of conglomerate, on the left of the path; one piece about a dozen feet high, being called the **Great Bear**, as it somewhat resembles a large animal in a sitting posture. On, a ways farther the path is near the ledge, but then it turns and ascends it, and by quite a circuit to the left reaches a ledge above and turns to the right underneath it, through a fissure—the **Lemon Squeezer**, or, the **Elfin Pass**—passing **Fairy Spring**. It soon ascends the ledge to Star Rock. The return is made by way of Pudding-stone Hall, the same as in the walk by direct path to the top.

This makes a walk of about a mile and a fourth.

CATSKILL LAKES.
WALK IN THE MT. HOUSE REGION.

The Catskill Lakes are a half mile west of the Mountain House. They are distinguished as North and South Lake, and lie close on either side of the road to Kaaterskill Falls and Haines' Falls. The North one has an area of about twenty acres, and the South one some thirty-five acres. The water from them flows to the south-west over the Kaaterskill Falls. Their elevation is 2,138 feet. They are bordered by forest—one side of the South one by the side of South Mountain—and the Shore of the North one is covered with a cranberry marsh. Before reaching the Lakes by way of the road, a path turns off to the left and strikes the shore of South Lake at the boat-house.

Till death the tide of thought may stem,
  There's little chance of our forgetting
The highland lake, the water gem,
  With all its rugged mountain setting.—*Milnes.*

A few yards east of the Lakes, close on the south side of the road, is a large rock with a crevice in one end resembling the open jaws of an Alligator, and hence called **Alligator Rock.**

ARTIST' ROCK, AND PROSPECT LEDGE.
WALK IN THE MT. HOUSE REGION.

It is a walk of half a mile from the Mountain House to **Artist's Rock,** which is a bowlder on the brow of the mountain north of the house. The way is down the mountain road to the top of the second small hill, where two paths start on the left. The right hand path gradually ascends a ledge, giving a sight of the valley below, and soon reaches Artist's Rock, from where the scenic beauty is seen with increased extent.

After ascending some steps in the rocky way it is only a few yards to **Prospect Ledge**. At this place the high wall of rock facing the valley curves farther out than at any other point near, and thus greatly extends the view both north and south. The Hudson valley is spread to view form [from] Albany to West Point. Down to the left and

View on South Lake.

near is Sleepy Hollow, while just over it is Cairo Round Top—a prominent round hill. This is an attractive walk.

On, three-eighths of a mile are

SUNSET ROCK, JACOB'S LADDER, AND BEARS' DEN.

From Prospect Ledge the path soon ascends a short hill,—called Red Hill, from the color of the earth,—at the top of which stands a bowlder on the right of the path, known as **Sunset Rock**. The views from this point are interesting. Stone steps and a ladder—**Jacob's Ladder**—permit of the next ledge being ascended, and to the left of the top are deep clefts in the rock, constituting the **Bears' Den**. To the south appear the Mountain House resting against South Mountain, with High Peak and Round Top looming up in the distance. Close down to the west lie the Catskill Lakes and a dozen miles beyond appear Stony Mountain, Hunter Mountain, and Rusk Mountain. This spot commands a varied scenery that is well worth viewing.

The path continues to

NEWMAN'S LEDGE,

Which is a mile and three-fourths from the Mountain House. After winding along a ways it ascends quite a steep hill, and near the top of this hill it turns to the right to **Newman's Ledge**. (The path which continues up the hill leads to The Outlook.) The scenes presented from this Ledge are similar to those seen from Prospect Ledge except that the northern horizon has receded and the southern drawn nearer. The Ledge was named after Rev. Newman Hall. It has a perpendicular height of about one hundred feet.

THE OUTLOOK, ON NORTH MT.

The Outlook is two miles and three fourths from the Mountain House. Following the path from where the one branches to Newman's Ledge beyond the Bears' Den, a small hollow is crossed in which, on the left, is a depression called **The Cellar**. The way is now mostly through an unbroken forest; at one place through a clump of tall, straight spruce up the slope of the mountain, with the ground exceedingly smooth and free from brush—as beautiful a piece of wood as is often met with. The path through the forest is clearly shown by marked trees.

There are two points for observation from The Outlook, called the First and Second Outlook. This brow of North Mountain on which they are situated is extremely steep.

From the First a broad, steep basin lies below and in its depths are the Catskill Lakes. In successive order, beyond are the Mountain House, South Mountain, and High Peak—the latter seen just to the left of the curve in the mountain forming the other Outlook. Round Top is hidden by this curve. From here a good idea may be obtained of the route and distance traveled to reach this point.

The Second Outlook is a few rods farther along the path. Its elevation is 3,108 feet. The view is similar to that obtained from the First, with some portions increased in beauty and extent.

The return route is usually by a nearly direct and plain path from the Second Outlook down through the forest, striking the road just west of the Lakes.

WALK FROM THE CATSKILL MT. HOUSE TO KAATERSKILL FALLS.

BY PATH SOUTH OF SOUTH LAKE.

The distance is a mile and a half. The path starts by the barns, passes Hygeia Spring three-eighths of a mile along and continues most of the way through the woods to Scribner's. Here it passes front of the house, and beyond the saw-mill crosses the creek at Glen Mary and comes out by the Laurel House Laundry. This is the shortest path between these places and gives a charming walk; but some parts of the way are usually muddy just after rains.

BY PATH ALONG NORTH SHORE OF SOUTH LAKE.

This route is a mile and three-fourths long. From on the road, west of the Lakes, near the charcoal pit, a well worn path follows through the woods, near the Lake, and comes to the road to Scribner's, and opposite this point is a small house. The path continues close by this house, on the right, across a field and over Spruce Creek by the Laundry.

SLEEPY HOLLOW.

The spot known as Sleepy Hollow, and said to be the place where Rip Van Winkle took his twenty years' nap, is on the Mountain House road two miles down the mountain.

The illustration showing Rip at home is from the piece of statuary by John Rogers. Irving says: "The children of the village, too, would shout with joy whenever he approached. Whenever he went dodging about the village, he was surrounded by a troop of them, banging on his skirts, clambering on his back, and playing a thousand tricks on him with impunity; and not a dog would bark at him throughout the neighborhood."

Endnotes

1. J.B. Beers, ed., *History of Greene County* (New York: J.B. Beers & Co., 1884), 78.

2. Olmsted and Vaux were the most important landscape architects of the period. They designed Central Park in New York City, as well as scores of other parks throughout the country. Downing, who died at the dawn of this movement, had great influence on architectural taste and design. Before his partnership with Olmsted, Vaux worked in Downing's design studio at Newburgh, New York.

3. "American Highland Scenery. Beacon Hill," *New-York Mirror* 12 (March 14, 1835), 293-94, as quoted by David Schuyler.

4. The following is an account by Jervis McEntee of a walk that he took with his brother-in-law, Calvert Vaux, shortly after the death of McEntee's wife, Gertrude. The account is at once touching and informative. They have driven by carriage from Rondout through Kaaterskill Clove, and after seeking lodging in Haines Falls finally took a room at the Laurel House, where they stayed the night of Friday, November 1, 1878: "The twenty fourth anniversary of our marriage. I thought I must go home so as to be there at least a part of the day. Calvert seemed to want to stay and finally it seems to me that it would be a great satisfaction in this day to take some of the walks which were so familiar to and so much enjoyed by her. It was a warm still day most rare for this season. After breakfast, about 9 we started for the Mountain House intending to make the circuit of South Mountain. We stopped at Scribner's and saw the old lady who seemed not to have changed a fraction unless for the better. ... We walked through the familiar pasture fields and the favorite woodpath toward the Mountain House where Gertrude so often walked and with which she seemed so intimately identified and where I could so plainly recall her in her wood dress that the whole place was hallowed by her presence. We did not stop at the Mountain House but passed on down the road intending to go by 'Moses Rock' but we missed it getting however upon a pleasant path below the mountain House which we followed to the cliffs above Palenville, then up to the top of South Mountain to Fairy Spring. All along the way on the Mountain House path and from the Fairy Spring back I gathered ferns and wood plants to set out in our cemetery lot, it seemed pleasant to have them from these places. ... After we got back we went out to Sunset Rock. The whole day had been consecrated to thoughts of Gertrude so that I do not know how more satisfactory or appropriately I could have dreamed it." The Jervis McEntee papers, 1850-1905, Archives of American Art, Smithsonian Institution. Author's transcription of Jervis McEntee's diary entry for November 2, 1878. The handwritten diary and other papers of Jervis McEntee are available online.

5. Calvert Vaux, *Villas and Cottages: A Series of Designs Prepared for Erection in the United States* (New York, 1857), 155, as quoted by Francis R. Kowsky.

6. Michael Kudish, "Forest History of the Kaaterskill Region," essay in Mountain Top Historical Society, *Kaaterskill: From the Catskill Mountain House to the Hudson River School* (Hensonville, N.Y.: Black Dome Press, 1993).

7. We will also encounter remnants of a logging operation from the 1910s that included a small railroad for hauling logs, and a children's amusement ride from a mid-twentieth-century vacation attraction.

8. John M. Ham and Robert K. Bucenec, *Light Rails and Short Ties through the Notch* (Hunter, N.Y.: Stony Clove and Catskill Mountain Press, 2002), 13.

9. Postcard in the collection of Justine and Hillard Hommel.

10. The road is a small part of an early turnpike—the Little Delaware Turnpike—that was intended to reach from the village of Catskill to the Delaware River in the town of Delhi. Beers, History of Greene County, 45; and Alf Evers, *The Catskills: From Wilderness to Woodstock* (Garden City, N.Y.: Overlook Press, 1972), chapter 43. Evers is a good source for the early history of the road.

11. As tempting as it may look, this is too difficult a climb for all but the most fit and avid Catskill enthusiasts. The Otis traveled over a concrete trestle at a particularly difficult portion of its route. The trestle still stands and is a dangerous obstacle for anyone who attempts the climb.

12. R. Lionel DeLisser, *Picturesque Catskills* (Northampton, Mass.: Picturesque Publishing Co., 1894; reprint, Cornwallville, N.Y.: Hope Farm Press, 1971), 65.

13. Roland Van Zandt's description of the Old Mountain Road is in chapter 4 of his classic, *The Catskill Mountain House* (Hensonville, N.Y.: Black Dome Press, 1993). The chapter is filled with period descriptions of the journey. See especially pages 95–97 for Van Zandt's discussion of the Rip Van Winkle house and shanty.

14. Charles Dudley Warner, "Their Pilgrimage," Harper's *New Monthly Magazine,* Vol. LXXII, No. 432 (1886), 885–98.

15. On a recent attempt to reach Rip's Ledge we found the trail difficult to follow. We had a number of inexperienced hikers with us, so we abandoned the attempt. The ledge is a long cliff on the north side of Sleepy Hollow and is visible from Newman's Ledge on North Mountain. A trail from the Winter Clove hotel in Round Top leads to Rip's Ledge from the north.

16. 1902 Ulster and Delaware brochure.

17. This section of the modern trail is not the classic climb, which Van Loan calls the "direct path," nor the popular walk known as the Circuit of South Mountain. The modern trail was described in the 1891 edition of Van Loan's *Catskill Mountain Guide.* Earlier Mountain House guests took either the "direct path" or the Circuit of South Mountain.

18. Don't get confused; one hill, two ledges! The reason for the apparent disappearance of a first ledge is that the modern trail is slightly east of the direct path described by Van Loan. Just to the west of the blue trail, the climb would take you over two smaller ledges. Remnants of a water tower that served the Mountain House can still be found at the top of the second ledge. Uphill from the tower is the first conglomerate layer—the Pudding-Stone Hall layer.

19. This is the only reference to this rock of which I'm aware. The name is rather mundane compared to the more romantic names of most sites on South Mountain, but it describes the rock very well. I had been trying to find the name of this rock since I started work on this book. My thanks go to Scott Koster, who e-mailed me two days before I completed the manuscript and asked me if I could identify a rock shown on a postcard in his collection. Scott, a former resident of Poughkeepsie, now lives in Comstock Park, Michigan. He and his family camped for many summers at North Lake.

20. Of particular interest are the names S. Root and those of several members of the Dreer family. The date is 1855. A rare photo of the back of the Mountain House in Raymond Beecher's book, *Kaaterskill Clove: Where Nature Met Art* (Hensonville, N.Y.: Black Dome Press, 2004), 111, depicts members of the Dreer family (an Internet search seems to imply that Dreer was a jeweler from Philadelphia). The photo was taken by S. Root in 1854. This same combination of names can also be found at the original Sunset Rock (also called Lake View Pinnacle) on the approach to Bear's Den. Root's name can also be found carved on a rock at the end of the trail to Kaaterskill Falls.

21. The view from the eroded path is partially obscured by trees and is not as good as the view from the easily accessed ledges above. In many places the path is on loose rock above a very steep and slippery slope. After working my way out a little too far along the path and turning around to return, I found the trail seemed somehow much more intimidating than it had been on the way out. There is no good way from here up to the blue trail until you reach the area below Boulder Rock. I did scramble up by US Signal, but it wasn't easy. To be plain and simple—without climbing experience and equipment, don't go here! Even then, the rock here is shale and conglomerate and does not provide good holds.

22. It may be of interest that Ed West referred to the area just right of the blue trail at the top of the Pudding-Stone Hall ledge as Lovers' Retreat. I don't think that fits, because Van Loan has us pass this spot on a different walk and makes no mention of it there. The location is also too high for Van Loan's and Rusk's descriptions.

23. Until the fall of 2003, the blue trail went straight uphill. Erosion of the trail caused the Department of Environmental Conservation to put a zigzag in the path as it climbs to the second ledge.

24. William Cullen Bryant, ed., *Picturesque America, or, The Land We Live In* (New York: Appleton, 1872–74), 127.

25. Philip Quilibet, "Driftwood," *The Galaxy,* vol 24, issue 4 (October 1877), 554. One of a very large collection of primary documents at Cornell University's *Making of America* web site: http://cdl.library.cornell.edu

26. Loeffler published two stereoviews of the Lemon Squeezer (numbers 334 and 335) in the fifth series of *Catskill Mountain Scenery.* I have yet to see a copy of number 335. Number 334 may have served as the model for an illustration in a souvenir folder, which is the only other image of the Lemon Squeezer that I've seen.

27. *Guide to Rambles from the Catskill Mountain House* (Catskill, N.Y.: Joesbury, 1863), 2–3.

28. *Guide to Rambles,* op. cit., 3. Rusk agrees that Elfin Pass and Lemon Squeezer are the same place, but he implies that it is a fissure along the bottom of the ledge.Van Loan is vague on this point. Both Rusk and Van Loan climb the ledge after passing Fairy Spring.

29. The trails in this area have changed. DEC recently obliterated a trail from the base of Kaaterskill

Falls because of excessive erosion. To see the falls from the base, you will need to start on Route 23A. A much longer time ago—before the fire that killed Frank Layman—the trail in this area took a more easterly direction and went directly toward Sunset Rock. It is still possible to bushwhack in that direction, but take a map and compass since GPS may not work under tree cover.

30. Bryant, *Picturesque America,* 130.

31. Robert Titus, *The Catskills in the Ice Age* (Fleischmanns, N.Y.: Purple Mountain Press, 1996), chapter 6.

32. Scribner's was a small cottage that often took overflow guests from the Catskill Mountain House. Alf Evers, in *The Catskills,* states that Henry David Thoreau stayed there, and the diaries of Jervis McEntee speak of a visit to Scribner's by McEntee and Calvert Vaux, the architect of Central Park.

33. There is another Indian Head—a mountain along the Devil's Path. That mountain, together with Twin Mountain and Sugarloaf, forms the "Sleeping Giant." The giant can be seen from the eastern approach to the Rip Van Winkle Bridge. An illustration of it appears in Rusk's guide, included in this book.

34. This information comes from a letter in the files of the Mountain Top Historical Society, in which an undated newspaper article by Roscoe Craft in the *Catskill Examiner Recorder* is quoted.

35. Evers, *The Catskills,* 89–90, 266.

36. I recently received an e-mail from a researcher in England who asked about the connection between Rev. Hall and the Mountain House. The Greene County Historical Society was able to locate Rev. Hall's signature in the Mountain House register for 1867.

37. Michael Kudish, *The Catskill Forest: A History* (Fleischmanns, N.Y.: Purple Mountain Press, 2000), 134.

38. Ibid., 134.

39. This location was pointed out to me by Edward West, who as a former director of land acquisition for NYSDEC was in a position to know.

40. James Anthony Ryan, *Frederic Church's Olana: Architecture and Landscape as Art* (Hensonville, N.Y.: Black Dome Press, 2001), 28–29.

41. There is a trail in Saugerties that leads to the lighthouse. It is located near the Coast Guard station.

42. W. D. Mulholland, *Catskill Trails* (Albany, N.Y.: State of New York Conservation Department, 1953). The painted name, "Lake View Pinnacle," is still visible, though difficult to read as of fall 2004.

43. *Guide to Rambles,* op. cit., 1. Also in Van Loan, *Catskill Mountain Guide* (1879), 17.

44. The actual location of Jacob's Ladder is off the present trail at the base of the conglomerate ledge and near the eastern escarpment. With a GPS unit you can find it at [N 42° 12.318′ – W 74° 1.823′], but this way is no longer a good approach to the top of Bear's Den and I include it only for historical interest. The anonymous *Guide to Rambles* mentions this in 1863. I've seen reference to a different Jacob's Ladder below Haines Falls.

45. According to Van Loan the ledge is named for Rev. Newman Hall of London. Recent correspondence with Dave Shaw, a researcher in the United Kingdom, indicates that Hall was a leading figure in the Congregational Church in the nineteenth century. Hall visited the United States in 1867. I have not been able to determine his exact connection with Newman's Ledge.

46. Kudish, *The Catskill Forest,* op. cit., 15.

47. Ibid.

48. Mulholland, *Catskill Trails,* op. cit.

49. Beecher, *Kaaterskill Clove,* op. cit., 182–187.

50. Francis Overbaugh, *The Hotel Kaaterskill: Clippings from the Past* (Privately printed, circa 1968), 3.

51. Beers, *History of Greene County,* op. cit., 7.

52. "Haunts of Rip Van Winkle," souvenir brochure for the Hotel Kaaterskill, 1884 and 1888.

53. Robert Titus, "The Great Cascade," *Kaatskill Life,* fall 2001.

54. For reference, I measured the GPS coordinates of this bridge to be [N 42° 10.603′ – 74° 2.264′ – elev. 652 ft.]

55. Beers, *History of Greene County,* op. cit., 45.

56. N.Y.S.D.O.T. Project Assessment and Project Proposal—Route 23A Haines Falls to Palenville Greene County, (draft, March 1980), 6.

57. Robert Titus discusses this interesting feature in "The Great Cascade," op. cit.

58. I have not been able to find the view depicted in that painting. I suspect that it is a composite of several scenes, but the scene depicted is certainly reminiscent of Kaaterskill Clove.

59. Beecher, *Kaaterskill Clove,* op. cit., 209.

60. N.Y.S. D.O.T. Project Assessment, op. cit., 2.

61. Kudish, *The Catskill Forest,* op. cit., 158; Van Zandt, *The Catskill Mountain House,* op. cit., 125; Beers, History of Greene County, op. cit., 343.

62. A. (Annie) E.P. Searing, *The Land of Rip Van Winkle* (New York: G.P. Putnam's Sons, 1884), 50.

63. See Delisser, *Picturesque Catskills,* op. cit., 46, for a photo from the 1890s.

64. If we stay on the road, we will pass some of the foundations of a small community called East Hunter [N 42° 1.046′ – W 74° 4.235′ – elev. 1,105 ft.] and eventually reach the site of Lake Creek Bridge. From there we may go downstream and rejoin the hike, or proceed upstream, skipping Delmura Falls, and climb to Bastion Falls and Route 23A.

65. Kudish, *The Catskill Forest,* op. cit., 167. This is listed as #274 on Kudish's map. He apparently refers to what I call Lake Creek as Spruce Creek, which is the tributary that enters Lake Creek above Kaaterskill Falls. I was not aware of the sawmill here and didn't look for it when I walked the area in late summer 2002.

66. Period stereoviews of Bastion Falls show only the top falls.

67. Robert Titus, "Piracy," *Kaatskill Life,* fall 2002, 56.

68. Creek names get muddled here. There are three: Lake, Spruce, and Kaaterskill creeks. I call the creek that flows from South Lake over Kaaterskill Falls and into the clove near Santa Cruz Ravine, "Lake Creek." The creek over Haines Falls and through the clove I call "Kaaterskill Creek." "Spruce Creek" enters Lake Creek just above Kaaterskill Falls near the Laurel House.

69. Kudish, *The Catskill Forest,* op. cit., 136.

70. Bryant, *Picturesque America,* op. cit., 125.

71. Rev. Charles Rockwell, *The Catskill Mountains and the Region Around* (New York: Taintor, 1867; reprint, Cornwallville, N.Y.: Hope Farm Press, 1973), 291.

72. James Fenimore Cooper, *The Pioneers.*

About the Author

Robert A. Gildersleeve was born and grew up in the mid-Hudson River Valley city of Newburgh, New York. He moved to the Catskill Mountains in 1972 when he started teaching at Hunter–Tannersville Central School. Soon after moving to the Catskills, Mr. Gildersleeve became involved with the Mountain Top Historical Society, serving first as treasurer, then as vice president. He has worked on the historical society's publications, including the book *Kaaterskill: From the Catskill Mountain House to the Hudson River School,* for which he wrote the introduction, and he has been a leader of the society's hiking program since the mid-1970s. Mr. Gildersleeve has hiked throughout the Catskills and the surrounding areas, but it is the area around the Pine Orchard site of the Catskill Mountain House that has drawn him more than any other location. His lifelong study of science and technology has enabled him to bring a scientific and technical background to bear on the exploration of this historic and cultural landscape. Now retired from teaching, Mr. Gildersleeve and his wife Maria live in Maplecrest, New York, near a system of hiking trails that interconnect with the historic trails that are the subject of this book.

Bibliography

Beach, Charles, editor. *The Scenery of the Catskills.* Facsimile edition, Astoria, N.Y.: J. C. & A. Fawcett, 1994.

Beecher, Raymond. *Kaaterskill Clove: Where Nature Met Art.* Hensonville, N.Y.: Black Dome Press, 2004.

Beers, F.W. *Atlas of Greene County, New York.* New York: Beers, Ellis & Soule, 1867; reprint, Churchville, N.Y.: Martin Wehle, 1976.

Beers, J.B., editor. *History of Greene County.* New York: J.B. Beers & Co., 1884.

Bryant, William Cullen, editor. *Picturesque America*: or, *The Land We Live In.* NewYork: Appleton, 1872–74. As notable for its illustrations by Harry Fenn as for its text.

The Catskills. New York: Wittemann Brothers, 1884. A souvenir album containing photo-views by the Louis Glasser process.

DeLisser, R. Lionel. *Picturesque Catskills.* Northampton, Mass.: Picturesque Publishing Co., 1894; reprint, Cornwallville, N.Y.: Hope Farm Press, 1971.

Evers, Alf. *The Catskills: From Wilderness to Woodstock.* Garden City, N.Y.: Overlook Press, 1972.

Guide to Rambles from the Catskill Mountain House. Catskill, N.Y.: Joesbury, 1863. Written by "a visitor." Similarities between this and Van Loan's guide make me suspect that the "visitor" may have been Van Loan.

Ham, John M. and Robert K. Bucenic. *Light Rail and Short Ties through the Notch.* Hunter, N.Y.: Stony Clove and Catskill Mountain Press, 2002.

Helmer, William F. *Rip Van Winkle Railroads.* Hensonville, NY: Black Dome Press, 1999.

Kudish, Michael. *The Catskill Forest: A History.* Fleischmanns, N.Y.: Purple Mountain Press, 2000.

Mountain Top Historical Society. *Kaaterskill: From the Catskill Mountain House to the Hudson River School.* Hensonville, N.Y.: Black Dome Press, 1993.

Mulholland, W. D. *Catskill Trails.* Albany, N.Y.: State of New York Conservation Department, 1953.

N.Y.S.D.O.T. Project Assessment and Project Proposal—Route 23A Haines Falls to Palenville Greene County. (Draft) NYSDOT, March 1980.

Overbaugh, Francis. *The Hotel Kaaterskill: Clippings from the Past.* Privately printed, circa 1968.

Quilibet, Phillip. "Drift-wood." *The Galaxy* (October 1877). On the Cornell University "Making of America" website: http://cdl.library.cornell.edu/moa/

Ryan, James Anthony. *Frederic Church's Olana: Architecture and Landscape as Art.* Hensonville, N.Y.: Black Dome Press, 2001.

Rockwell, Rev. Charles. *The Catskill Mountains and the Region Around.* New York: Taintor, 1867; reprint, Cornwallville, N.Y.: Hope Farm Press, 1973.

Rusk, Samuel E. *An Illustrated Guide to the Catskill Mountains with Maps and Plans.* Catskill, N.Y.: Rusk, 1879.

Searing, A. (Annie) E. P. *The Land of Rip Van Winkle.* New York: G. P. Putnam's Sons, 1884.

Titus, Robert. *The Catskills: A Geological Guide.* Fleischmanns, N.Y.: Purple Mountain Press, 1993.

———. *The Catskills in the Ice Age.* Fleischmanns, N.Y.: Purple Mountain Press, 1996.

———. "Dance Floors." *Kaatskill Life* (Winter 1998–99).

———. "The Glaciers and the Park." *Kaatskill Life* (Winter 2000).

———. "The Great Cascade." *Kaatskill Life* (Fall 2001).

———. "Piracy." *Kaatskill Life* (Fall 2002).

———. "Where Is Puddingstone Hall?" *Kaatskill Life* (Summer 1996).

Van Loan, Walton. *Catskill Mountain Guide.* Catskill, N.Y.: 1879; facsimile edition, Astoria, N.Y.: J.C. & A. Fawcett, 1994.

Van Zandt, Roland. *The Catskill Mountain House.* Hensonville, N.Y.: Black Dome Press, 1993.

Warner, Charles Dudley. "Their Pilgrimage." *Harper's New Monthly Magazine*, Vol. LXXII, No. 432 (1886): 885–98.

West, James. Letter to Justine Hommel, August 28, 1992.

Index

Page numbers in italics indicate an illustration.